ESL
Grammar Workbook 2

for intermediate speakers and writers of english as a second language

HIGH-INTERMEDIATE

ALLAN KENT DART

New York University

REGENTS/PRENTICE HALL, Englewood Cliffs, New Jersey 07632

Library of Congress Cataloging in Publication Data

DART, ALLAN KENT, 1937
   ESL grammar workbook.

   CONTENTS: 1. Low-intermediate.—2. High-intermediate.
   1. English language—Text-books for foreigners.
2. English language—Grammar—1950- I. Title.
PE1128.D345   428'.2'4076   77-25316
ISBN 0-13-283663-7 (v. 1)
ISBN 0-13-283671-8 (v. 2)

TO MY MOTHER,
AND
IN MEMORY OF MY FATHER

 © 1978 by Prentice-Hall, Inc.
A Simon & Schuster Company
Englewood Cliffs, New Jersey 07632

Printed in the United States of America
20 19 18

ISBN 0-13-283671-8

Prentice-Hall International (UK) Limited, *London*
Prentice-Hall of Australia Pty. Limited, *Sydney*
Prentice-Hall Canada Inc., *Toronto*
Prentice-Hall Hispanoamericana, S. A., *Mexico*
Prentice-Hall of India Private Limited, *New Delhi*
Prentice-Hall of Japan, Inc., *Tokyo*
Simon & Schuster Asia Pte. Ltd., *Singapore*
Editora Prentice-Hall do Brasil, Ltda., *Rio de Janeiro*

CONTENTS

4 ADVERBIAL CLAUSES, 104

5 NOUN CLAUSES, 150

6 -ING FORMS AND INFINITIVES, 181

PREFACE

Book 2 of *ESL Grammar Workbook* is the continuation of a survey of the English language for intermediate students of English as a second language. The material has been designed primarily for students in colleges, universities, and adult education programs.

Books 1 and 2 may be used as a complete course of study for an intensive one-semester program of approximately 175 hours, or the work may be divided for a two-semester program. However, Book 1 is not a prerequisite to Book 2, for the two books have been designed as separate textbooks.

The material in this text has been tested by me and other teachers at New York University over a period of three years. This book (in a somewhat different form) was tested with three different pilot groups in a sixty-hour program designed for the New York Telephone Company. Thus, the material has been intensively tested both with students who were preparing for future university studies, and with non-academic students in an industrial setting who were studying English to improve their performance on the job.

There are many people I want to thank for the constructive criticism, encouragement, and interest they showed during the development of the manuscript. Unfortunately, space does not permit me to thank them all. For their many suggestions and the strong motivating force that they provided, I would particularly like to thank Clarice Wilkes Kaltinick, Rosalie Yarmus Lurie, Fred Malkemes, Jr., Linda Rooney Markstein, and my good neighbor, Anna M. Halpin. I would also like to thank Milton G. Saltzer, Director of the American Language Institute, New York University, for permitting me to test the material in my classes.

To the following at Prentice-Hall, I wish to express my appreciation: Marylin Brauer, Ilene McGrath, and Teru Uyeyama.

I want to express my special indebtedness to my friend Gary-Gabriel Gisondi, librarian at the Performing Arts Research Center of the New York Public Library at Lincoln Center. Without his assistance and inspiration, this book could not have been written.

My deepest gratitude must go to the hundreds of students I have had over the years who have made my teaching career so enjoyable and meaningful. An especially strong feeling of gratitude is felt toward those who participated in the shaping of the final draft of the manuscript: Alcira Derevizus (of Argentina); Jose Concepcion (of Cuba); Ronna Estrada and Martha Mejia (of Colombia); Ho-Foo Hui (of Curaçao); Josefina Rivera (of the Dominican Republic); Armelle Mathurin and Nicole Villejoint (of Haiti); Angelina Goldamez (of Honduras); Swandayati (Lin) Aliwarga (of Indonesia); Raymond Malkomian (of Iran); Abdel Jaber Tarik (of Palestine); Tazuko Hosaka (of Japan); Hae-Kyoung Cha (of Korea); Hilda Avalos (of Peru); Reinaldo Franqui (of Puerto Rico); Tull Syvanarat (of Thailand); Eddy Dieguez (of Uruguay); and Orlando Angarita, Nary Barrios, and Clemilde (Cleo) Beltran (of Venezuela).

Allan Kent Dart

INTRODUCTION

This textbook is for high-intermediate students of English as a second language who have completed Book 1 of this work, or another text containing comparable material. The book begins with the perfect tenses and a review of the material covered in Book 1.

The explanations and exercises are carefully sequenced and graded, so I recommend that the order of the chapters be followed as closely as possible since past material is constantly being reviewed within the context of the new material that is being presented.

Exercises are usually preceded by grammar explanations so that various points of the explanation may be easily referred to by everyone in the class. As an effective introduction to the exercises that are to follow, I suggest that the instructor read the grammar explanations out loud to the students. This short period of reading descriptions and examples (the examples may be used for choral practice) will allow the students to practice the pronunciation of various grammatical terms, and it will also help ensure that everyone will have a clear understanding of the Focus that is to appear in the following exercise.

Every Grammar Exercise in this book contains complete exercises which focus on a specific topic. For best results, it is essential that everyone keep his or her mind on the Focus that is stated at the top of each exercise. The Focus is there to give control to the lesson and direction to the group.

Most of the exercises are designed so that they may be used as a plan for a guided period of conversation by the group. For example, in a Grammar Exercise with the Focus of *yes-no* questions, the list of questions may be used as a script by the instructor for conducting a drill. Depending on the group and its teacher, during such drills it might be best for the students to keep their books closed.

The exercises can also be used as quizzes, as homework, or for writing assignments during a class. A particularly effective procedure is for the students not to use a pen or pencil while they are doing an exercise in class. Then the exercise may be given as a homework assignment. While the students are doing their homework, they will be testing themselves to see what they have remembered, or may have forgotten, from the previous meeting.

It will be noted that the pages of this book are perforated and easy to tear out. If the students wish, at the end of this course they may remove all of the pages (including those not submitted to the teacher), and reassemble them in a binder or folder. By doing this, they will create their own presentation, which will add a personal touch to their book. Also, it will be a convenient way for them to review the corrections the teacher has made in their assignments.

Sometimes during an exercise, a student will find *s/he*, a "word" that can mean *she* or *he* — for example, *S/he lives in Boston* (she); or *S/he lives in Boston* (he).

Sentences like *S/he took his/her wife/husband out to dinner on his/her birthday* also sometimes occur. With such a sentence, one can say or write *S/he took his/her wife/husband out to dinner on his/her birthday;* or *S/he took his/her wife/husband out to dinner on his/her birthday*.

Note: Primarily, the use of these devices is to help the students develop their skills in using pronouns and possessive adjectives. Secondarily, it reflects the author's attempt to create a nonsexist atmosphere for a group meeting.

Notes and reminders are some of the other learning devices used throughout this book. A Note supplies new information, and a Reminder helps a student remember something that has already been discussed.

The terms FORMAL and INFORMAL are frequently used in grammar explanations in this text. Formal usage is that style found in formal writing — for example, a letter to an ambassador, a scientific report, or a doctoral thesis. An informal style of writing would most likely be used in a letter to an old school friend, a quick note to a neighbor, or an article in a newspaper about a football game.

Because the emphasis in this book is on spoken English, the material in the exercises most frequently represents an informal style of writing, and the model sentences reflect the style of speaking that is used by educated people in an informal situation. I hope that students and teachers will find their experience with this book interesting and enjoyable.

THE PRESENT PERFECT TENSE

1.1

A REVIEW OF VERB TENSES

Before we discuss the present perfect tense, a short review of the verb tenses covered in Book 1 of this work will prove helpful to those students who were not with us, and will serve as a review for those students who were.

1. The SIMPLE PRESENT TENSE is used for (a) a generally known fact or condition: *There **are** 360 degrees in a circle; Water **contains** no nitrogen;* (b) a state of being: *They **are** in love; The giraffe **is** the tallest of existing animals;* and (c) a habitual activity or occurrence: *Many animals **hibernate** every winter; The sun always **rises** in the east; Leap year **comes** every four years.*

2. Though not discussed as such in Book 1, the simple present tense is sometimes used for future time: *The ship **sails** at dawn; The sun **rises** at 6:18 tomorrow morning; The bank **opens** at nine o'clock tomorrow morning.*

3. The PRESENT CONTINUOUS TENSE is used for (a) an event that is occurring at this moment (now): *We **are beginning** this book; You **are looking** at this page now;* (b) an event that is taking place temporarily: *The patient **is taking** penicillin; She **is living** in a hotel for the time being* (temporarily); and (c) an event in future time: *The astronauts **are leaving** for the moon tomorrow; The curtain at the theater **is rising** at 8:30 tomorrow night.*

4. *Be going to* + a base form is also used for a coming event: *We're **going to learn** a lot of new things in this course; He's **going to take** another course after this one.*

5. *Be going to* + *be* + a present participle is used to emphasize the duration of a future event: *We **are going to be studying** together for several months; The earth **is going to be revolving** around the sun for millions of more years.*

6. The SIMPLE PAST TENSE is used for an event at a definite point of time in the past: *Jesus **died** on the Cross almost two thousand years ago; Buddha **lived** from c. 563 to 483 B.C.; Columbus **discovered** America in 1492.*

7. The PAST CONTINUOUS TENSE is used (a) to emphasize an event at one point in past time: *Everyone **was sleeping** at the time of the earthquake; Everyone in the theater **was crying** at the end of the movie;* and (b) to emphasize the duration of an event in past time: *His grandfather **was working** hard from the beginning to the end of the day; They **were celebrating** their victory at the Olympics all night long.*

8. The past continuous tense is most frequently used in complex sentences where the past continuous time (in a main clause) is interrupted by a definite past action (in a subordinate clause): *They **were talking** about me when I **interrupted** their conversation; The sun **was shining** when the climbers **reached** the top of Mt. Everest.*

9. Besides simple futurity, the FUTURE TENSE is used to express (a) promise: *I **will always love** you; I **will never break** this promise;* (b) determination: *We **will never give up** our freedom; We **will die** for our religion;* (c) inevitability: *The twentieth century **will come** to an end; Spring **will bring** new life;* and (d) prediction: *It **will rain** tomorrow; Everyone in the class **will speak** English well.*

1.1 (Continued)

10. The FUTURE CONTINUOUS TENSE is used (a) to emphasize an event at one point in future time: *I'll be seeing you at the beginning of the game; Our plane will be taking off in a few minutes;* and (b) to emphasize the duration of an event in future time: *He will be thinking about only his girlfriend until she returns; I will be working all day long.*

11. Like the past continuous tense, the future continuous tense is used in complex sentences where the future continuous time (in a main clause) is interrupted by a definite future action (in a subordiante clause): *It will probably be raining when we get to the beach; I will be waiting for you at the airport when your plane comes in.*

1.2

GRAMMAR EXERCISE   Name _____ Date _____

Focus: Reviewing Verb Tenses Covered in Book 1: the Present (Continuous) Tense, the Past (Continuous) Tense, the Future (Continuous) Tense, *Be going to* + a base form, *Be going to* + *be* + a Present Participle

Reminder: *Be going to* and the future tense are essentially interchangeable.

Fill in the blanks with appropriate verb forms (affirmative or negative) of the base forms given in the parentheses.

EXAMPLES: a. (have) Our little boy always <u>has</u> a good time at the zoo.
b. (drive) A friend of mine <u>is driving</u> a taxi for the time being.
c. (eat) When Mary is on a diet, she <u>doesn't eat</u> potatoes.

1. (rain) When I left the house this morning, it _____.

2. (have) I didn't take a vacation because I _____ any money.

3. (win) Who _____ in the next election?

4. (rise) The sun _____ at 6:38 yesterday morning.

5. (live) They _____ in an apartment temporarily because they can't find an inexpensive house.

6. (eat) I _____ Italian food only once in a while.

7. (ring) The bell _____ and the class began.

8. (blow) A hard wind _____ while we were climbing the mountain.

9. (understand) He _____ anything at the last meeting.

10. (enter) Who _____ the university next September?

11. (talk) When I came into the room, everyone _____ about me.

12. (give) How often does your teacher _____ the class a quiz?

1.2 (Continued)

Name _____ Date _____

13. (go) We _____ anywhere in particular next weekend.

14. (fight) We _____ our enemy until our last man falls.

15. (talk) My secretary _____ on the phone right now.

16. (begin) The movie _____ soon.

17. (take) When he goes on a business trip, he usually _____ his wife.

18. (set) The sun never _____ in the east.

19. (set) The sun _____ at 5:48 tomorrow afternoon.

20. (enter) The patient _____ the operating room at this very moment.

21. (fall) Our little girl _____ down and hurt herself seriously.

22. (take) Who _____ care of your children now?

23. (speak) I _____ to anyone on the phone last night.

24. (make) I _____ a few mistakes on the last examination.

25. (shine) When I get up tomorrow morning, the sun _____.

26. (be) The assassination of President Kennedy _____ a shock to the world.

27. (be) We _____ at the beginning of this book.

28. (live) Few people _____ in the Sahara Desert.

29. (fall) Listen! Some rain _____ on the roof.

30. (fall) The leaves usually _____ from the trees in October.

31. (graduate) He _____ from the university next June.

32. (get) Everyone in my office usually _____ to work by 9:30.

33. (be) People _____ sometimes difficult.

34. (find) She won't quit her present job until she _____ a new one.

35. (blow) We didn't go sailing in our boat because the wind _____.

36. (keep) He _____ a car because it's too expensive.

37. (take) A very important meeting _____ place at the White House a couple of days ago.

38. (go) We _____ to the beach tomorrow because the weather isn't going to be nice.

39. (think) A selfish person always _____ about only himself.

40. (be) Everyone at the last meeting _____ surprised by the president's decision to resign.

41. (be) There _____ no one in the house when I got home last night.

1.2 (Continued)

42. (be) The party _____ a success because there weren't enough people.

43. (enter) Everyone will stand up when the King _____ the room.

44. (feel) I didn't go to work because I _____ well.

45. (be) The chicken _____ any good at dinner last night.

46. (arrive) When the telegram _____, please let me know immediately.

47. (make) During the examination, he was angry at himself because he _____ a lot of mistakes.

48. (take) Everyone in my office usually _____ a coffee break in the middle of the afternoon.

49. (be) When I got to work, nobody _____ there.

50. (fly) We _____ on Air France when we went on our last trip.

51. (take) He never _____ his car when he goes to work.

52. (sleep) When I got home, the children _____.

53. (be) All of us _____ a little nervous when we came into this room today.

54. (do) When the phone rang, I _____ anything in particular.

55. (come) The world _____ to an end tomorrow.

56. (learn) We _____ a lot of new things in this book.

57. (be) Good health _____ our most precious possession.

58. (finish) We _____ this exercise now.

59. (mail) He _____ the package in time for his sister's birthday.

60. (hike) We _____ up the northwest trail on our last attempt.

1. The PRESENT PERFECT TENSE is used to express the duration of an event that began at a definite point in past time and has continued to the present and will probably continue into future time: *The earth **has existed** for millions of years; Elizabeth II **has been** the Queen of the United Kingdom since 1952.*

2. To form the present perfect tense, we use the verb *have* as an auxiliary and a PAST PARTICIPLE as the main verb of a verb phrase. *Have* occurs as an *-s* form in the third person singular.

	Singular		Plural	
First person	I	} have worked	we	} have worked
Second person	you		you	
Third person	he		they	
	she	} has worked		
	it			

3. Regular past participles are formed by adding *-ed* to a base form (simple form) of a verb. The rules for spelling regular past participles are the same as those for spelling regular past forms:

    (a) When a regular base form ends in *-y* preceded by a consonant, change the *-y* to *-i* and add *-ed*: (*bury*) *They have **buried** many people since the beginning of the famine;* (*carry*) *I have **carried** my boss's responsibilities since he became sick.*

    (b) When the final *-y* is preceded by a vowel, no change is made: (*stay*) *He has **stayed** home for two weeks;* (*play*) *The children have **played** all day long.*

    (c) When a regular base form ends with a single consonant preceded by a single stressed vowel, the consonant is doubled before adding *-ed*: (*stop*) *My watch has **stopped**;* (*permit*) *The police have **permitted** us to pass through the barricades.*

    (d) When a regular base form ends in *-e*, only *-d* is added: (*change*) *Life in Cuba has **changed** since the revolution;* (*smoke*) *He has **smoked** since he was eighteen.*
    Note: A list of commonly used irregular verbs appears in the Appendix.

4. When we express the duration of an event from past to present time, the preposition *for* is used in a prepositional phrase when the amount of time is given: *He has been here **for three hours**; I have lived in this country **for seven years**.* The use of *for* is optional: *He has been here (for) three hours; I have known her (for) seven years.*

5. A prepositional phrase with *since* is used when the exact moment, time, day, or year that the event began is given: *They have been here **since one o'clock yesterday afternoon**; They have been married **since 1973**; They have lived in London **since 1974**.*

1.3 (Continued)

6. When one event follows another, the preposition *since* also occurs: *Life in Lebanon has been different **since the civil war**; They have been happy **since their marriage**; His parents have lived in Hong Kong **since the end of the war in Vietnam**.*

7. *Since* occurs as a subordinate conjunction when it introduces a past time clause (subordinate clause) to a sentence: *He has made a lot of money **since he started work at the company**; They have lived in San Francisco **since they arrived in the United States**.*
   Reminder: A time phrase never has a subject or a verb, but a time clause always does. Compare:

Time Phrase	Time Clause
. . . *since the beginning of the party.*	. . .*since **the party began**.*
. . . *since the end of the war.*	. . .*since **the war ended**.*

8. The adverb *ago* appears with the simple past tense only: *His grandfather **died many years ago**.* However, *ago* may appear in a time clause or phrase introduced by *since* when the verb phrase in the main clause of a sentence is in the present perfect tense: *He has been in the hospital **since he got sick five weeks ago** (since the beginning of his illness five weeks ago.)*
   Special Note: The simple present tense is never used for the duration of an event from past to present time. Compare:

Wrong	Correct
I am married for five years.	*I **have been** married for five years.*
She lives here since 1973.	*She **has lived** here since 1973.*

1.4

GRAMMAR EXERCISE   Name _Meriyana_   Date _8. Feb. 1994_

Focus: The Duration of an Event

Supply *have* or *has* in the first blank and *since* or *for* in the second.

EXAMPLES: a. The United States <u>has</u> been independent <u>since</u> 1776.
   b. We <u>have</u> had the problem of pollution <u>for</u> many years.

1. The earth __*has*__ been in existence __*for*__ millions of years.

2. Cuba __*has*__ been a socialist country __*since*__ 1959.

3. Korea and Germany __*have*__ been divided nations __*for*__ quite a few years. (*Quite a few* means *many;* the expression may modify countable nouns only: *They have had quite a few problems.*)

4. Latin __*has*__ been a dead language __*since*__ the decline of Rome.

5. Bill and his best friend __*have*__ known each other __*for*__ many years.

6. Life in China __*has*__ been very different __*since*__ the People's Revolution. The people __*have*__ changed.

7. Israel __*has*__ been a state __*since*__ 1948.

8. Canada and Australia __*have*__ been a part of the British Commonwealth __*for*__ quite a few years.

9. Islam __*has*__ been the most important religion in the Middle East __*for*__ approximately 1,400 years.

10. Life __*has*__ been a magnificent puzzle __*since*__ the beginning of time.

11. All of the students __*have*__ studied hard __*since*__ the beginning of the course. The class __*has*__ been in session __*since*__ September 1.

12. Buddhism __*has*__ been a major religion in the Far East __*for*__ more than two thousand years.

13. The sun __*has*__ been in the center of our solar system __*for*__ millions and millions of years.

14. My parents __*have*__ had their house __*for*__ quite a few years.

15. Washington, D.C., __*has*__ been the capital of the United States __*since*__ 1800.

16. I __*have*__ known my best friend __*since*__ I was six.

17. The Eiffel Tower __*has*__ been a famous tourist attraction __*since*__ the time of its erection for the Paris Exhibition in 1889.

18. Relations between those two countries __*has*__ been bad __*since*__ the end of the last war.

19. Christianity __*has*__ been an important religion __*for*__ almost two thousand years.

20. The Red Cross __*has*__ been an important international organization __*since*__ 1864. It __*has*__ helped people __*for*__ many years.

21. The Soviet Union __*has*__ been a socialist state __*since*__ 1917.

GRAMMAR EXERCISE   Name *Miryang*   Date *9. Feb. 94*

Focus: Duration with the Present Perfect Tense

Fill in the first blank with an appropriate verb phrase in the present perfect tense and supply *since* or *for* in the second. Use past participles made out of the base forms in the following list: be, do, have, know, live, love, speak, work.

EXAMPLES: a.   She has spoken English since she was a little girl.
  b.   They have been married for seventeen years.

1.   I _have had_ my car _for_ three years.

2.   We _have been_ in this classroom _since_ ten o'clock.

3.   S/he _has loved_ him/her secretly _for_ many years.
     Reminder: Indicate your choice of pronouns.

4.   He _has had_ a great deal of money _since_ the day he was born. (*A great deal of* means *much*. The expression modifies only uncountable nouns: *There is a great deal of money in his account.*)

5.   My best friend _has lived_ in New York _since_ he was born.

6.   They _have had_ a great deal of trouble with their car _since_ the day they bought it.

7.   The weather _has been_ beautiful _since_ the beginning of the month. We _have had_ sunshine _for_ almost three weeks.

8.   The President _has been_ in office _for_ some years.

9.   Bill and his father _have worked_ together in the same company _for_ more than ten years.

10. Everyone _has done_ well _since_ the beginning of the course.

11. Our little boy _has had_ an infection in his ear _since_ he went swimming in the lake a couple of weeks ago.

12. I _have spoken_ English _for_ only a couple of years.

13. My next-door neighbor _has been_ very inactive _since_ she became ill.

14. He _has had_ a great deal of trouble with his boss _since_ he started working for the company.

15. Betty Smith, a good friend of mine, _has been_ a very unhappy woman _since_ the death of her husband.

16. My house plants _have done_ much better _since_ I fed them with a new kind of organic fertilizer.

17. I _have known_ my best friend _for_ more than fifteen years.

18. My parents _have had_ their car _since_ 1951. It has become an antique.

19. We _have been_ in this room _for_ about an hour and a half.

1.6

CONTRACTIONS, THE NEGATIVE FORM, AND *ALWAYS/NEVER*

1. Contractions of *have* or *has* with subject pronouns occur in informal usage: *They've been sick for days; She's lived by herself for years.*

	Singular	Plural
First person	I've	we've
Second person	you've	you've } been
Third person	he's } been	they've
	she's	
	it's	

2. It is sometimes difficult for students to determine whether the contraction *'s* is *has* or *is*. Two general rules to follow are: (a) When a past participle (sometimes preceded by an adverb) follows *'s,* it is the contraction of *has;* for example, *It's (has) been a beautiful day; He's (has) already had his car for three years; She's (has) spoken French since she was little.* (b) When *'s* is followed by articles, adjectives, and *-ing* forms, it is the contraction of *is;* for example, *It's (is) a beautiful day; He's (is) homesick; She's (is) talking about her vacation.*
Reminder: Some past participles occur as adjectives: *He's (is) tired; It's (is) broken; He's (is) drunk.*

3. A negative verb phrase is formed by inserting *not* between the auxiliary and main verb: *I **have not spoken** Spanish since I returned to Toronto from Mexico; She **has not spoken** to me since we had that argument three weeks ago.*

I you } have not been	we you } have not been
he she } has not been it	they

4. The contractions *haven't (have not)* and *hasn't (has not)* occur in informal usage: *I **haven't** done anything about my visa problem; My father **hasn't** played football for years.*

5. The adverbs *always* and *never* are also inserted between the auxiliary and the main verb: *My mother **has always driven** a Ford car; I **have never known** a person as nice as you are.*

1.7

GRAMMAR EXERCISE   Name _____ Date _____

Focus: Contractions and *Always/Never*

Fill in the blanks with appropriate verb phrases in the present perfect tense containing the adverbs *always* or *never*. Practice using contractions. Use past participles made out of the base forms in the following list.

be	eat	live	obey	see	study	work
drink	have	love	respect	sing	use	worry
drive	like	make	run	speak	want	

EXAMPLES: a. I've never run in an election for a public office.
b. She's never sung in a church choir.
c. They've never studied English at a school, but they speak it well.

1. I _____ my parents.

2. Unfortunately, they _____ a great deal of trouble with their son.

3. I _____ in a tropical climate.

4. He _____ a Rolls-Royce.

5. They _____ a lot of money in their business.

6. It _____ cold at the North Pole.

7. She _____ a selfish/generous person.

8. I _____ to take a trip around the world.

9. John _____ to go on a trip through the Sahara.

10. I _____ my mother's favorite child.

11. You _____ respect for yourself.

12. She _____ an excellent student.

13. Ann _____ a poor student.

14. He _____ English well.

15. We _____ English during the classes.

16. They _____ each other very much.

17. Fortunately, she _____ good health.

18. I _____ wine with my meals.

19. We _____ Japanese food.

20. They _____ about their son.

21. I _____ hard drugs. (*Hard drugs* means any of the addictive drugs such as *heroin, morphine,* or *opium.*)

22. I _____ a woman as beautiful as she is.

23. Jim _____ for General Motors.

24. We _____ in Los Angeles.

25. I _____ to go to the dentist a lot.

1.8

GRAMMAR EXERCISE

Name *Mariyana. S.* Date _____

Focus: Negative Verb Phrases

Fill in the blanks with appropriate negative verb phrases in the present perfect tense. Use past participles made out of the base forms in the following list.

appear	call	drink	feel	have	rain	send	take
be	do	drive	get	occur	see	speak	work

EXAMPLES: a. I <u>haven't felt</u> well since I got up this morning.
   b. She <u>hasn't been</u> in her hometown since she was a little girl.

1. I _<u>haven't had</u>_ time to sit down for a second since I got to work.

2. Grandpa's health _<u>hasn't felt</u>_ good for years.

3. Grandma _<u>hasn't been</u>_ able to walk well since she fell down and broke her hip two years ago. It _<u>was</u>_ easy for her.

4. That actor _<u>hasn't</u>_ in a movie for quite a few years.

5. A major earthquake _<u>hasn't been</u>_ in San Francisco since 1906.

6. It _____ for more than a month, and the countryside is very dry.

7. Bill _____ since he retired four years ago.

8. She's worried because her boyfriend _____ her for more than a month.

9. I _____ a really good movie for a long time.

10. In spite of the inflation, they _____ many financial problems. They _____ any vacations, however.

11. That student _____ any homework since the beginning of the course.

12. That unfortunate person _____ happy since the day she was born. (The *exaggeration* here is used for emphasis.)

13. Life _____ easy for him since he lost his job.

14. The doctor is extremely busy, and she _____ the chance (opportunity) to go to bed since early yesterday morning.

15. I _____ the chance to sit down since I got up this morning.

16. We _____ good weather since the beginning of the year.

17. I _____ any alcohol since I started taking penicillin.

18. Because he is angry at his brother, he _____ to him for more than a year.

19. I _____ in my native country for two years.

20. Because of his poor vision (eyesight), my grandfather _____ a car for quite a few years.

21. I _____ my parents for quite a long time.

22. This _____ a difficult exercise.

1.9

Focus: Time Clauses with *Since*

The adverb *ever* may occur as an intensifier of the subordinate conjunction *since: He's been madly* (very much) *in love with her **ever since** he first met her; I've felt wonderful **ever since** I stopped smoking; She's been unhappy **ever since** her husband died.*
Note: This pattern is used more informally than formally.

Fill in the blanks with past forms made out of the base forms given in the parentheses.

EXAMPLES: a. (lose) Germany has been a divided nation ever since it <u>lost</u> the war.
b. (fall) Berlin has been a divided city ever since it <u>fell</u>.

1. (inherit) She's been a difficult person ever since she <u>*inherited*</u> a great deal of money.

   (happen) Her life has changed completely ever since this <u>*happened*</u>.

2. (take) The patient has felt much better ever since he <u>*took*</u> the new drug. (begin)

   Everyone in his family has felt much better ever since his condition <u>*began*</u> to improve.

3. (drop) They've been worried about their son ever since he <u>*dropped*</u> out of school. (*To drop out of* means *to quit.* The idiom is most often used in reference to quitting school. A person who drops out of school is called a *dropout.*)

4. (move) Dick has been happy ever since he <u>*moved*</u> to New York.

5. (win) His father has had a great deal of luck ever since he <u>*won*</u> a lot of money in the lottery.

6. (break) She's been unhappy ever since he <u>*broke*</u> his promise to her.

7. (enter) Their daughter has been a very good student ever since she <u>*enter*</u> school.

   (leave) Her life has been completely different ever since she <u>*left*</u> home for the university.

8. (be) They've been in love with each other ever since they <u>*was*</u> children in school.

9. (get) They've been very happy ever since they <u>*got*</u> married.

10. (introduce) His company has been very successful ever since it <u>*introduced*</u> a new mouse-trap to the market.

11. (buy) My life has been different ever since I <u>*bought*</u> a new car.

12. (meet) We've had a lot of fun together ever since we <u>*met.*</u>.

13. (graduate) Their son has made a lot of money ever since he <u>*graduated*</u> from the university.

14. (arrive) My life has been very different ever since I <u>*arrived*</u> in this country.

1.10

INTERROGATIVE SENTENCES (Questions)

1. *Yes-no* questions in the present perfect tense are formed by putting the subject of a sentence after the auxiliary: ***Have they*** *been happy since their marriage?* ***Has time*** *gone fast since the beginning of the course?*

	Singular		Plural	
First person	have $\left\{\begin{array}{l} \text{I} \\ \text{you} \end{array}\right.$		have $\left\{\begin{array}{l} \text{we} \\ \text{you} \\ \text{they} \end{array}\right\}$ gone	
Second person				
Third person	has $\left\{\begin{array}{l} \text{he} \\ \text{she} \\ \text{it} \end{array}\right\}$ gone			

2. *Always* and *never* follow the subject in *yes-no* questions: *Have **we always** had pollution? Have **you never** been in Europe?*

3. In negative questions, *haven't* or *hasn't* precedes the subject: ***Haven't you*** *eaten anything since last night?* ***Hasn't your father*** *found a job? Why **haven't you** been busy at work?*

4. In formal usage in negative questions, *have (has)* and *not* are not contracted, and *not* follows the subject: *Has **she not** broken her promise to you? Have **I not** done the right thing? Why has **the government not** done more for the poor?*
   Reminder: Negative questions are used to show anger, surprise, or irritation.

5. In *yes-no* answers, *have* or *has* follows the subject of the answer: *Have you been back to your hometown since 1975? Yes, **I have**; No, **I haven't**; Has she always lived here? Yes, **she has**; No, **she hasn't**.*

6. In tag questions, *have* or *has* occurs in the tag endings: *You've been at this school for quite a few months, **haven't you**? She has never studied English, **has she**? John hasn't been sick, **has he**?*

7. To ask for the length of an event that began in the past and has continued to the present, the information words *how long* occur in information questions with the present perfect tense. As in *yes-no* questions, the subject follows *have* or *has*: *How long **have you** known your best friend?* The preposition *for* may precede *how long*, but its use is optional: *(For) how long has he been a teacher? How many* + years, days, etc., also occurs: ***How many years*** *have you been married?* ***How many days*** *has the class been in session?*

1.11

Focus: The Length of an Event

Pronunciation Note: *How long have* sounds like *how long-of; how long has* sounds like *how long-iz* (*longz*). Written contractions of noun subjects and *have* or *has* do not occur; however, *children have* may sound like *children-of; Mary has* may sound like *Marys.*

Supply appropriate past participles in the blanks.

EXAMPLES: a. How many years have your parents <u>been</u> married?
           b. For how long have we <u>known</u> each other?

1. How long has the United States _____ an independent nation?
2. How long has pollution _____ a serious world problem?
3. How many days have they _____ out of town?
4. For how many years has Cuba _____ a socialist government?
5. For how many years have you _____ your best friend?

Now make appropriate information questions with *how long* and *how many*. The following "pretends" will indicate the questions that may be asked.

EXAMPLES: c. Pretend you are talking to a friend about his or her car. *How many years have you had your car?*
           d. Pretend you are talking to a little girl. *How long have you had your doll?*

6. Pretend you are talking to a little boy or girl.
7. Pretend you are talking to someone about his or her best friend.
8. Pretend you are a doctor talking to a patient.
9. Pretend you are a lawyer talking to a client.
10. Pretend you are talking to a person about religion.
11. Pretend you are talking to another student at school.
12. Pretend you are having a conversation about politics.
13. Pretend you are talking to the President.
14. Pretend you are talking to a scientist about the world in general.

Now complete the following sentences.

15. How many years have_____?
16. How many days has _____?
17. For how long have _____?
18. How many weeks has _____?
19. How long_____?
20. For how long _____?
21. How many months _____?

EVENTS AT AN INDEFINITE TIME IN THE PAST

1. Besides expressing the duration of an event from a definite point in the past time to the present, the present perfect tense may also be used to describe an event at an <u>indefinite</u> time in the past: *I **have been** in Europe; She **has studied** French; They'**ve finished** the job.*

2. Even though these events occurred in past time, they are directly related to events in present time because they are the cause (reason) for situations that now exist. We call this relationship the *cause and effect* (reason and situation) relationship. Compare:

Cause (an event at an indefinite time in the past)	Effect (now)
It's rained a lot.	*The streets are all wet.*
I've eaten lunch.	*I'm not hungry now.*
I've spoken to my lawyer.	*I'm not worried about the problem now.*
I've been in Europe.	*I know what it's like.*

3. The present perfect tense is <u>never</u> used for an event at a definite point of time in the past. **Reminder:** The simple past tense is used for an event at a definite point of time in the past. Compare:

Wrong	Correct
*I **have been** there yesterday.*	*I **was** there yesterday.*
*I **have gone** two days ago.*	*I **went** two days ago.*
*She **has done** it last night.*	*She **did** it last night.*

Reminder: Adverbs such as *yesterday* and *ago* may appear in sentences that contain the present perfect tense but only in subordinate clauses (or time phrases) like those introduced by *since: She hasn't felt well **since she got up yesterday morning**; He has lived in Texas **since he graduated from Cornell University three years ago.***

4. Adverbs of indefinite time like *recently, finally,* and *just* are used in verb phrases containing the present perfect tense. Their usual position is following the auxiliary: *The military **has recently** overthrown the government; The mail **has finally** arrived; Her pet bird **has just** died.*

5. *Just* may appear only within a verb phrase, but *recently* and *finally* may appear in the initial or final position as well: ***Recently,** I have made a great deal of money; The children have come home **finally.***
   Punctuation Reminder: When an adverb occurs in initial position, a comma usually follows the word: *Finally, spring has come.*

6. A good response to a sentence like *He has recently finished school* is a question *How recent is recently? Recently* can mean a week ago, a month ago, perhaps a couple of months ago, or possibly even a year ago. The period of time is very indefinite.

7. *Just* is more specific than *recently.* We do not know exactly when the event has taken place, but we know that it has happened close to the present time—for example, *They have just arrived* (they still have on their coats and are talking about the cold weather). When we use *just,* we know that the event has taken place almost right before the moment of speaking.

8. *Finally* means more than just a sense of time; it suggests that we have been anticipating the event, and we are happy or relieved that it has happened: *The war has finally ended, and everyone in the nation is relieved that the soldiers can now come home.*

9. These adverbs also appear in verb phrases containing the simple past tense. When this occurs, adverbial expressions of definite time may follow *just* and *finally: He just got married* **last week;** *They finally arrived* **yesterday;** however, definite adverbs of time never appear with *recently: He recently got out of the hospital; His horse recently won an important race.*

10. When the adverb *ever* occurs in *yes-no* questions with the present perfect tense, it means *at any time in this life: Have you ever (at any time in this life) been in China?*

1.13

GRAMMAR EXERCISE   Name _____ Date _____

Focus: *Yes-No Questions with Ever and Always*

Supply *have* or *has* in the first blank and an appropriate past participle in the second; use past participles made out of the base forms in the following list. Practice *yes-no* answers.

be	cut	eat	keep	ride	see	take	wear
break	do	fall	live	ring	shake	talk	
catch	drive	have	play	rise	swim	tell	

EXAMPLES: a. Have you always kept your word (promise)?
              b. Has the sun always risen in the east?

1. _____ you ever _____ in love?

2. _____ your brother always _____ his homework for the class?

3. _____ you ever _____ a bone (for example, one of your arms)?

4. _____ you ever _____ the President's hand?

5. _____ your neighbor always _____ a Ford car?

6. _____ you ever _____ in the Pacific Ocean?

7. _____ you ever _____ a French film (movie)?

8. _____ the seat of the Catholic Church always _____ in Rome? _____ the Pope ever _____ in the Americas?

9. _____ you ever _____ Japanese food?

10. _____ Washington, D.C., always _____ the capital of the United States? _____ you ever _____ there?

1.13 (Continued)

11. _____ you ever _____ yourself seriously with a knife?

12. _____ you ever _____ a bikini (a brief bathing suit)?

13. _____ your phone ever _____ while you were in the shower?

14. _____ you ever _____ penicillin?

15. _____ you ever _____ on a horse?

16. _____ you ever _____ a serious lie?

17. _____ your teacher ever _____ about Shakespeare?

18. _____ your family always _____ in California?

19. _____ it always _____ hot at the Equator?

20. _____ you ever _____ a Rolls-Royce?

21. _____ you ever _____ a shark (a very big fish)?

22. _____ you ever _____ in an earthquake/a hurricane?

23. _____ you ever _____ a broken heart (disappointment in love)?

24. _____ your brother ever _____ on an important team?

Now complete the sentences.

25. Have you ever _____?

26. Has your father/mother/teacher ever _____?

27. Have your children always _____?

28. Has the community always _____?

29. Has Richard ever _____?

30. Have the students always _____?

31. Have the news media always _____?

32. Has it ever _____?

33. Has the convention ever _____?

34. Have they ever _____?

35. Has your garden ever _____?

1.14

GRAMMAR EXERCISE   Name _____ Date _____

Focus: *Just* in Verb Phrases

Fill in the blanks with *have* (*has*) + *just* + a past participle.

EXAMPLES: a. (get) They've just gotten back from a trip to Tibet, and they have a lot of wonderful photographs to show us.
b. (occur) An earthquake has just occurred somewhere in the Middle East. (hear) I've just heard about it.

1. (make) I _____ a very foolish mistake.

2. (spill) Darn it! I _____ a bottle of ink.

3. (inherit) You won't believe this, but I _____ a great deal of money. (become) I _____ a millionaire.

4. (get) Can you believe it? I _____ a telegram from the President. (give) My secretary _____ it to me.

5. (break) He's extremely upset. His girlfriend _____ her promise to marry him. (tell) He _____ me about it.

6. (hear) I _____ a very funny story about you.

7. (get) I must tell you about the wonderful news I _____ from home.

8. (lose) How terrible! Several people _____ their lives in a fire in a nearby hotel.

9. (meet) He _____ a new girl, and he wants to tell me about her. (enter) She _____ our school.

10. (find) It's hard to believe, but I _____ a hundred-dollar bill on the street. (have) I _____ a stroke of luck. (happen) It _____.

11. (hear) Congratulations! We _____ the news about your most recent success. (tell) Your boss _____ us.

12. (have) His wife _____ a baby, and he's very excited about it. (come) He _____ back from the hospital.

13. (get) Mary and Tom _____ married secretly, and all their friends are surprised. (hear) They _____ about it.

Now complete the sentences.

14. My best friend_____.

15. The rain _____.

16. The sun _____.

17. I'm still sleepy because _____.

18. Hurry up! The class _____.

1.15

GRAMMAR EXERCISE   Name _____ Date _____

Focus: *Finally* in Verb Phrases

Fill in the blanks with *have (has)* + *finally* + a past participle.

EXAMPLES: a. (win) How exciting! My favorite team <u>has finally won</u> a game.
b. (find) At last! I've <u>finally found</u> my wallet. (*At last* means *finally*.)

1. (come) It's about time! It's three o'clock in the morning, but our son _____ _____ home. (*It's about time!* means *finally!*)

2. (become) It's hard to believe, but our cat and dog _____ good friends. (stop) They _____ fighting.

3. (come) At last! The guests _____; now we can have cocktails. (begin) The party _____.

4. (become) It's about time! The weather _____ nice after a long hard winter. (come) Spring _____.

5. (become) After many years of study, their daughter _____ a medical doctor. (graduate) She _____.

6. (find) Bob _____ an interesting job. (come) His long search _____ to an end.

7. (improve) We're very relieved. Our mother's health _____.

8. (finish) It took a long time, but I _____ the project.

9. (get) At last! I _____ a letter from my parents.

10. (be) Fortunately, he _____ able to stop smoking. (break) He _____ his dirty habit.

11. (come) At last! The war _____ to an end.

12. (decide) At the age of seventy-four, my grandfather _____ to retire.

13. (graduate) It's about time! All of our children _____ from the university. (realize) We _____ our dreams.

14. (get) What a surprise! Tom and Marilyn _____ married.

15. (become) After more than twenty years, his father _____. _____ the president of the company.

Now complete the sentences.

16. At last! The movie _____.

17. It's about time! The bus _____.

18. Well, the children _____.

19. Their son/daughter _____.

20. The rain/snow _____.

1.16

GRAMMAR EXERCISE   Name _____ Date _____

Focus: *Recently* in Verb Phrases

Fill in the blanks with *have* (*has*) + *recently* + a past participle.

EXAMPLES: a. (have) Their son has recently had a very serious operation.
             b. (put) She's recently put on a lot of weight. (*To put on weight* means *to gain weight.*)

1. (lose) He _____ a lot of weight. (see) I _____ him, and he looks terrific (wonderful).

2. (develop) A research team at the hospital _____ a new kind of treatment for cancer. (read) I _____ about it.

3. (lose) They _____ their house in a fire, so they're living in a hotel for the time being.

4. (inherit) A friend of mine _____ a great deal of money.

5. (graduate) Their son _____ from Oxford University.

6. (develop) A scientist in my company _____ a new method for collecting solar energy. (receive) He _____ a grant (a sum of money) from the Federal government.

7. (paint) They _____ their house, and it looks wonderful.

8. (read) I _____ a wonderful book about animal life in Africa. (write) The same author _____ a book about insect life.

9. (receive) She _____ an important literary prize.

10. (have) His wife _____ a baby, and he is still bragging (boasting) about it.

11. (quit) He's taking it easy because he _____ his job.

12. (find) We _____ a faster way to get up to our cabin in the mountains. (A *cabin* is a *small house* or *cottage.*)

13. (buy) We _____ a cottage beside a lovely lake.

Now complete the sentences.

14. My mother/father _____.

15. My sister/brother _____.

16. The President/Queen _____.

17. A friend of mine _____.

18. My boss/teacher/roommate _____.

1.17

GRAMMAR EXERCISE   Name _____ Date _____

Focus: Clauses of Reason with *Because*

We often use the present perfect tense in a clause of reason introduced by the subordinate conjunction *because: She's extremely sad **because she's just lost a very old friend.***
Reminder: A *because* clause usually occurs in the final position of a sentence (see above example), but we may also put it in the initial position. When we do this, a comma follows the clause: ***Because we haven't had much rain,*** *all of the flowers in our garden are dying.* Remember that a *because* clause always tells *why:* **Why is he a success?** . . . *because he's worked long and hard.*

Fill in the blanks with *have* (*has*) (+ *not*) + **a past participle.**

EXAMPLES: a. (inherit) He's excited because he <u>has inherited</u> a fortune.
              b. (eat) I don't have an appetite because I<u>'ve eaten</u> lunch.

1. (come) The children are excited because their father _____ home. (have) We're
   all hungry because we _____ our dinner.

2. (find) I'm thrilled because I _____ a wonderful new job. (decide) My present boss
   is angry because I _____ to quit.

3. (score) Everyone is cheering because our team _____ a point.

4. (get) I'm worried because I _____ any news from my parents. (write) Because I
   _____ any letters to them, I haven't received any. (hear) Because they _____
   from me for a long time, they're beginning to get worried.

Now complete the sentences with appropriate *because* **clauses.**

EXAMPLES: c. They're extremely worried <u>because their son has become an alcoholic</u>.

5. I'm in a very good/bad mood today _____.

6. _____, I am very happy/unhappy.

7. S/he's excited _____.

8. _____, my parents are very angry at me.

9. I am worried about a friend of mine _____.

10. He's a failure _____.

11. She's a great success _____.

12. I'm angry at myself_____.

13. I'm hungry/thirsty _____.

14. S/he speaks English well _____.

15. _____, the team is ready.

1.18

ALREADY AND YET

1. When the adverb *already* occurs in a verb phrase containing the present perfect tense, it usually suggests recent to fairly recent time in the past: *They've already gone home* (an hour ago); *My birthday has already passed* (a couple of weeks ago). However, in some circumstances *already* may occur in statements about the distant past: *I don't want to go to Mexico; I've already been there* (fifteen years ago).

2. Like other adverbs (e.g., *just, finally, not*), *already* is inserted between the auxiliary and the main verb: *They've **already had** three children, but she wants one more; They've **already done** their homework, so they can watch TV.*

3. In less formal usage, *already* occurs in the final position of a sentence: *The mailman has come and gone **already**; The children have gone to bed **already**.*

4. The adverb *yet* usually occurs in the final position of a simple sentence or in the final position of a main clause in a complex sentence: *The rain hasn't started **yet**; I haven't made a decision **yet**, but I will soon. Yet* is used in negative verb phrases and *yes-no* questions only. **Note:** In more formal usage, and sometimes informal, one could say: *Rain hasn't **yet** started; I haven't **yet** made a decision.*

5. *Yet* shows expectation (something that we plan to do) and is closely related to a coming event in future time: *We haven't reached the top of the mountain **yet**, but with luck and determination we will soon; Our child hasn't begun to speak **yet**, but he will soon.*

6. *Yet* occurs in *yes-no* questions more frequently than the other adverbs of indefinite time: *Have you had lunch **yet**? Hasn't your team won a game **yet**?* Besides the usual *no* answers, the response *No, not **yet**,* may occur in response to a *yes-no* question.

7. Abridged (shortened) main clauses containing *will, be going to,* and *hope to* often occur in sentences with *yet: We haven't done anything about the problem yet, but we **will*** (do something); *They haven't arrived yet, but they're **going to*** (arrive) soon; *I haven't seen that movie yet, but I **hope to*** (see it).

8. This kind of abridgment also occurs with the verbs *like* and *want: Her boyfriend doesn't like to dance, but she **likes to*** (dance); *I haven't gone to Japan yet, but I **want to*** (go).

1.19

GRAMMAR EXERCISE   Name _____ Date _15.02.1994_

Focus: *Already* in Verb Phrases

Fill in the blanks with *have (has)* + *already* + a past participle.

EXAMPLES: a. (eat) Bob isn't eating with us because he's already eaten.
b. (come/go) She hasn't gotten here yet, but her husband <u>has already come</u> and <u>gone</u>.
Reminder: In compound verbs with the conjunction *and,* the subject, the auxiliary, and the adverb are not repeated after the conjunction.

1. (eat/leave) The guests ___*have already eaten*___ and ___*left*___.

2. (write/send) I ___*have already written*___ and ___*sent*___ the letter.

3. (have) No, thank you, I don't care for another drink because I ___*have already had*___ four. (get) I ___*have gotten*___ a little drunk.

4. (go) Jack is still here, but his wife ___*has already gone*___ home.

5. (see) I don't want to see that movie because I ___*I'v already seen*___ it.

6. (rise) Please let's go home. The sun ___*has already risen*___ and I'm dead tired (very tired). (leave) Most of the other guests ___*have already left*___. (be) We ___*have been*___ here for ten hours.

7. (take) Don't worry about the problem because I ___*have already taken*___ care of it. (speak) I ___*have already spoken*___ to my lawyer about it.

8. (hear) You don't have to tell me about the scandal because I ___*have already heard*___ about it. (be) It ___*was*___ in all the newspapers; (cover) even television ___*has covered*___ it.

9. (speak) I ___*have already spoken*___ to her about the matter, and I'm not going to speak to her about it again.

10. (do) Fortunately, I ___*have already done*___ my homework, so I can go out with you.

11. (have) Bill hasn't taken his vacation yet, but his sister ___*has had*___ one. (come/go) She ___*has already come*___ home and ___*gone*___ back to work.

12. (be) I don't want to go to Rome again on my vacation because I ___*have already been*___ there five times. I want to go some place new.

13. (blossom) It's only the middle of March, but the cherry trees in Washington ___*has already blossomed*___

14. (get) It's only the beginning of October, but it ___*has already gotten*___ cold. (have) We ___*had*___ a few snowfalls.

15. (set) Let's go home. The sun ___*has already set*___ and it's getting late. (leave) Everyone in the office ___*has already left*___ for home.

1.20

GRAMMAR EXERCISE   Name _____ Date _____

Focus: Negative Verb Phrases and *Yet*

Fill in the blanks with *have* (*has*) + *not* + a past participle.

EXAMPLES: a. (catch) I <u>haven't caught</u> a cold this winter, yet, but I will.
b. (get) She <u>hasn't gotten</u> over her cold yet, but she will. (*To get over* can mean *to recover from.*)

1. (get) He _____ over his recent divorce yet, but he will.

2. (arrive) The guests _____ yet, but I expect them any minute. (*Any minute* means *very soon.*)

3. (sit) We _____ down to dinner yet, but we're going to any minute now. (*Now* may be added to *any minute.*)

4. (enter) Their son _____ the army yet, but he wants to.

5. (get) He _____ over his last love affair yet, but he eventually will. (find) He _____ a new girlfriend yet.

6. (see) I _____ that movie yet, but I hope to.

7. (begin) The movie _____ yet, but it will any minute.

8. (call) I _____ my boss yet, but I will in a few minutes.

9. (write) I _____ my parents yet, but I will tomorrow.

10. (go) My headache _____ away yet, but it will because I've taken a few aspirins. (take) They _____ effect yet.

11. (begin) It _____ to rain yet, but it will any minute.

12. (get) I _____ any news from the university about my application yet, but I will any day now.

13. (do) I _____ anything about the problem yet, but I will.

14. (choose) We _____ a name for our new baby yet, but we will by the end of today.

15. (fall) Our enemies _____ yet, but they will soon.

16. (get) They _____ married yet, but they expect to very soon.

17. (set) The sun _____ yet, but it will in a few minutes.

18. (meet) I _____ her new boyfriend yet, but I expect to tonight. (introduce) She _____ him to her family yet, but she's going to soon. (propose) He _____ to her yet, but he wants to. (make) She _____ up her mind yet.

19. (grow) We _____ any tomatoes in our garden yet, but we plan to next summer. (have) We _____ time yet.

20. (deliver) They _____ our new refrigerator yet, but they will any day now.

1.21

GRAMMAR EXERCISE   Name _____ Date _15.02.94_

Focus: *Still and Yet*

A negative response with *yet* frequently follows an affirmative statement with *still: He's still single; he hasn't found a wife yet.*

Fill in the blanks with *have* (*has*) + *not* + a past participle.

EXAMPLES: a. (rise) It's still dark outside; the sun <u>hasn't risen</u> yet.
  b. (make) Our cat and dog are still fighting; they <u>haven't made</u> up yet. (*To make up* means *to become reconciled.*)

1. (make) Jack and Tina are still angry at each other; they _____ up yet.

   (reconcile) They _____ their differences yet, but they will.

2. (make) The actress is still not ready to go on the stage; she _____ up yet.
   (*To make up* can also mean *to apply cosmetics to one's face: Little girls often like to make up with their mothers' cosmetics.*)

3. (make) I still don't want to go home; I _____ up a good excuse to give my parents yet. (*To make up [a story/excuse/alibi] means to invent*—sometimes used meaning *to lie.*)

4. (make) I'm still waiting for my wife; she _____ up yet.

5. (make) I still don't know where I'm going on my vacation; I _____ up my mind yet. (*To make up one's mind* means *to make a decision.*)

6. (get) His mother is still in the hospital; she _____ over her serious illness

   yet. (recover) She _____ yet.

7. (come) We're still waiting for the bus; it _____ yet.

8. (get) He's still very unhappy; he _____ over the loss of his wife yet.

9. (finish) The students are still writing; they _____ the exam yet. (reach)

   They _____ the hard part yet.

10. (hear) He's still worried about his mother; he _____ from her yet. (get)

    He _____ any news yet.

11. (eat) I'm still hungry; I _____ enough yet.

12. (make) I'm still waiting for an answer; they _____ up their minds yet.

    (come) They _____ to a decision yet.

13. (fix) My watch is still broken; they _____ it yet.

14. (come) The leaves are still on the trees; fall _____ yet.

15. (sleep) I'm still tired; I _____ enough yet.

16. (open) The bank is still closed; it _____ yet.

1.22

Focus: *Yes-No Questions with Yet and Already*

Make (aloud and/or in writing) appropriate *yes-no* questions with *yet* or *already*. The "pretends" in the parentheses will indicate the questions that can be asked.

EXAMPLES: a. (Pretend it is six o'clock in the evening.)
                <u>Have you eaten dinner yet?</u>
         b. (Pretend you are at an office at nine o'clock in the morning.)
                <u>Has your boss already gotten to his office?</u>

1. (Pretend it is one o'clock in the afternoon.)

   _____?

2. (Pretend it is 11:30 at night.)

   _____?

3. (Pretend you are at a train station.)

   _____?

4. (Pretend you are at a newsstand. [A *newsstand* is a place to buy newspapers and magazines.])

   _____?

5. (Pretend you are a nurse talking to a doctor.)

   _____?

6. (Pretend it is seven o'clock in the morning.)

   _____?

7. (Pretend you are at a radio and TV repair shop.)

   _____?

8. (Pretend it is in the middle of summer.)

   _____?

9. (Pretend you are giving a party.)

   _____?

10. (Pretend you are standing at the box office of a theater.)

    _____?

11. (Pretend you are talking to the police.)

    _____?

12. (Pretend you are talking to a friend about another friend.)

    _____?

13. (Pretend it is Christmas Eve. [*Christmas Eve* is the evening before Christmas Day.])

    _____?

14. (Pretend you are sitting in a classroom.)

    _____?

1.23

REPEATED EVENTS IN THE PAST

1. A third and frequent use of the present perfect tense is to express events that have taken place once or more than once in past time: *He **has been** married once, but now he's divorced; There **have been** two world wars in this century; Many countries **have become** independent nations since the end of World War II.*

2. When the present perfect tense is used for repeated events in past time, there is the expectation that the event may occur again in future time: *We have gone to Europe three times* (and we expect to go again); *There have been many little wars over the past forty years* (and there will probably be more); *She's fallen in love only twice* (and she will probably fall in love again.)

3. When we express repeated events in past time with the simple past tense, there is no expectation that the event will be repeated. Compare:

The Simple Past Tense	The Present Perfect Tense
There were many national revolutions in Latin America during the nineteenth century. (the nineteenth century is over)	*There have been many national revolutions since the beginning of the twentieth century.* (the twentieth century hasn't ended yet)
I saw two movies last month. (last month is over)	*I have seen two movies this month.* (this month hasn't ended yet)

Note: When *never* is used with the simple past tense, the expectation is reversed. *I **never** went to Europe* implies you will continue not to go; *I **have never gone** to Europe* implies there is still a chance you will go.

4. The information words *how many times* or *how many* + nouns may occur in information questions when we ask about repeated events in past time: *How many revolutions has Bolivia had? How many times have you been in China? How many times has the earth revolved around the sun? How many cookies have you eaten today?*

1.24

GRAMMAR EXERCISE   Name _____ Date _____

Focus: Repeated Events in the Past

Fill in the blanks with *have* (*has*) + a past participle. Supply appropriate words in the parentheses. Do not use negative forms in this exercise.

EXAMPLES: a. (be) There <u>have been (two)</u> major world wars in this century. Will there be another one?
  b. (have) The United States <u>has had</u> about 40 presidents.

1. (be) Jane _____ married only once.

2. (live) I _____ in (_____) countries.

3. (have) My mother _____ (_____) children.

4. (see) I _____ (_____) movies this month.

5. (go) She _____ (not) _____ to the dentist (_____ times) this year.

6. (ring) My telephone _____ at least fifty times since I got to work this morning (*At least* means *the minimum of.*)

7. (have) His father _____ at least thirty jobs since he started working.

8. (have) Steve _____ (_____) jobs since he started working.

9. (fall) I _____ (never) _____ in love once/twice/(_____ times).

10. (be) He _____ (never) _____ in Europe (_____).

11. (be) The President of the United States _____ (never) _____ in Argentina/France/England (_____).

12. (be) One of the most beautiful women in the world _____ married (_____).

13. (be) One of the most famous men in the world _____ in my native country (_____).

14. (be) There _____ very little rainfall recently.

15. (send) I _____ (_____) letters this month.

16. (deliver) Dr. Smith _____ around two thousand babies since he started practicing medicine twenty-seven years ago.

17. (have) My best friend and I _____ many good times together, and we expect to have more.

18. (do) We _____ (_____) exercises in this chapter.

19. (make) Since the beginning of this course, I _____ (_____) new friends.

20. (see/do) Since I arrived in this country, I _____ and _____ many interesting things.

1.25

GRAMMAR EXERCISE   Name _____ Date _____

Focus: Repeated Events in the Past

Supply *have* or *has* in the first blank and an appropriate past participle in the second, using the verbs in the following list.

attend	borrow	fall	fly	lend	receive	see
be	break	feed	go	lose	ride	speak
bet	do	find	have	make	rob	win

EXAMPLES: a. How many presidents <u>has</u> the United States <u>had</u>?
   b. How many times <u>have</u> you <u>been</u> to Europe?

1. How many times _____ you _____ in love?

2. How many times _____ that fellow _____ a woman's heart?

3. How many times _____ [supply name] _____ _____ married?

4. How many times _____ you _____ to the doctor this year?

5. How many countries _____ you _____ in?

6. How many times _____ you _____ on Pan American?

7. How many trips _____ your father _____ around the world?

8. How many jobs _____ you _____ since you started working?

9. How many academic degrees (e.g., *B.A., M.A., Ph.D.*) _____ you _____? How

   many schools _____ you _____?

10. How many exercises _____ we _____ in this chapter?

11. How many houses _____ the thief _____?

12. How many times _____ s/he _____ money?

13. How many times _____ you _____ sugar from your neighbor?

14. How many times _____ your friend _____ money in the lottery?

15. How many times _____ you _____ ice skating?

16. How many times _____ your sister _____ money to you?
    Note: We *borrow from* and we *lend to*.

17. How many times _____ you _____ money on a horse?

18. How many times _____ Alice _____ her earrings?

19. How many times _____ the President of the United States _____ in your native

    country? How many times _____ you _____ him?

20. How many dogs, cats, or birds _____ you _____ in your lifetime?

21. How many movies _____ Jan _____ this month?

22. How many times _____ your boss _____ to his laywer about the problem?

23. How many times _____ you _____ on a horse?

24. How many times _____ Kim _____ the cat today?

1.26

Focus: Irregular Past Participles

Fill in the blanks with *have* (*has*) + a past participle.

EXAMPLES: a. (throw) <u>Have</u> you ever <u>thrown</u> a party for a hundred people? (*To throw a party* means *to give a party.*)

b. (make) <u>Have</u> you ever <u>made</u> a bet on a game.

1. (blow) Darn it! One of our tires _____ out.

2. (hide) Where _____ you _____ your money?

3. (bite) _____ a dog ever _____ you? (sting) _____ a bee ever _____ you?

4. (freeze) How many pounds of meat _____ you _____?

5. (forbid) Why _____ your father _____ you to go to the party?

6. (lend) _____ your bank recently _____ money to the government?

7. (find) It's about time! I _____ my shoes under my bed.

8. (bet/won) How many times _____ you _____ and _____ money on a long shot? (A *long shot* is a bet made at and against great odds, as in a horse race, with only a slight chance of winning.)

9. (throw) Why _____ the baby suddenly _____ up? Is she sick? (*To throw up* means *to vomit.*)

10. (grow) _____ you ever _____ roses in your garden?

11. (hold) _____ your teacher ever _____ the class in the park?

12. (hang) Where _____ your father _____ up his jacket?

13. (hit) How many homeruns _____ your favorite player _____ this season. (make) How many fouls _____ he _____?

14. (fight) _____ your favorite boxer ever _____ with the world champion?

15. (feed) _____ you always _____ your dog that kind of food?

16. (understand) _____ your parents always _____ your problems?

17. (beat) At last! My favorite team _____ finally _____ its most important rival. (win) It _____ finally _____ a really big game. (lose) For a change, it _____ not _____.

18. (sing) _____ your favorite soprano ever _____ for the Metropolitan Opera Company in New York?

19. (grind) _____ you _____ up the coffee/meat/chicken yet? (*To grind up* means *to grind completely.*)

20. (hurt) His recent actions _____ his parents' feelings.

21. (begin) Hurry up! The movie _____ already _____.

22. (keep) _____ your boyfriend always _____ his word?

1.27

THE PRESENT PERFECT CONTINUOUS TENSE

1. To form the PRESENT PERFECT CONTINUOUS TENSE, we use *have* and *been* (as a second auxiliary) and a present participle as a main verb. *Have* occurs as an *-s* form in the third person singular. *Not* is inserted between *have* and *been* in negative verb phrases.

	Singular		Plural	
First person	I	} have (not) been going	we	} have (not) been going
Second person	you		you	
Third person	he		they	
	she	} has (not) been going		
	it			

2. In *yes-no* and information questions, a subject follows *have:* **Have you** *been working on any interesting projects lately? How long* **have you** *been studying English?*

3. The form is used to emphasize the duration of an event that began at a definite point of time in the past and has continued to the present and possibly into the future: *She has been studying English* **for several years;** *It's been raining hard* **since last night.**

4. Also, we may use the form for repeated events in the past: *We've been going to* **a lot of interesting places** *recently; They've been going* **to the theater a lot** *this month.*

5. Sometimes, the form is used to express a temporary situation: *They've been living* (or *are living*) *in a hotel for the time being; I've been using* (or *am using*) *John's typewriter temporarily.*

6. *Just* and *recently* may occur in verb phrases with the present perfect continuous tense: *I've* **just** *(recently) been talking to the police about the matter;* however, *never, already, finally,* and *how many times* never occur with the form.

7. For expressing the duration of an event, the present perfect tense and its continuous form are essentially interchangeable; the continuous form only emphasizes the duration: *They have been living* (or *have lived*) *in Rome since 1971; I have been smoking* (or *have smoked*) *since I was sixteen; I have been driving* (or *have driven*) *for a long time.*

8. As in the present continuous tense, nonaction verbs such as *be, cost, need, prefer,* and *want,* etc., do not usually occur in the present perfect continuous tense; however, when we express a temporary feeling or action, a nonaction verb occurs as a main verb in a phrase: *This vacation* **has been costing** *a lot* (but *our vacations* **have always cost** *a lot*); *I've* **been wanting** *to tell you the secret ever since I heard it last week* (but *I* **have always wanted** *to travel around the world*).

9. *Have* does not occur as a main verb in the present perfect continuous tense when it means possession only (*I* **have had** *my car for three years*). However, the verb occurs idiomatically with certain nouns: *I have been having a lot of* **luck** *lately; He's been having* **trouble** *with his boss; They've been having* **problems** *with their son; We've been having a good (bad)* **time** *on this vacation; We've been having a lot of* **parties** *recently; We've been having very cold* **weather** *this year; She's been having private English* **lessons.**

1.27 (Continued)

10. The expressions *so far, up to now,* and *until now* are used in sentences containing verb phrases in the present perfect (continuous) tense. They usually occur at the end of a sentence, but they are sometimes put at the beginning and followed by a comma: *We've been enjoying ourselves on this vacation **so far;** **So far,** we've been having wonderful weather;* ***Up to now,** everything has been great.*

11. *Now* (meaning *so far*) is also used with the present perfect (continuous) tense: *They've been living in Paris for seven years **now** (so far); He's been at the university for three years **now** (so far).*

SPELLING BEE (CONTEST)

Transform the base forms in the following list into present participles.

EXAMPLES: a. do <u>doing</u>
             b. try <u>trying</u>

1. carry _____
2. lie _____
3. begin _____
4. hit _____
5. stop _____
6. die _____
7. stay _____
8. run _____
9. get _____
10. cry _____
11. drip _____
12. beg _____
13. omit _____
14. leave _____

1.28

GRAMMAR EXERCISE   Name _____ Date 22.02.94

Focus: The Present Perfect Continuous Tense

Fill in the blanks with *have* (*has*) + *been* + a present participle.

EXAMPLES: a. (wait) I've been waiting for my wife for more than an hour, and she hasn't shown up yet. (*To show up* can mean *to arrive.*)

b. (have) They have been having a lot of problems with their son lately.

1. (wear) Our daughter _____ lipstick since she was sixteen.

2. (rain) It _____ steadily for three days now.

3. (take) I _____ care of my neighbors' cats while they're away. (feed) I _____ them twice a day.

4. (have) We _____ a lot of problems with our new car lately. (burn) It _____ too much gas.

5. (worry) Everyone in the world _____ about the situation in the Middle East for years. (happen) A lot of things _____ there recently.

6. (play/win) We _____ cards for the past couple of hours, and everyone except me _____ money so far.

7. (fight) Dick and Janet _____ with each other ever since the day they were married.

8. (wait) She's angry because her boyfriend hasn't shown up yet, and she _____ for more than three hours.

9. (talk) He _____ about me behind my back, and I don't like it. (spread) He _____ rumors about me.

10. (work) We _____ on a lot of interesting projects lately.
    Note: We *work on* projects, but we *do* work or a job.

11. (have) We _____ beautiful weather this month so far.

12. (study) Our daughter _____ at the university for three years now.

13. (get) The children _____ on my nerves. (make) They _____ too much noise. (*To get on one's nerves* means *to make one nervous.*)

Now complete the sentences.

14. I/you/my father _____.

15. My teacher/doctor _____.

16. S/he _____.

1.29

GRAMMAR EXERCISE   Name _____ Date _____

Focus: The Present Perfect Continuous Tense

Fill in the blanks with *have* (*has*) + *not* + *been* + a present participle.

EXAMPLES: a. (have) She <u>hasn't been having</u> much luck in her new job.
              b. (work) She <u>hasn't been working</u> hard enough.
              Reminder: *Hard enough* means *with enough interest* or *effort.*

1. (feel) I'm tired because I _____ well lately.

2. (have) We _____ any problems with our car so far.

3. (go) She _____ with anyone for a long time. (*To go with someone*
   means *to have a romantic relationship with someone: She's been **going with her boss** for
   some time now.*)

4. (have) Unfortunately, I _____ much luck in the lottery lately.

5. (go) The weather hasn't been very nice lately, so we _____ to the
   beach much.

6. (make/try) My company _____ much money for the past couple of
   years because it _____ hard enough.

7. (get/study) He _____ good grades on his tests for the course because
   he _____ hard enough.

8. (get/send) I _____ any letters lately because I _____
   _____ any. I haven't had the time.

9. (go) He _____ with anyone since he broke up (ended his relationship)
   with Janet.

10. (sleep) I'm tired because I _____ enough lately.

11. (take) The patient _____ penicillin for several days now. (get)
    However, his condition _____ worse.

12. (work) I haven't been able to listen to the weather forecasts because my radio _____
    _____. My TV _____, either.

13. (feel) My grandfather _____ well lately.

14. (win/practice) Our team _____ any games for a long time because it
    _____ hard enough.

15. (live) His mother and father _____ together for quite a few years
    now. (speak) They _____ to each other for years.

16. (think) You're making mistakes because you _____ hard enough.

17. (ride) Chris _____ for several days now, and she misses her horse.

1.30

GRAMMAR EXERCISE   Name _____ Date _____

       Focus: *Yes-No and Information Questions*

Fill in the blanks with present participles.

EXAMPLES: a. (do) Well, hello! How are you? What have you been <u>doing</u> lately?
              b. (take) What kind of medicine has the patient been <u>taking</u>?

   1. (feel) How have you been _____ since your operation?

   2. (take) Who has been _____ care of your children?

   3. (do) Why haven't you been _____ your homework for the class? (waste) Haven't you

       been _____ your time?
       Pronunciation Note: (a) *What have* sounds like *what-of;* (b) *How have* sounds like *how-of;*
       (c) *Who has* sounds like *hooze;* (d) *Who have* sounds like *who-of.*
       Reminder: *Haven't you* sounds like *haven't-chew.*

   4. (play) Why hasn't your team been _____ more games this season?

   5. (lose) How much money have you been _____ on this new project? (make) Why

       haven't you been _____ any?

Now supply present or past participles in the blanks.

   6. (do) What has the government been _____ about the problem?

   7. (explain) Why hasn't your lawyer _____ the problem to you?

   8. (live) Where are you _____ for the time being?

Now practice making appropriate questions in response to the following "pretends." Use the present perfect (continuous) tense only.

   9. Pretend you are talking to a friend about his or her job.
  10. Pretend you are discussing the weather with somebody.
  11. Pretend you are talking to your teacher about his or her professional career.
  12. Pretend you are talking to a doctor/lawyer/teacher/scientist.
  13. Pretend you are talking to a taxi driver/secretary/architect.
  14. Pretend you are talking to a friend about his or her new romance.
  15. Pretend you are talking to a writer/dancer/painter/actor.
  16. Pretend you are a newspaper reporter, and you are talking to a well-known movie star.
  17. Pretend you are talking to yourself about your school/your job.
  18. Pretend you are talking to your neighbor about a new recipe.
       Pronunciation Note: *Have I* following information words like *how long, what,* etc., may
       sound like *of-I.*

1.31

     Name _____ Date _____

        Focus: *Situation* and *Reason*

Do the exercise aloud, and/or on a separate piece of paper write appropriate statements to follow the situations and remarks listed below. Use only the present perfect tense (or the present perfect continuous tense when appropriate).

EXAMPLES: a. He doesn't speak English very well. *He's never studied it.*
             b. I can't go out with you tonight. *I haven't finished my homework yet.*
             c. The garden looks beautiful. *It has been raining a lot lately.*

1. I'm hungry/thirsty/tired.
2. Unfortunately, all the plants in the garden are dying.
3. S/he feels a little foolish.
4. Everyone in Mary's family is relieved.
5. Our neighbors are going to get a divorce.
6. All of the flags in the nation are at half mast. (A flag at *half mast* is a flag halfway up a flagpole.)
7. My mouth and throat are unusually dry.
8. S/he's going to get the best grade in the course.
9. Everything in our house is damp. (*Damp* means *wet.*)
10. My apartment is messy and dirty. (*Messy* means *not neat.*)
11. Sh! The curtain is rising. (Pretend you are at a theater.)
12. We are waiting for the teacher.
13. Everyone is cheering/applauding/booing/whistling.
14. There is a long line of people standing at the corner.
15. No, I'm sorry, I don't know the temperature outside.
16. S/he's very anxious and nervous.
17. I'm in a wonderful mood, and I must tell you about it.
18. The newspaper says the man will go to prison for life.
19. I'm beginning to get bored/worried.
20. No one is at home next door.
21. Everyone at school/work is excited/worried/surprised/angry/relieved.
22. S/he's angry at him/her.
23. I'm not going to take a vacation this year.
24. No thank you, I don't care for anything else to eat/drink. (*I don't care for* means *I don't like* or *I don't want.*)
25. S/he's going to enter the university soon.
26. Everybody is laughing/crying.
27. All the trees in the park are blossoming/falling.
28. I must go to the bank right away.
29. Everyone understands the present perfect tense much better now.

1.32

GRAMMAR EXERCISE

Name *Miryang S.* Date *8.02.94*

Focus: The Simple Past Tense versus the Present Perfect Tense

Fill in the blanks with verbs in the simple past tense or the present perfect tense.

EXAMPLES: a. (teach) He <u>taught</u> English in Hong Kong from 1974 to 1976.
b. (teach) He <u>has taught</u> at the University of Hawaii since 1976.

1. (learn) We <u>*have learned*</u> a lot of new things in the class so far.

2. (go) They <u>*went*</u> to Texas on their vacation last year.

3. (speak) She <u>*has spoken*</u> French since she was a little girl.

4. (speak) I <u>*spoke*</u> to my lawyer about the problem a couple of days ago. (take) He <u>*has taken*</u> care of it since then.

5. (get) Everyone <u>*got*</u> to work late yesterday morning.

6. (have) We <u>*have had*</u> a lot of luck with our car until now.

7. (have) We <u>*had*</u> a good time when we were in Iran.

8. (be) Her childhood <u>*has been*</u> a very happy one so far.

9. (spend) My father <u>*spent*</u> his childhood on a farm in Kansas.

10. (begin) Sh! The movie <u>*has begun*</u>. It <u>*began*</u> a few minutes ago.

11. (ring) The bell <u>*has rung*</u>, and the class is beginning.

12. (live) They <u>*have lived*</u> in San Francisco since they moved to California a couple of years ago. They <u>*lived*</u> in Seattle, Washington, before they made their move.

13. (be) They <u>*have been*</u> very happy with their new home ever since. (visit) I <u>*visited*</u> them on my last vacation.

14. (be) There <u>*was*</u> a good musical program on television last night. There <u>*has been*</u> quite a few lately.

15. (accept) At last! My girlfriend <u>*has accepted*</u> my proposal.

16. (know) Dick and Sally <u>*have known*</u> each other ever since they were in elementary school. I <u>*knew*</u> both of them then.

17. (have) Our son and daughter-in-law <u>*have had*</u> three children.

18. (break) He <u>*broke*</u> his leg in a skiing accident last winter.

19. (win) My favorite team <u>*has won*</u> three games out of seven so far.

20. (win) They <u>*won*</u> every game last year.

21. (be) The weather <u>*has been*</u> very hot lately.

22. (take) I <u>*have taken*</u> three courses in French so far.

23. (have) He <u>*has had*</u> many jobs since he graduated from school.

24. (be) Last summer <u>*was*</u> the hottest summer on record.

GRAMMAR EXERCISE   Name _____ Date _22.02.94_

        Focus: Reviewing Verb Tenses

Fill in the blanks with verbs in the simple present tense or the present perfect tense. Do not use negative forms.

EXAMPLES: a. (live) They <u>live</u> in Montreal.
            b. (live) They <u>have lived</u> in Montreal since they immigrated.

1. (work) His father _____ from nine to five every day.

2. (work) He _____ for the same company since he was eighteen.

3. (go) Bill _____ to the movies once in a while (occasionally).

4. (be) The weather _____ good until now.

5. (have) A sailor often _____ a girlfriend in more than one port.

6. (win) Our team _____ the game, and everyone is cheering.

7. (go) Sh! The baby _____ to sleep.

8. (take) He _____ a nap every afternoon.

9. (enjoy) I _____ a cocktail from time to time (occasionally).

10. (be) Grandpa _____ asleep for several hours now (so far).

11. (have) My boss _____ three wives.

12. (meet) I _____ that woman at parties from time to time.

Now the present continuous tense may also be appropriate.

EXAMPLES: c. (do) We <u>are doing</u> an exercise now.

13. (do) I _____ my homework for the class already.

14. (do) She usually _____ her homework in the library.

15. (live) Bob and Gloria _____ in a hotel for the time being.

16. (be) The formula for water _____ H_2O. There _____ no change in the formula since it was formulated many years ago.

17. (work) Bill occasionally _____ on Sunday. He _____ today.

Now the past or past continuous tense may also be appropriate.

EXAMPLES: d. (do) I <u>did</u> my homework last night.
            e. (do) When you called me last night, I <u>was doing</u> my homework.

18. (go) We _____ to church every Sunday.

19. (go) They _____ to Europe five times in the last three years.

20. (go) I _____ to work on the bus temporarily.

21. (rise/wake) The sun _____ just as I _____ up yesterday morning.

22. (meet) I _____ a very interesting person at the last meeting.

1.34

GRAMMAR EXERCISE

Focus: Reviewing the Simple Present Tense

Using the following "pretends" as a guide, make up, on a separate piece of paper, appropriate information questions in the simple present tense.

EXAMPLES: a. Pretend you are talking to your teacher about his or her life.
How often do you teach? What kind of car do you have?
b. Pretend you are talking to someone about food.
What kind of food do you like? How often do you eat Chinese food?

1. Pretend you are a newspaper reporter interviewing a famous baseball player, a movie star, or a world-famous scientist.
2. Pretend you are talking to a friend about his/her wife/husband.
3. Pretend you are talking to a friend about his/her daily schedule.
4. Pretend you are shopping at a department store.
5. Pretend you are talking to someone about different members of his or her family.
6. Pretend you are lost and you are asking for directions.
7. Pretend you are angry at someone.
8. Pretend you are talking to someone you have just met.

1.35

GRAMMAR EXERCISE   Name _____ Date _____

Focus: Reviewing the Simple Past Tense

Make up appropriate information questions in the simple past tense.

EXAMPLES: a. Pretend you are talking to a friend about yesterday.
What did you do yesterday? Where were you last night?
b. Pretend you are talking to a friend who is sick in the hospital.
How did you break your leg?

1. Pretend you are talking to a friend about his/her last vacation.
2. Pretend you are interviewing an important politician.
3. Pretend you are a mother or father, and you are talking to one of your children.
4. Pretend you are talking about a football/soccer/basketball game.
5. Pretend you are talking to a woman about her former husband.
6. Pretend you are talking to yourself about your past mistakes.
7. Pretend you are talking to one of the richest people in the world.
8. Pretend you are talking to a notorious criminal.
9. Pretend you are talking to your teacher about his or her professional career. Pretend you are the teacher.
10. Pretend you are angry at someone in your class.
11. Pretend you are talking to the ghost of Napoleon Bonaparte/William Shakespeare/Mao Tse-tung/Che Guevara/Christopher Columbus/Adolf Hitler/Romeo/Martin Luther/Joan of Arc.

1.36

GRAMMAR EXERCISE   Name _____ Date _____

Focus: Reviewing Tag Questions

Supply appropriate tag endings in the blanks. **Reminder:** When the statement in a tag question is positive, the tag ending is negative: *She's gone, hasn't she?* When the statement is negative, the tag ending is positive: *She hasn't gone, has she?* During the exercise, practice using the down intonation pattern: *hasn't she?*

EXAMPLES: a. You'll never be a millionaire, <u>will you</u>?
             b. They've left for the beach, <u>haven't they</u>?
             c. She has to study hard, <u>doesn't she</u>?
             d. It's not cold outside today, <u>is it</u>?

1. You've never been in Hawaii, _____?

2. She's not going to have to take another course, _____?

3. She shouldn't smoke, _____?

4. He's had many different kinds of jobs, _____?

5. He's an engineer for a government agency, _____?

6. Bob and Mary have to go home now, _____?

7. Bill and Henry have gone, _____?

8. She's recently been ill, _____?

9. There's something cooking on the stove, _____?

10. You had a good time at the game, _____?

11. It'll be cold tomorrow, _____?

12. He's always lived by himself, _____?

13. He's never on time to work, _____?

14. There were a lot of people at the concert, _____?

15. I'm going to be with you tomorrow night, _____?
    Reminder: *Am I not?* is formal; *Aren't I?* is informal.

16. Mary had to cook dinner, _____?

17. John has had several operations this year, _____?

18. We've studied a lot of things so far, _____?

19. You weren't at the last meeting, _____?

20. They've never had a child, _____?

21. I'll be seeing you tomorrow, _____?

22. You can type well, _____?

23. I'm not pronouncing your name correctly, _____?

24. She hasn't been enjoying herself lately, _____?

25. I should do something about the problem at work, _____?

26. He hurt himself in the accident, _____?

27. You couldn't be cruel to animals, _____?

1.37

GRAMMAR EXERCISE　　　　　　　　Name ＿＿＿＿＿＿＿＿＿＿ Date ＿＿＿＿＿＿

Focus: Reviewing *Too, Either, And,* and *But*

Supply appropriate words in the blanks.

EXAMPLES:　a.　You'll never make a million dollars, and I <u>won't either</u>.
　　　　　　　b.　He can't speak English, but she <u>can</u>.

1.　I don't particularly care for travel, but my wife ＿＿＿＿＿＿.

2.　I should vote for her in the elections, and you ＿＿＿＿＿＿.

3.　She'll be at the meeting, and her husband ＿＿＿＿＿＿.

4.　She cut class, and I ＿＿＿＿＿＿. (*To cut class* means *not to attend a scheduled class at school.*)

5.　I've never been there, but everyone else in my family ＿＿＿＿＿＿.

6.　Life without love isn't easy, and life with love ＿＿＿＿＿＿.

7.　We have a good reason to complain about the problem, but they ＿＿＿＿＿＿.

8.　I've already sent out my Christmas cards, and he ＿＿＿＿＿＿.

9.　She's not been well lately, and her husband ＿＿＿＿＿＿.

10.　The city has a lot of pollution, but the country ＿＿＿＿＿＿.

11.　I speak with a foreign accent, and she ＿＿＿＿＿＿.

1.38

GRAMMAR EXERCISE

Focus: Reviewing *So* and *Neither*

Supply appropriate words in the blanks.

EXAMPLES:　a.　I couldn't kill a defenseless animal, and <u>neither could</u> you.
　　　　　　　b.　She has to work on Sundays, and <u>so does</u> her husband.

1.　He doesn't like to travel, and ＿＿＿＿＿＿ his wife.

2.　I've never been late to work, and ＿＿＿＿＿＿ you.

3.　I have to do a lot of homework, and ＿＿＿＿＿＿ everyone else.

4.　A nice house isn't cheap, and ＿＿＿＿＿＿ a nice apartment.

5.　Their daughter hasn't graduated yet, and ＿＿＿＿＿＿ their son.

6.　I made a few mistakes in the last test, and ＿＿＿＿＿＿ the others.

7.　I must take care of my health, and ＿＿＿＿＿＿ you.

8.　I should stop smoking, and ＿＿＿＿＿＿ she.

9.　He couldn't go to the party last night, and ＿＿＿＿＿＿ his wife.

10.　I'm not having lunch today, and ＿＿＿＿＿＿ my boss.

1.39

        Focus: Contrasting the Present (Continuous) Tense, the Past (Continuous) Tense, the Future (Continuous) Tense (or *Be Going to*), and the Present Perfect (Continuous) Tense.

Supply appropriate verb phrases (affirmative or negative) in the blanks.

EXAMPLES: a. (begin) This exercise has begun.
                b. (begin) It is beginning now.

1. (do) I _____ my homework yet.

2. (be) My parents _____ here two weeks from today.

3. (shine) When I got up, the sun _____.

4. (go) She _____ to the doctor once a year for a physical.

5. (wear) When I graduate, I _____ a black robe.

6. (exist) The earth _____ for millions of years.

7. (go) We _____ anywhere special last weekend.

8. (work) She _____ for an airline company temporarily.

9. (have) We _____ a wonderful vacation in France in 1975.

10. (listen) Sh! Someone _____ to our conversation.

11. (see) I _____ that movie yet, but I want to.

12. (make) I _____ only a few mistakes in the last quiz.

13. (sit) Nobody _____ in the room when I came in.

14. (be) No one _____ there when I get home tomorrow night.

15. (begin) Look! It _____ to snow.

16. (buy) I _____ anything at the store yesterday.

17. (live) My parents _____ in Florida since my father retired.

18. (live) Our son _____ in Germany until he gets out of the army. (be) He _____ in the army since he was twenty-two.

19. (dance) Everyone _____ when I got to the party.

20. (rain) It _____ for several days now.

21. (feel) The patient _____ well lately.

22. (speak) He sometimes forgets *-s* forms when he _____.

23. (defend) We _____ our city until our last man falls.

24. (eat) Don't call at six tomorrow night because we _____.

25. (know) He _____ anything about the realities of life.

26. (take) The plane _____ off at seven o'clock tomorrow evening.

27. (tell) She _____ me anything about the situation since last week. (have) And she _____ much to say at that time.

GRAMMAR EXERCISE   Name _____ Date _____

Focus: Reviewing Prepositions

Supply appropriate prepositions in the blanks.

about	at	for	into	on	to
above	during	in	of	since	under

EXAMPLES: a. My boss was sitting at his desk when I got to work.
b. We arrived in Paris in early morning.
c. We arrived at the airport at 7:30 in the morning.
   Reminder: We arrive *in* a city or a town. We arrive *at* a place such as a school, an office, or a station.

1. Many people couldn't believe it when man landed _____ the moon. Everyone _____ the world was thrilled _____ that moment.

2. Look _____ all the birds _____ the sky.

3. The best location _____ a business is _____ the middle _____ town.

4. We haven't been _____ Europe _____ 1974.

5. You'll find your gloves _____ the bottom drawer _____ the desk.

6. They've been living _____ 495 Park Avenue _____ about ten years.

7. When I came _____ the room, no one was here.

8. His father owns a shop _____ Fifth Avenue.

9. I have just recently read an interesting article _____ the *New York Times*. The article was _____ elephants in India.

10. My mother first met my father _____ an elevator.

11. There are a lot _____ ships _____ the bottom _____ the ocean.

12. We arrived _____ London _____ the 25th of April and left _____ the first day _____ May.

13. He came _____ the United States _____ 1973. He went back _____ Argentina _____ May 16, 1975.

14. They've been living _____ a hotel _____ the time being.

15. There was a sudden thunderstorm while they were _____ their way _____ the top _____ the mountain.

16. I ran _____ an old friend of mine while I was shopping. (*To run into someone* means *to meet someone by accident*.)

17. He hasn't felt well ever _____ his operation.

18. The people _____ the apartment _____ ours are very noisy.

19. Your name is _____ the top _____ this page.

20. I never like to sit _____ the first row _____ a movie theater.

1.41

HAVE GOT

1. The verb phrase *have got* is used idiomatically in the present perfect tense to show possession in the same way that we use the verb *have: I **have got** (have) a slight temperature; She **has got** (has) eleven children.*
    Note: The past participle *gotten* never occurs in this form.

2. The form is very informal and does not ordinarily occur in formal writing. Because of its informality, *have* (*has*) and subject pronouns most often occur in a contracted form: ***I've got** a secret; **She's got** a problem with her daughter.*

3. Negative verb phrases with *have got* are often heard: *I **haven't got** time to fool around at school; He **hasn't got** much money in the bank, but he's a happy man; They **haven't got** a car, but they're getting one soon.*

4. *Yes-no* and information questions with *have got* sometimes occur: *Have you got time to help me with this project? How much money have you got in your pocket?* However, the use of *have got* in questions is more frequent in British usage; a North American (particularly in the United States) is more likely to say: ***Do you have** time to help me with this project? How much money **do you have** in your pocket?*

5. We cannot show possession with *have got* in past time; however, we may express possession with *have got* for the future: *I've got a dentist appointment **tomorrow**; I've got a date for the dance **next Saturday night**.*
    Pronunciation Note: *Got a* sounds like *gotta* when we are speaking very quickly.
    Reminder: Never use the past participle *gotten* in this form.
    Note: *Have got to* + a base form for expressing necessity is discussed in the chapter on modal auxiliaries.

1.42

GRAMMAR EXERCISE   Name _____ Date _____

Focus: Using *Have Got* to Show Possession

Fill in the blanks with *have* (*has*) (+ *not*) + *got.*

EXAMPLES: a. We've <u>got</u> the desire to speak and write English well.
            b. I <u>haven't got</u> any money left in my bank account.

1. _____ you _____ the time by any chance?

2. She _____ any time to enjoy herself.

3. I _____ a wonderful idea; let's get married right away.

4. He _____ any imagination.

5. We _____ enough bread to make sandwiches.

6. How many brothers and sisters _____ you _____?

1.42 (Continued)

7. They _____ any money in the bank, and they don't care. (*Don't care* means *don't mind* or *it doesn't make any difference.* Do not confuse *don't care* with *don't care for,* which means *don't like* or *don't want.*)

8. I _____ a great suggestion; let's take a break.

9. _____ your sister _____ any children?

10. You _____ any children, have you?

11. We _____ the time to complete the project, but we _____ the equipment.

12. I _____ a problem with my lawyer, and he _____ one with his. You _____ a lawyer, have you?

13. She _____ a British accent, hasn't she?

14. I'm very lucky because I _____ any financial worries.

15. They _____ five sons, but they _____ a daughter.

16. S/he is very upset because s/he _____ a problem with his/her Husband/wife. They _____ a good understanding.

17. Excuse me, _____ you _____ a match?

18. I _____ a secret, and I'm not going to tell anyone.

19. He _____ a lot of good ideas, but he's lazy.

20. She _____ a very boring job, but she _____ the time to look for a new one.

21. They _____ a brand new (very new) car, but it isn't working well. They _____ a lemon (a bad product).

22. We _____ time to do another exercise, have we?

23. How much money _____ you _____? _____ you _____ a dime?

24. _____ we _____ time to take a little break before we go on to the next exercise?

1.43

Focus: Reviewing Information Words as Subjects

Reminder: When an information word(s) is the subject of an information question, the usual question form does not occur: *Who invented the electric light bulb?* (but *When did Edison invent it?*); *What happened to the dog?* (but *Where did the dog go?*); *How many people came to the party?* (but *How many people did you invite?*).

1.43 (Continued)

Fill in the blanks with appropriate information words.

EXAMPLES: a. <u>Who</u> gave you your watch?
b. <u>What</u> happened to you last night?

1. _____ people went to the concert?

2. _____ people live in your hometown?

3. _____ has happened in the world this week?

4. _____'s got a long tail, is rather small, and likes to eat cheese?

5. _____ animal is the tallest in the world?

6. _____ ate my sandwich?

7. _____'s done it?

8. _____'s happened to my pen? _____'s taken it?

9. _____ people live in your house?

10. _____ lives with you?

1.44

GRAMMAR EXERCISE   Name _____ Date _____

Focus: *How Come*

How come means *why*. It precedes the subject in questions (usually negative) in informal usage: ***How come*** *he hasn't done anything for his family?* However, note that with *how come* the subject precedes the verb, but with *why* the sentence is in the question form: *How come **he is** here? Why **is he** here? How come **you didn't do** your work? Why **didn't you** do your work?*

Fill in the blanks with appropriate negative verb phrases.

EXAMPLES: a. (take) How come he <u>hasn't taken</u> care of the problem yet?
b. (have) How come she <u>doesn't have</u> any friends?

1. (come) How come you _____ to school yesterday?

2. (have) How come you _____ any money in the bank?

3. (be) How come you _____ here tomorrow?

4. (pay) How come you _____ your phone bill last month?

5. (come) How come the mailman _____ yet? He's late.

6. (eat) How come you _____ any dinner last night?

7. (drive) How come you _____ your car to work yesterday?

8. (go) How come the children _____ to school yet?

9. (take) How come you _____ a vacation this coming summer? (take) How come you _____ one last summer?

10. (send) How come you _____ any Christmas cards last year?

1.45

Focus: *Be Going to* + a Base Form in Past Time

When *be going to* + a base form is used for an event in past time, it means the event was planned but did not take place; in other words, it was an unrealized plan: *We **were going to** take a trip to Europe last summer, but we decided to go to the Orient instead.*

Fill in the blanks with appropriate verb phrases.

EXAMPLES: a. We weren't going to attend the reception yesterday afternoon, but at the last moment we finally decided to (attend it).

b. They were going to get married, but much to everyone's surprise, they suddenly decided against it.

1. Jack _____ married to Patricia, but at the last moment he married her sister instead.

2. We _____ another exercise, but there wasn't enough time.

3. We _____ our children with us on our last trip to Vancouver, but we finally decided to.

4. I _____ yesterday's meeting, but I didn't feel well enough to get out of bed.

5. He _____ to the convention in Chicago, but he couldn't because the airlines were on strike.

6. We _____ at the conference before it began, but we got lost on our way to the conference hall.

7. Harriet _____ to the prom (a class dance) with Bob, but at the last moment she decided to go with Bill.

8. Dick _____ a course in French last semester, but he finally decided to.

9. We _____ a Japanese car, but we changed our minds and bought a German one instead.

10. Daniel _____ to the University of California at Berkeley, but he won a scholarship to Harvard.

11. I _____ to the movies last night, but I changed my mind.

12. Bill _____ computer science, but he went into engineering instead.

13. We _____ our vacation in Spain last summer, but we decided on Italy instead.

14. Sandra _____ a nurse, but she became a medical doctor instead.

15. I _____ anything at the store yesterday, but I did when I found a pair of nice-looking shoes.

THE PAST PERFECT TENSE

2.1

EVENTS PRECEDING EVENTS IN PAST TIME

1. The PAST PERFECT TENSE is used to express an event that occurred before another in past time: *When the war in Vietnam finally ended, Saigon **had fallen** to the Communists* (before the war ended).

2. To form the past perfect tense, *had*, the past form of *have*, is used as an auxiliary, and a past participle occurs as the main verb in the verb phrase: *Before I got to the doctor, my pain **had gone** away.*

	Singular		Plural	
First person	I		we	
Second person	you } had gone		you } had gone	
Third person	he		they	
	she			
	it			

Note: The auxiliary in third person singular is *not* an *-s* form.

3. In less formal usage, contractions of *had* and subject pronouns occur: *By the end of the game (when the game ended),* **he'd** *made thirty-two baskets; By the end of the tennis season,* **she'd** *won more matches than anyone else on her school team.*

I'd		we'd	
you'd } gone		you'd } gone	
he'd		they'd	
she'd			

Pronunciation Note: There is no contracted form for *it had;* however, in speaking *it had* sounds like *it-hid.*

4. Negative verb phrases are formed by inserting *not* between the auxiliary and the main verb: *Before the French Revolution, the aristocrats **had not paid** any attention to the demands of the people, and many of them paid for their mistake with the loss of their heads.*

I		we	
you } had not gone		you } had not gone	
he		they	
she			
it			

5. *Hadn't*, the contraction of *had not*, occurs in informal usage: *He **hadn't** prepared for the final examination, so he got a very low grade.*

6. As in the present perfect tense, such adverbs as *already, finally, just,* and *recently* appear in verb phrases containing the past perfect tense; they immediately follow the auxiliary: *When Japan surrendered to the Allies on September 2, 1945, Germany **had already** surrendered five months before; When the armistice was signed in 1918, the First World War **had finally** come to an end; When our son graduated from high school, the war in Vietnam **had just** ended; When I bought my used car, it **had recently** been painted.*

7. The adverb *yet* most often appears in its usual position at the end of a clause or sentence containing a negative verb phrase: *When the United States won its independence from Great Britain, the French Revolution had not taken place **yet**; At midnight, her son had not come home **yet**.*

8. The past perfect tense is also used to express the duration of an event that preceded another in past time: *When John Fitzgerald Kennedy was assassinated in Dallas on November 22, 1963, he had been the President **for less than three years**; When their baby was born, they had been married **for five years**.*

9. The form may also be used for repeated events before another single event in past time: *When the American Civil War finally ended, hundreds of thousands of people had lost their lives; By the time he was forty, he had written many books.*

10. Because the past perfect tense is most often used for an event preceding another in past time, the form usually occurs in a complex sentence containing a main and subordinate (*when*) clause. In such sentences, the simple past tense is used in the *when* (time) clause, and the past perfect tense occurs in the main clause. The event in the main clause preceded the event in the subordinate (*when*) clause. Compare:

Subordinate Clause	Main Clause
When Jesus died on the Cross,	*he **had lived** for only thirty-three years.* (before he was crucified)
When Jimmy Carter became the President,	*there **had already been** thirty-eight Presidents.* (before he became the President)

11. The past perfect tense sometimes occurs in subordinate clauses introduced by *after* and *before*, but in modern usage, speakers and writers often replace the form with the simple past tense: *After I had **spoken** (spoke) to you, I got a letter from David; Before the robber **had gone** (went) very far, the police caught him.*

12. The form also occurs in subordinate *because* clauses to give the reason for a situation that is expressed in the main clause of a complex sentence: *Richard Nixon left the Presidential office in disgrace because he **had lied** to the American people; Dwight D. Eisenhower became a national hero because he **had led** the American forces to victory in the Second World War.*

13. When the past perfect tense is used in a complex sentence, adverbs of time like *yesterday, last night,* and *ago* must take a different form in order to keep the sentence logical: (yesterday) *When I last saw Alex, he had just taken an important examination **the day before**;* (last year) *I didn't want to go to Paris because I'd been there **the year before**;* (this morning) *I was very tired the other day because I'd gotten up early **that morning**;* (two days ago) *Jonathon was still excited because he'd just graduated from the university **two days before**.*

14. In *yes-no* and information questions, the subject follows the auxiliary *had:* **Had you** *finished the examination yet when the bell rang? How long **had you** had your car when you finally decided to sell it?* In *yes-no* answers, *had* follows the subject: *Yes, **I had**; No, **I hadn't**.*

15. Negative questions are used to express confirmation, surprise, or irritation: *Hadn't you locked the door before you left the house? Why hadn't the government done something about the problem before it got so serious?*
    Note: Questions containing the past perfect tense usually occur only in very formal usage. A speaker is more likely to use the simple past tense in a main clause combined with a subordinate clause introduced by *before: Did (didn't) you lock the door before you left the house? Why didn't the government do something about the problem before it became so serious?*

2.2

Focus: Contrasting the Past Continuous Tense with the Past Perfect Tense

Read each sentence aloud twice, once using the past continuous tense in blank (a), and once using the past perfect tense in blank (b). **Reminder:** The past continuous tense is used for an event that was taking place at the same time as another event occurred. The past perfect tense is used for an event that preceded another event in past time.

EXAMPLES: a. When we got to the theater, the movie (a) was beginning (b) had begun.
　　　　　　 b. When I got to the garage, the mechanic (a) was fixing (b) had fixed my car.

1. When I got home my mother (a) _____ (b) _____ dinner.

2. When I woke up this morning, the sun (a) _____ (b) _____.

3. When the doctor finally arrived, the patient (a) _____ (b) _____

　　 _____.

4. When I went home yesterday afternoon, the sun (a) _____ (b) _____

　　 _____.

5. When I got to the station, the train (a) _____ (b) _____.

6. When I last saw the baby in her crib, she (a) _____ (b) _____

　　 _____ to sleep.

7. When his father got out of the army, the war (a) _____ (b) _____

　　 _____.

8. When we got to the airport, our plane (a) _____ (b) _____

　　 off.

9. When I got to the party, all of the guests (a) _____ (b) _____.

10. When I got back to the dormitory, my roommate (a) _____ (b) _____

　　 _____ his homework.

11. When I called Mary the other night, she (a) _____ (b) _____

　　 to bed.

12. When I first met their son, he (a) _____ (b) _____ to

　　 medical school.

13. When the bell rang, the teacher (a) _____ (b) _____

　　 into the room.

2.3

GRAMMAR EXERCISE   Name _____ Date _28.02.94_

Focus: Verb Phrases with *Just*

Fill in the blanks with *had* + *just* + a past participle. Practice using contractions of subject pronouns and *had*.

EXAMPLES: a. (rise) When I woke up, the sun had just risen.
              b. (sit) When you called, we'd just sat down to dinner.

1. (set) When we got to the cocktail party, the sun _____.

2. (begin) When I arrived at the meeting, it _____.

3. (end) When we entered the theater, the movie _____.

4. (rise) When we got to our seats, the curtain _____.

5. (have) Everyone _____ dinner when we got to the party.

6. (end) When he was born, the Second World War _____.

7. (get) I _____ into the shower when I realized I had forgotten the soap.

8. (ring) When I walked into the classroom, the bell _____.

9. (finish) I _____ my dinner when a friend called and asked me to eat out at the best restaurant in town.

10. (leave) We _____ the elevator when the electricity went out. (get) We _____ out in the nick of time (at exactly the right time).

11. (go) I _____ to sleep when the phone rang, and it was a wrong number.

12. (sit) We _____ down to dinner when the doorbell rang.

13. (read) I _____ the story in the paper when I suddenly heard it on the radio.

14. (leave) His father _____ the doctor's office when he fell and broke his leg.

15. (borrow) He _____ fifty dollars from me when he asked me for fifty more.

16. (start) When I arrived in Paris, a transportation strike _____.

17. (get) I _____ out of bed when my mother called me for breakfast.

18. (start) The fire _____ when the firemen got there.

19. (close) The bank _____ when I got there.

20. (leave) When his office called with an emergency, he _____ for his vacation.

21. (turn) I _____ on the radio when the news about the election came on.

22. (leave) I _____ the house when the rain started.

23. (send) I _____ a letter to my mother when she called me.

24. (end) The war _____ when we arrived in Saigon.

25. (get) I _____ into the room when the class began.

2.4

GRAMMAR EXERCISE   Name _____ Date _____

Focus: Verb Phrases with *Already*

Fill in the blanks with *had* + *already* + a past participle.

EXAMPLES: a. (take) When I got to the airport, my friend's plane <u>had already taken off</u>, so I couldn't say good-bye to her.
Note: *Good-by* (*bye*) is a contraction of *God be with you*.

b. (eat) When I got home, everyone <u>had already eaten</u> dinner.

1. (die) The patient _____ when the doctor arrived.

2. (know) He _____ Mary for five years when he suddenly, much to his surprise, fell in love with her.

3. (be) He didn't know it, but she _____ in love with him since the day they first met.

4. (ring) When I got to school, the bell _____.

5. (set) When I got home last night, the sun _____.

6. (fall/be) By the end of October, the leaves _____ from the trees, and there _____ a few snowfalls.

7. (do) When we started this exercise, we _____ two.

8. (be) When they got married, she _____ married once before.

9. (rise) When I got up, the sun _____.

10. (raise) When they celebrated their twenty-fifth wedding anniversary, they _____ _____ their children.

11. (study) He _____ a little bit of English when he started this course.

12. (arrive) When I got to the meeting late, the chairperson _____. (A *chairperson* is a person who leads a meeting.)

13. (leave) When I arrived, my wife _____.

14. (have) When he got to the party, he _____ a lot to drink.

15. (have) When I was born, my mother _____ two children.

16. (go) When I got into bed, my wife _____ to sleep.

17. (be) When my alarm rang, I _____ awake for a few minutes; (begin) my day _____.

18. (tell) Unfortunately, when she asked me to keep the information a secret, I _____ _____ everyone.

19. (leave) When I got up, my roommate _____ for school.

20. (make) When he asked her to marry him, she _____ up her mind; (decide) she _____ to say no.

21. (make) When they offered me the job, I _____ up my mind not to accept it.

2.5

GRAMMAR EXERCISE   Name _____ _____ Date _____

Focus: Negative Verb Phrases and *Yet*

Fill in the blanks with *had not* (*hadn't*) + a past participle.

EXAMPLES: a. (rise) When I got up the sun <u>hadn't risen</u> yet.
             b. (speak) When I spoke to her, she <u>hadn't done</u> anything about the problem yet.

1. (take) When I spoke to my lawyer, he _____ care of my tax problem yet. (do) He _____ anything about my problem with my wife yet, either.

2. (set) When I left my office, the sun _____ yet.

3. (fall) By late September, the leaves _____ yet.

4. (die) When the doctor got to the hospital, the patient _____ yet.

5. (fix) When I got to the TV shop, they _____ my TV yet.

6. (be) When World War II started, I _____ born yet.

7. (write) When my boss asked me about my report, I _____ it yet.

8. (begin) When we got to the theater, the movie _____ yet.

9. (meet) When my father graduated from high school, he _____ my mother yet. (finish) My mother _____ elementary school yet. (begin) Their life together _____ yet.

10. (discover) In 1490, Columbus _____ America yet.

11. (invent) When my grandfather was young, the Wright brothers _____ the airplane yet.

12. (start) When I got to the stadium, the game _____ yet.

13. (become) When Jimmy Carter was fifty, he _____ the President yet.

14. (feed) When I got home, my wife _____ the baby yet.

15. (blossom) In early April, the cherry trees _____ yet.

16. (end) When I was in school, the war in Vietnam _____ yet.

17. (have) When I got home, the family _____ dinner yet.

18. (have) When I got to work, I _____ breakfast yet.

19. (finish) When he was twenty, he _____ his studies yet.

20. (get) When I knew Mary in Chicago, she _____ married yet.

21. (fix) When I got to the garage, they _____ my car yet.

22. (ring) When I got to school, the bell _____ yet.

23. (finish) When the bell rang, I _____ the examination yet.

24. (go) When you called, I _____ to sleep yet.

25. (start) When she was fifteen, she _____ wearing lipstick yet.

26. (begin) When he was fifteen, he _____ to go out with girls yet.

2.6

GRAMMAR EXERCISE   Name _____ Date _____

Focus: Verb Phrases with *Never*

Supply appropriate verb phrases containing the adverb *never*. Notice the use of *before* in this exercise.

EXAMPLES: a. When I went to the Metropolitan Opera last night, I <u>had never heard</u> an opera before.
b. When I had dinner the other night at Tazuko's, I'd <u>never eaten</u> Japanese food before.

1. When I first came to New York, I _____ on a subway before.

2. When I went to Central America on my vacation, I _____ a banana tree before.

3. When I went to the wedding on Saturday, I _____ champagne before.

4. When Mary became John's girlfriend, he _____ a girlfriend before.

5. When I voted in the last election, I _____ before.

6. Before Jose went out with Alice, he _____ out with a North-American woman before.

7. When I came to the United States last December, I _____ here before.

8. When his father had the heart attack, he _____ sick a day in his life. (*A day in his life* in this sentence means *in his whole life.*)

6. When Mary went out with Carlos, she _____ out with a Latin-American man before.

10. When he fell in love with Anne at the age of thirty-eight, he _____ in love before.

11. When I went to Haiti on my vacation, I _____ in a tropical climate before.

12. When I went to Africa on my vacation, I _____ elephants in their natural habitat before.

13. When my grandmother flew to Europe last summer, she _____ on a plane before.

14. When I met Enrique, I _____ a person from Argentina before.

15. When our son had a physical examination the other day, he _____ one before.

16. When he started school, he _____ English before.

2.7

GRAMMAR EXERCISE   Name _____ Date _____

Focus: Clauses of Reason with *Because*

Fill in the blanks with *had* (+ *not*) + a past participle.

EXAMPLES: a. I got wet during the rainstorm because I had forgotten my umbrella.
            b. I was angry at myself because I had put my foot in my mouth. (*To put one's foot in one's mouth* means *to say something that is embarassing or is not appropriate for the occasion.*

1. I was very tired because I _____ well the night before. I couldn't sleep because I _____ too much coffee.

2. I didn't get a good grade because I _____ hard enough.

3. They were proud of their son because he _____ very high honors at the graduation ceremonies.

4. She was angry at herself because she _____ a foolish mistake.

5. I felt wonderful because I _____ good news from home.

Now complete the sentences.

6. I wasn't at home when you called _____.

7. He had a stomach ache _____.

8. I had a headache _____.

9. I was furious _____.

10. I felt (didn't feel) well_____.

11. She was happy _____.

12. I was angry at my lawyer/secretary _____.

13. [supply name] _____ was angry at me_____.

14. I was very thirsty/hungry/tired_____.

15. My parents were proud of me _____.

16. The people of the nation were disappointed _____.

17. I felt wonderful _____.

18. The garden was very dry _____.

19. I didn't have an appetite last night _____.

20. I was late to school _____.

21. I missed my bus _____.

22. I had a bad sunburn _____.

23. I couldn't pay last month's phone bill _____.

24. I was laughing when you saw me out in the hall _____.

25. I got up very late_____.

2.8

GRAMMAR EXERCISE   Name _____ Date _____

Focus: *Yes-No* and Information Questions

Supply appropriate past participles in the blanks.

EXAMPLES: a. How long had they <u>known</u> each other before they finally got married?

b. How much money had the company <u>lost</u> before they finally went out of business? (*To go out of business* means *to close a business forever.*)

1. How long had the patient _____ sick before she was cured?

2. How long had the movie _____ on when you arrived at the theater?

3. Had you ever _____ in Europe before you went last year?

4. Had the sun already _____ when you got up this morning?

5. Hadn't the children _____ their dinner before nine o'clock last night?
   Reminder: Negative questions have the sense of surprise or irritation.

6. Why hadn't the police _____ the criminal before he stole all that money?

7. Hadn't you ever _____ champagne before the wedding last Saturday? I'm surprised!

8. Why hadn't you _____ your taxes before you got into all that trouble with the government?

9. Why hadn't the children _____ their breakfast before they went to school?

Now supply appropriate base forms in the blanks in the following questions containing the simple past tense. Reminder: Questions containing the past perfect tense usually occur in only very formal usage.

10. Did you _____ your homework before you went to bed?

11. Why didn't the children _____ their breakfast before they left?

12. How much money did the company finally _____ before it went bankrupt? (We use the expression *to go bankrupt* to describe a situation when a business is not able to pay its bills and is forced *to go out of business.*)

13. How much money did the city government _____ before it went broke? (*To go broke* means *to go bankrupt.*)

14. How long did they not _____ to each other before they finally made up?

15. How many courses did you _____ before you started this one?

2.9

GRAMMAR EXERCISE   Name _____ Date _____

Focus: The Past Perfect Tense in Main Clauses

On a separate piece of paper (or orally in class), complete the following sentences with appropriate main clauses containing the past perfect tense.

EXAMPLES: a. When I got to school, *none of the other students had arrived yet.*
(Note that an affirmative verb phrase follows *none.*)
  b. When I woke up this morning, *the sun had already risen.*
  c. When he told me the gossip about his boss, *I had just heard about it from his boss's secretary.* (*Gossip* means *idle talk about other people* or *sensational rumors of a personal nature.* The word may also be used as a verb: *Who gossips more, men or women?*)

1. When I spoke to my attorney (lawyer) about the problem, . . .
2. When I arrived at the wedding late, . . . (Use the words *bride* and *groom.*)
3. When the police arrived at the scene of the crime, . . . (Use *criminal* and *escape.*)
4. When I got to the airport/train station/dock, . . .
5. When I got home very early/late last night, . . .
6. When I left the house for work this morning, . . .
7. When I got to work, . . .
8. When I got to the bank, . . .
9. When we finally got to our seats in the theater, . . .
10. When our teacher arrived, . . .
11. When I got to class, . . .
    Note: *To get to* may mean *to arrive at;* however, *get to* is followed by the destination: *We got to* **the concert** *late;* but *arrive* (without *to*) may occur without the destination: *We arrived late*.
12. When I started this course, . . .
13. When I got up this morning, . . .
14. When I went to bed last night, . . .
15. When the train arrived at the station, . . .
16. When Timothy and Gloria went to Greece on their vacation, . . .
17. When I had Russian food at the party the other night, . . .
18. When I went to California on my vacation last year, . . .
19. When I bought my automobile, . . .
20. When I went to the exhibition of Indian art at the museum, . . .
21. When the Queen arrived at the Palace, . . .
22. When I arrived at the doctor's office, . . .
23. When Hassan went out with an American girl from San Francisco, . . .

2.10

THE PAST PERFECT CONTINUOUS TENSE

1. The PAST PERFECT CONTINUOUS TENSE is used to emphasize the duration of an event preceding another in past time: *When we finally arrived in San Francisco, we* **had been driving** *our car for more than six days; When the book was finally published, the author* **had been working** *on it for around twelve years.*

2. To form the past perfect continuous tense, we use *had* and *been* as auxiliaries and a present participle as the main verb of a verb phrase.

	Singular		Plural	
First person	I		we	
Second person	you } had been going		you } had been going	
Third person	he		they	
	she			
	it			

3. Negative verb phrases are formed by inserting *not* between *had* and *been: When the hurricane suddenly struck the city, people* **had not been** *expecting it; When I finally took my car to the garage, it* **hadn't been** *working well for a couple of months.*

I			we		
you	} had not been going		you	} had not been going	
he			they		
she					
it					

4. In *yes-no* and information questions, the subject of a sentence follows the auxiliary *had:* **Had she** *been looking for a very long time when she finally found a good job? How long* **had Columbus and his crew** *been sailing before they finally landed in the New World?*

   Note: Adverbs like *just, recently,* and *finally* do not occur in verb phrases containing the past perfect tense.

   Special Note: Adverbial expressions of time almost always appear in sentences containing the past perfect continuous tense: *When my guests finally sat down to dinner, I'd been cooking* **for three hours;** *She'd been working for the company* **for twenty-eight years** *when she finally retired.*

2.11

GRAMMAR EXERCISE   Name _____ Date _____

Focus: The Past Perfect Continuous Tense

Fill in the blanks with *had* (*hadn't*) + *been* + a present participle.

EXAMPLES: a. (protest) When the war in Vietnam finally ended, people all over the world <u>had been protesting</u> against it for many years.

b. (get) Everything in our garden was dying because we <u>hadn't been getting</u> any rain for more than five months.

1. (go) Fred and Peggy _____ together for three years before they finally got married.

2. (make) He lost his job because he _____ (causing) trouble at the office. He was a real trouble maker.

3. (bother) I had to go to the dentist because a tooth _____ me for

a month; (take) I _____ care of myself.

4. (rain) When the monsoon finally ended, it _____ for more than a month.

5. (wait) When they finally had their baby boy, they _____ for more than seven years.

Now complete the following sentences orally or on a separate piece of paper.

EXAMPLE: c. I wasn't surprised by the Director's decision to suspend Jim from school because *he'd been making a great deal of trouble for a long time.*

6. When the rain finally stopped, . . .
7. When I finally found a good job, . . .
8. When our daughter finally became a medical doctor, . . .
9. My eyes were very tired last night because . . .
10. My feet were very tired last night because . . .
11. John's father had to go to the doctor because . . .
12. The patient wasn't feeling well because . . .
13. When we finally reached the top of Mt. Everest, . . .
14. When our plane finally landed at JFK (Kennedy Airport in New York), . . .
15. When my alarm clock rang, . . .
16. When my girlfriend/boyfriend finally got to our meeting place, . . .
17. When they finally got married, . . .
18. When the surgeon finally finished the operation, . . .
19. We were tired yesterday morning because our baby . . .
20. He was kicked out of (suspended from) school because he . . .
21. When the concert finally ended, . . .
22. When I finished my homework last night, . . .

2.12

Focus: The Simple Past Tense versus the Past Perfect (Continuous) Tense

Fill in the blanks with verbs in the simple past tense or the past perfect (continuous) tense. Do not use negative forms.

EXAMPLES: a. (get) I got to work at 9:30 yesterday morning.
         b. (get) When I got to work, my boss had already gotten there.

1. (immigrate) He _____ to Toronto five years ago.

2. (look) When he finally found a good job there, he _____ for more than a year.

3. (have) He was eventually able to find a good job because he _____ a good education in his native country.

4. (be) His first day at work _____ very exciting.

5. (see) I _____ a very good movie a couple of nights ago.

6. (see) We didn't want to watch the late movie on TV last night because we _____ it already at a theater.

7. (take) I _____ three aspirins an hour ago.

8. (take) My headache went away because I _____ some aspirins.

9. (eat) I _____ chicken for dinner last night.

10. (eat) When I got home late last night, everyone in my family _____ already.

11. (do) I _____ my homework last night.

12. (do) I was able to go to the game yesterday because I _____ my homework the night before.

13. (meet) My mother _____ my father at a Christmas party in 1957. (be) They _____ very young at the time.

14. (take) The patient felt better after she _____ the medicine.

15. (rain) When the storm was finally over, it _____ for more than a week. (be) Everything in the house _____ damp.

16. (look) When I finally found an interesting job, I _____ for a couple of years. (know) They hired me because I _____ a lot about their kind of business.

17. (forget) It was difficult for her to read the exercises because she _____ to bring her glasses with her to school.

18. (rain) It _____ for just a few minutes last night.

19. (go) When they finally got married, they _____ together for several years.

20. (rain) Everything in the house was damp because it _____ for more than a month.

21. (write) I _____ a couple of letters last night.

2.13

GRAMMAR EXERCISE   Name _____ Date _____

> Focus: Reviewing *Too, Either, And,* and *But*

Supply appropriate words in the blanks.

EXAMPLES: a. When we went to the Orient, my wife had already been there, but I <u>hadn't</u>.
            b. She didn't have to go to work yesterday, and I <u>didn't either</u>.

1. He has to do a lot of homework, and everyone else _____.

2. I've never made a million dollars, and you _____.

3. Mary is very popular at school, but her twin sister _____.

4. I have to work on Saturdays, but no one else in my family _____.

5. My roommate isn't going to go to school tomorrow, and I _____.

6. When they went to Europe, he had never been there, but his wife _____.

7. John has to take the bus to work, and his brother _____.

8. I couldn't go to the game yesterday, and my sister _____.

9. I don't care for Japanese food, and my wife _____.

10. This book cost a lot, and that one _____.

11. He had to attend an important meeting yesterday, and she _____.

12. I don't have to be at school tomorrow, but you _____.

13. She should stop smoking, and I _____.

2.14

GRAMMAR EXERCISE

> Focus: Reviewing *So* and *Neither*

Supply appropriate words in the blanks.

EXAMPLES: a. Before their wedding, she'd had a blood test, and <u>so had</u> he.
            b. She'd never been to Europe before, and <u>neither had</u> he.

1. She works for a bank, and _____ her husband.

2. My boss is working very hard, and _____ I.

3. Tomorrow will not be cold, and _____ the day after.

4. My roommate got good grades last semester, and _____ I.

5. I'd left the party by midnight, and _____ everyone else.

6. I didn't enjoy the concert and _____ everyone else.

2.14 (Continued)

7. You must try to do your best in the test, and _____ I.

8. I don't have to get up early tomorrow morning, and _____ my roommate.

9. She doesn't have any financial problems, and _____ he.

10. She'll do well on the final examination, and _____ you.

11. It was a wonderful trip; the weather in France was perfect, and _____ the food.

2.15

GRAMMAR EXERCISE   Name _____ Date _9. 03. 94_

Focus: Reviewing Prepositions

Fill in the blanks with appropriate prepositions. Do this exercise as a quiz.

at	during	in	off	since	up
between	for	into	on	through	with
down	from	of	out	to	

EXAMPLES: a. They've been going together <u>for</u> years.
b. The shortest distance <u>between</u> two points is a straight line.

1. We are now _____ the beginning _____ this exercise.

2. Their house is next _____ a small park.

3. _____ my office, Dick's desk is _____ front _____ mine.

4. The thief entered the house _____ an unlocked door.

5. We were tired from walking _____ the long hill.

6. It's difficult to put thread _____ the eye _____ a needle.

7. _____ exactly ten o'clock, the teacher walked _____ the classroom.

8. They arrived _____ Mexico City _____ June 1.

9. The boys like to skate _____ my driveway.

10. Jack has been going _____ Grace _____ they met _____ a party a couple _____ months ago. They're going to get married _____ June. They're going to get married _____ her parents' home.

11. _____ the hurricane, we stayed _____ our house _____ some friends _____ ours and had a party.

12. Please keep this information a secret _____ you and me.

13. Is it difficult to get _____ Columbia University?

14. Some very good friends _____ mine live _____ Fifth Avenue.

15. The Eiffel Tower is _____ the center _____ Paris.

16. We keep a lot _____ old things _____ the basement _____ our house.

17. The hostages were allowed to walk _____ the plane _____ nine o'clock yesterday morning.

MODAL AUXILIARIES

3

3.1

A SHORT REVIEW OF MODAL AUXILIARIES

1. The modal *can* shows (a) a physical ability: *He **can lift** about fifty pounds without strain; A human being **can go** without water for several days;* (b) a learned ability: *She **can speak** five languages; She **can sew, knit,** and **crochet** beautifully;* and (c) possibility: *Canada **can produce** millions of tons of wheat a year; You **can find** a list of irregular verbs at the back of this book.*
   Reminder: The idiom *be able to* is also used to show ability or possibility: *The doctor **is able to see** you now; The patient **isn't able to get** out of bed.*

2. *Could,* the past form of *can,* shows ability or possibility in past time: *I **couldn't carry** the package home because it was too heavy; We **could go** for a drive yesterday because our car was working.*

3. *Could* is also used to show slight probability (in a manner similar to *may*) in present time: *Where's the boss today? He **could be** sick, but I don't think so.*

4. *Could not* means impossibility: *This letter **couldn't be** from John Smith; he's been dead for ten years.*

5. *May,* and its other form *might,* also means slight probability in present time: *They **may** (**might**) **have** a lot of money, but I don't think so.*

6. *May* (and in very formal usage *might*) is also used for asking permission: ***May I** please open the door? **May I** leave?*
   Reminder: In less formal usage *can* may be used for asking permission: *Can (may) I please leave the table? **Can** (may) I open the window?*

7. The modal *must* means (a) necessity: *He's very ill and **must go** to the doctor immediately;* (b) strong recommendation: *You **must see** that movie; it's wonderful;* and (c) strong probability (deduction): *The President's job **must be** very difficult.*
   Reminder: *Must* for necessity has no past form.

8. The idiom *have to* also shows necessity; however, it does not show the feeling of necessity as strongly as *must: I **have to pay** $15.00 a month for my phone* (but *I **must pay** my taxes*).

9. *Have to* can appear in all verb tenses: *I **have to go** to work every day; I **had to go** to work yesterday; I **will have to go** to work tomorrow; I **have had to go** to work every day this week; He was angry because he **had had to go** to work earlier than usual.*
   Reminder: In the present and past tenses, *have to* requires the auxiliary *do* in questions and negatives: *Do you have to go to work? I didn't have to go to work yesterday.*

3.1 *(Continued)*

10. It is important to remember that *do not have to* means lack of necessity: *I don't have to eat because I'm not hungry;* while *must not* means prohibition: *I mustn't eat this food because it's spoiled.*

11. *Should* and *ought to* mean (a) expectation: *There **shouldn't be** crime in the city, but there is; Our children **ought to be** good all the time, but sometimes they're not;* (b) advisability: *You **should take** care of the problem now; You **ought to buy** a new dictionary;* and (b) recommendation: *You **should read** that book; You **ought to see** that movie.*
Reminder: (a) *Should* (*ought to*) does not express necessity and recommendation as strongly as *must.* (b) *Should* occurs more frequently than *ought to* in questions and negatives in American English.

3.2

GRAMMAR EXERCISE   Name _____ Date _____

Focus: Reviewing Modal Auxiliaries and Related Idioms

Supply appropriate base forms in the blanks.

EXAMPLES: a. There shouldn't <u>be</u> a discipline problem at the school, but there is. (expectation)
b. We might <u>run</u> out of money. (slight probability) (*To run out of* means *to deplete the supply of something.*)

1. I have to ___go___ to the store because I've run out of sugar. I have to ___buy___ it right away. (necessity)

2. I didn't have to ___take___ any medicine. (lack of necessity)

3. We must ___stop___ at the next gas station (necessity), or we might ___run___ out of gas. (slight probability)

4. You ought to ___see___ that program on TV tonight. (recommendation)

5. You should ___provide___ better care of your health. (advisability)

6. We must ___call___ the police about the crime. (necessity)

7. We must ___drink water___ to live. (necessity)

8. We mustn't _____ to eat. (prohibition)

9. You must ___reed___ this book; it's about the present political situation in your native country. (strong recommendation)

10. I don't have to ___reed___ the book because I know all about the situation from personal experience. (lack of necessity)

3.2 (Continued)

GRAMMAR EXERCISE   Name _____ Date _____

11. A camel can _live_ for days without water. (physical ability) —

12. A friend of mine can _speak_ seven languages. (learned ability)

13. Life in India for the poor must _be_ hard. (strong probability) — *jaa verolanely*

14. Dick may _be_ sick today, but I don't know. (slight probability)

15. May I please _come in_ the room? (polite request) — *rydoseu selxuseb*

16. Adjectives may _precede_ or _follow_ nouns. (possibility)

17. He must _have't_ a lot of money (strong probability) because he doesn't have to _pay_. (lack of necessity)

18. You mustn't _take_ that medicine; it's dangerous. (prohibition) — *zafuuco*

19. She could _be_ in love, but I don't know. (slight probability)

20. He couldn't _know_ everything about Europe; he's never been there. He's only read about it. (impossibility)

21. Everyone should _be_ honest, but some people aren't. (expectation)

22. I can't _eat_ sweets; they're fattening. (lack of physical ability)

23. She can't _speak_ well. (lack of learned ability)

24. I've run out of energy; I must _sit_ down. (necessity)

25. You mustn't _be_ lazy. (prohibition)

26. She doesn't have to _be_ lazy, but she is. (lack of necessity)

27. She is able to _do_ everything well. (ability)

3.3

PRESENT CONTINUOUS FORMS WITH MODALS

1. Modal auxiliaries may occur in verb phrases that contain the verb *be* (as a second auxiliary) and a present participle (as the main verb): *You **can be fixing** dinner while I am washing the dishes; Your lawyer **could be making** a mistake; Sh! The baby **may be sleeping;** Bob and Norma **might be coming** to the conference, but I don't know.*
   Note: It is customary to call *be* an auxiliary in a two- or three-word verb phrase.

2. Negative verb phrases are formed by putting *not* after the modal: *They **might not** be coming to tomorrow's lecture; You **shouldn't be** sitting on the floor, children.*

3. Subjects follow the modal in *yes-no* and information questions: ***Should I** be using this kind of paper in my typewriter? **Could he** be telling me the whole truth? What **should I** be doing now? Who **could he** be talking to on the phone at this late hour?*

4. In *yes-no* answers, *be* can occur along with the modal, but its use is optional: *Should she be doing that job now? Yes, she **should** (**be**); No, **she shouldn't** (**be**).*
   Special Reminder: (a) *May* (for slight probability) does not occur in questions. (b) *Might* in direct questions is very formal. (c) *Could* is the modal most often used for direct questions: *Could I be making an error? What could I be doing wrong?* (d) *Ought to* rarely occurs in questions in American usage. (e) *Must* (for strong probability) does not occur in questions.

SPELLING BEE   Name _____ Date _____

Make *-ing* **forms (present participles) out of the base forms.**

EXAMPLES: a. begin beginning
            b. do doing

1. put _____putting_____
2. study _____studying_____
3. occur _____occurring_____
4. die _____dying_____
5. stay _____staying_____
6. get _____getting_____
7. run _____running_____
8. hit _____hitting_____

9. turn _____turning_____
10. lie _____lying_____
11. buy _____buying_____
12. grin _____grinning_____
13. nap _____napping_____
14. chew _____chewing_____
15. kid _____kidding_____
16. drive _____driving_____

3.4

GRAMMAR EXERCISE　　　　　　　Name _____ Date _____

Focus: Present Continuous Forms with Modals

p. perf. tense

Supply appropriate present participles in the blanks.

EXAMPLES:　a.　Our guests should be coming any minute now (very soon).
　　　　　　b.　You must be kidding. I can't believe you've just inherited a million dollars. (*To kid* means *to joke* or *to deceive*.)

　　　　наследил

1. Our neighbors must be _sleeping_. All their lights are off.

2. The rich nations should be _helping_ more for the poor ones.

3. I might be _comming_ to school tomorrow, but I don't know.

4. He may be _making_ a lot of money with his company, but I don't think so.

5. The patient must be _feeling_ better because her appetite has improved greatly. She shouldn't be _taking_ penicillin any more.

6. Our neighbors upstairs must be _having_ a party. They shouldn't be _making_ so much noise.

7. I could be _____ a mistake in this matter, but I don't believe so.

8. The turkey should be _taking_ out of the oven any minute now.

9. Because their products are so terrible, his company mustn't be _____ much money.

10. They ought to be _taking_ better care of their children, but they're not. They should be _doing_ more for them.

11. The world's governments should be _taking care_ more about the problems of over-population and pollution.

12. What kind of paper should the students be _using_ for their compositions? Should they be _writing_ their papers (long compositions) in ink or with a pencil?

13. Hurry up! The plane should be _taking_ off any minute now.

14. When we go to Europe next summer, we may be _taking_ our children with us, but we don't know yet.

15. The bus should be _comming_ any minute; it's almost fifteen minutes late. It should be _running_ on schedule.

16. Where's Dad? He could be _sitting_ in the garden, but I don't think so.

17. The children are watching TV, but they should be _writing_ their homework. They shouldn't be _wasting_ their time.

18. Listen! It must be _raining_. Can't you hear the rain on the roof? Our garden furniture must be _____ wet.

19. Children, you shouldn't be _playing_ with matches.

PAST FORMS OF *SHOULD* AND *OUGHT TO*

1. When *should* and *ought to* are used for advisability and obligation in past time, it is understood that the advice was not followed or the obligation was not fulfilled: *The President* **should have listened** *to his advisers, but he didn't; Before the French Revolution, the aristocrats* **ought to have paid** *more attention to the needs of the common people, but they didn't.*

2. To form a past tense verb phrase, *have* (as a second auxiliary) and a past participle (as a main verb) follow *should* and *ought to*. In negative verb phrases, *not* follows the modal: *They* **should have done** *something about the problem before it got serious, but they didn't; I* **ought to have given** *my plants more water, but I didn't, so they all died; Nixon* **should not have listened** *to his advisers, but he did; They* **ought not to have submitted** *the proposal, but they did.*
   Note: *Not* is inserted between *ought* and *to*. *Ought not to* occurs more frequently in British English.
   Note: It is customary to call *have* a second auxiliary.

$$\left.\begin{array}{l} \text{I} \\ \text{you} \\ \text{he} \\ \text{she} \\ \text{it} \end{array}\right\} \text{should (not) have gone} \qquad \left.\begin{array}{l} \text{we} \\ \text{you} \\ \text{they} \end{array}\right\} \text{should (not) have gone}$$

   Remember: *Have* is never an *-s* form in this pattern; it is always in the base form.

3. *Should've* (sounds like *should-of*), the contraction of *should have,* occurs in spoken informal usage: *The children* **should've** *gone to bed much earlier than they did; I* **should've** *studied English when I was younger.*
   Note: *Should've* is not written unless dialogue is being quoted.
   Pronunciation Note: There is no written contraction for *ought to have;* however, it sounds like *ought-to-of.*

4. *Shouldn't have* (sounds like *shouldn't-of*) occurs in informal usage: *Our team* **shouldn't have** *lost the game, but they did; She* **shouldn't have** *drunk so much at the party, but she did.*

5. Subjects follow *should* in *yes-no* and information questions: **Should I** *have done it in a different way? What time* **should the guests** *have arrived?*
   Reminder: Questions with *ought to* in American English are seldom heard.

3.6

GRAMMAR EXERCISE   Name _____ Date _____

Focus: *Should* and *Ought to*

Fill in the blanks with past participles made out of the base forms given in the parentheses.

EXAMPLES: a. (drive) We should have <u>driven</u> up to the mountains, but we didn't.
          b. (ask) You ought to have <u>asked</u> your boss for a raise.

1. (put) I should have ____*put*____ on my gloves when I left the house, but I forgot to. (wear) I ought to have ____*worn*____ a heavier coat, too.

2. (do) The children should have ____*done*____ their homework before they went to bed. (be) I should have ____*been*____ more strict with them.

3. (install) They should have ___*installed*___ our new stove last week, but they didn't. (call) I ought to have ____*called*____ the store manager.

4. (write) You should have ___*written*___ to your parents. Why didn't you?

Now supply *should* (*ought to*) + *have* + a past participle.

5. (go) I'm tired out (completely tired). I ___*should have gone*___ to bed earlier than I did. (stay) I ___*should have stayed*___ in bed.

6. (put) This soup tastes bland. I ___*ought to have put*___ more salt in it.

7. (get) Darn it! I ___*should have gotten*___ a haircut yesterday, but I didn't have time.

8. (leave) We ___*ought to have left*___ the party before the fight started.

9. (practice) Our team ___*should have practiced*___ more before they played the champions. (try) They ___*should have tryed*___ harder.

10. (wear) He ___*ought to have worn*___ a better-looking suit to the job interview.

11. (take) The children ___*ought to have taken*___ a nap yesterday afternoon.

12. (water) I ___*should have watered*___ my house plants more than I did. (give) I ___*should have given*___ them better care.

13. (wear) I ___*should have wored*___ my glasses during the movie, but I forgot to put them on. (remind) You ___*should have reminded*___ me.

14. (drink) I ___*should have drunk*___ less coffee last night. I didn't sleep a wink (at all).

15. (study) I ___*should have studied*___ English when I was younger.

16. (use) You ___*should have used*___ a dictionary when you wrote the composition. (type) Even better, you ___*should have typed*___ it.

17. (get) I ___*should have gotten*___ to the meeting on time, but my bus was late. (take) I ___*should have taken*___ a taxi.

18. (have) The children ___*should have had*___ breakfast before they went to school.

3.7

GRAMMAR EXERCISE   Name _____ Date _____

Focus: *Should* in Negative Verb Phrases

Fill in the blanks with *should* + *not* + *have* + a past participle. **Pronunciation Reminder:** *Shouldn't have* sounds like *shouldn't-of*.

EXAMPLES: a. (buy) I don't like my car. I shouldn't have bought it.
           b. (spend) I'm complete broke (without money). I <u>shouldn't have spent</u> so much money last weekend.

1. (be) I <u>shouldn't have been</u> so foolish with my money.

2. (waste) You <u>shouldn't have wasted</u> so much time yesterday.

3. (wear) My feet ache. I <u>shouldn't have worsen</u> those new shoes when I went Christmas shopping.

4. (have) I'm a little drunk. I <u>shouldn't have had</u> that last cocktail.

5. (wear) I'm so warm. I <u>shouldn't have worsen</u> this heavy coat.

6. (listen) I <u>shouldn't have listened</u> to the weather forecast.

7. (pay) I <u>shouldn't have paid</u> any attention to the weatherman.

8. (reveal) He <u>shouldn't have revealed</u> the information to the authorities.

9. (cook) This meat is tough. I <u>shouldn't have cooked</u> it so long.

10. (get) Bob and my sister <u>shouldn't have gotten</u> married. They never got along before they were married, and now it's even worse.

11. (bet) I <u>shouldn't have bet</u> any money on that horse. Now I'm broke.

12. (make) I <u>shouldn't have made</u> so many mistakes on the test.

13. (permit) We <u>shouldn't have permited</u> the children to see that movie.

14. (go) I caught a bad cold. I <u>shouldn't have gone</u> outside without a jacket. (take) I <u>shouldn't have taken</u> a walk in the rain.

15. (listen) The German people <u>shouldn't have listened</u> to Hitler.

16. (drop) The United States <u>shouldn't have dropped</u> an atomic bomb on Japan.

17. (cheat) Your boss <u>shouldn't have cheated</u> on his income tax.

18. (join) Patricia Hearst <u>shouldn't have joined</u> the guerillas.

19. (permit) The government <u>shouldn't have permited</u> inflation to get so bad. (happen) It <u>shouldn't have happened</u> but it did.

20. (pardon) The President <u>shouldn't have pardoned</u> that criminal.

21. (make) The judge <u>shouldn't have made</u> that decision.

22. (sign) I <u>shouldn't have sung</u> that contract without reading it more carefully.

23. (put) I <u>shouldn't have put</u> so much garlic in the stew.

24. (waste) I <u>shouldn't have wasted</u> so much time yesterday.

3.8

WRITING EXERCISE   Name _____ Date _____

> Focus: *Should and Ought to*

Compose (aloud and/or in writing) appropriate statements in response to the following stated situations. Use *should (not)* or *ought (not) to have* + a past participle in your sentences.

EXAMPLES: a. They served a sweet white wine with the steak at dinner.
                   <u>They ought to have served red wine.</u>
             b. I'm very tired today.
                   I shouldn't have stayed up so late last night. (*To stay up* can mean *not to go to bed: How long are you going to stay up? We're going to stay up until our son gets home.*)

1. Even though he had a high fever, he went to work yesterday.
    He shouldn't have gone to work yesterday

2. She wore a red dress to the funeral last week.
    She ought to have worn a dark dress.

3. He put the milk on the shelf, and it spoiled.
    He shouldn't have put milk on the shelf.

4. I used a pencil when I did my homework.
    I ought to have used a ball-pen.

5. They served wine and beer at the wedding reception on Saturday.
    They should not have served wine and beer together.

6. When he wrote the letter to the President, he used an informal style of writing.
    he shouldn't have wrote informal style of writing.

7. He cooked the chicken for three hours.
    He ought not to have cooked chicken for three hours.

8. It was a beautiful day, but we stayed inside.
    We should have gone outside.

9. They served a large ham for dinner on Thanksgiving Day.
    They shouldn't have served

10. They were in France for a month, but they only visited Paris.
    _____

11. She put the cat and the dog in the same room, and they had a big fight.
    She shouldn't have put the cat and dog.

12. I gave him a beautiful present, and he said nothing.
    He shouldn't have said nothing.

13. I got up late and missed the train.
    I

14. It was very important news, but they sent a letter.
    _____

3.9

        Focus: Questions with *Should*

Supply appropriate past paticiples in the blanks. When doing the exercise aloud, practice using the short answers: *Yes, I should* (*have*); or *No, I shouldn't* (*have*). **Pronunciation Reminder:** *Should have* sounds like *should-of,* and *shouldn't have* sounds like *shouldn't-of.*

EXAMPLES: a. Why shouldn't she have <u>married</u> that man?

           b. Should I have <u>sent</u> a telegram to the company instead of a letter? No, you shouldn't have.

1. How much should I have _paid_ the waiter last night? I didn't want to tip him too much.

2. Why shouldn't our children have _gone_ to that movie? Was it too violent or porno- graphic?

3. Should she have _woren_ a different kind of dress to the job interview? Yes, she should have.

4. We're lost! What road should we have _used_ at the last intersection? Should we have _____ to the right instead of the left? Should we have _asked_ for directions at a gas station? Yes, we should have.

5. You didn't like the chicken, did you? How should I have _kneuv_ it? What else should I have _____ on it?

6. Should I have _____ it in butter instead of oil?

7. Should I have _woren_ a blue jacket instead of a brown one?

8. Why shouldn't you have _bought_ a Christmas present to yourself?

9. Why shouldn't you have _asked_ your boss for a raise? You're not making enough money to live on, are you? (Note the idiomatic expression *money to live on: Everyone needs* **money to live on;** *Do you have enough* **money to live on?**)

10. Why shouldn't I have _____ Jim's typewriter? It doesn't belong to him; it belongs to the company.

11. You didn't enjoy the party last night, did you? Where should we have _been_ instead?

12. I didn't like the chicken at the restaurant last night. What should I have _aten_ instead?

13. I don't like my Ford. What kind of car should I have _liked_ instead? Should I have _liked_ a European one?

14. You didn't like the movie, did you? What movie should we have _liked_ to instead?

3.10

PAST FORMS OF MAY AND MIGHT

1. The past form of *may* (*might*) is used to express slight probability, uncertainty, or conjecture (guess) about an event in past time.

Event in Past Time	Conjecture
She didn't come to work yesterday.	*She **may** (**might**) **have been** sick.*
He didn't say hello to me.	*He **may** (**might**) **have been** angry.*

2. As with past forms of *should* and *ought to, have* in the base form (as an auxiliary) and a past participle (as a main verb) follow *may* (*might*) in a verb phrase. *Not* follows the modal in negatives: *When I made that remark, **I may** (**might**) **have said** the wrong thing; He **may** (**might**) **not have answered** me right away because he hadn't understood my question.*

	Singular		Plural	
First person	I	⎫	we	⎫
Second person	you	⎬ may (might) (not) have gone	you	⎬ may (might) (not) have gone
Third person	he	⎭	they	⎭
	she			
	it			

3. *Might've* (sounds like *might-of*), occurs in spoken informal usage: *The baby **might've** eaten something bad; We **might've won** the game.*
   Note: *Might've* is not written unless dialogue is being quoted. *Mayn't* and *mightn't,* the contractions of *may not* and *might not,* seldom occur in American English.
   Pronunciation Note: The following contractions occur in speaking: (a) *may have* sounds like *may-of;* (b) *may not have* sounds like *may-not-of;* and (c) *might not have* sounds like *might-not-of.*
   Reminder: (a) *May* does not occur in questions (only in requests). (b) Direct questions with *might* (e.g., *Might the Ambassador have left?*) are very formal. (*May* and *might* in indirect questions will be discussed in the chapter on noun clauses.)

Practice reading the following sentences aloud.

1. She may have (*may-of*) been angry at me.
2. I might have (*might-of*) made a few mistakes in the last test.
3. The children might not have (*might-not-of*) had enough to eat.
4. They may not have (*may-not-of*) taken the right bus.
5. You may have had the wrong number when you tried to make the call.
6. The test might not have been difficult enough for the students.
7. You may not have had the right formula.
8. The team might not have practiced enough.
9. You may have taken the wrong road.

GRAMMAR EXERCISE   Name _____ Date _____

Focus: Slight Probability and Conjecture with *May/Might*

Fill in the blanks with *may* (*might*) + *have* + a past participle.

EXAMPLES: a. (be) He didn't say hello to me. He may have been angry at me.
  b. (have) The experiment was a flop. I might have had the wrong formula. (*Flop* is informal for *failure*.)

1. (eat) I have a little bit of a stomach ache. I _may have drunk_ something bad. (drink) I _may have used_ polluted water.

2. (have) She was absent yesterday. She _may have had_ a problem at home. (be) One of her children _may have been_ sick.

3. (be) The children didn't enjoy the animal film much. It _might have been_ too difficult for them. (be) They _might have been_ tired.

4. (be) I was calling him all day, but I always got a busy signal. His phone _may have been_ out of order. The receiver _might have been_ off the hook. (have) I _may have had_ the wrong number.

5. (forget) They didn't get my letter. I _might have forgotten_ to put a stamp on it, but I don't think so. (use) I _may have used_ the wrong address, but I doubt it (don't think so).

6. (be) Life _may have been_ better seventy-five years ago, but it's hard to say. Because there were few taxes, it _may have been_ better for the rich.

7. (make) I _may have made_ a mistake when I asked my supervisor (boss) for a raise. (ask) I _may have asked_ for too much. ✓

8. (cheat) He won every game when we played cards the other night. He _might have cheated_ but it's hard to believe. (be/get) He _might have been_ lucky and just _he might have gotten_ good cards.

9. (cheat) A few of the students _might have cheated_ on the final examination, but the teacher doubts it.

10. (have) The cake was a flop. I _might have had_ the wrong recipe. ✓

11. (fall) He's suddenly changed. He _might have fallen_ in love.

12. (be) The wine at dinner wasn't very good. It _might have been_ a bad vintage (year).

13. (put) Why did I say that? I _might have put_ my foot in my mouth. (say) I _might have said_ something indiscreet. ✓

14. (censor) The news about the scandal isn't in the newspapers. The government _might have censored_ it. (be) The publishers _might have been_ afraid to publish it.

3.12

GRAMMAR EXERCISE   Name _____ Date _____

handwritten: 14 af.

Focus: Slight Probability and Conjecture with May/Might

Fill in the blanks with *may* (*might*) + *not* + *have* + a past participle.

EXAMPLES: a. (invite) Our party was not a big success. We <u>may not have invited</u> the right kind of people.
b. (put) Isn't this soup a little bland? I <u>may not have put</u> enough salt in it.

1. (use) I *might not have used* the right kind of spices.

2. (have) We looked for a couple of minutes, but we couldn't find their house. We *might not have had* the right address. (look) We *might not have looked* long enough.

3. (get) My car isn't working right. I *might not have gotten* the right kind of gas when I filled her (it) up last. (*To fill up* means *to fill completely.*)

4. (put) These chocolates are a little bitter. I _____ in enough sugar when I made them. (have) I _____ the right recipe. (have) I _____ good chocolate. (follow) I _____ the directions as carefully as I should have [followed them].

5. (make) I _____ the right decision, but I'm a much happier person now, so I must have done something right.

6. (have) He doesn't appear to be a happy man, does he? He _____ a happy childhood.

7. (like) My boss _____ my decision to quit my job, but I don't care.

8. (make) I _____ any mistakes in the last test, but I'm not sure; there were only a few hard questions.

9. The movie wasn't entirely successful. (be) The music _____ right for the theme of the film. The actress _____ quite right for her role as a queen. (organize) The director _____ the plot carefully enough. (be) The actor's role _____ large enough. (have) The producer _____ enough time to supervise the production. (have) They _____ enough money to make a truly successful film. But it was still a fine movie.

10. (take) Are we lost? I _____ the right turn at the last intersection.

11. (use) This paint isn't going on the wall smoothly. I _____ enough paint thinner. (mix) I _____ the paint long enough.

WRITING EXERCISE   Name _____ Date _____

Focus: Slight Probability and Conjecture with *May/Might*

Compare (aloud and/or in writing) appropriate statements containing verb phrases with may (*might*)
(+ *not*) + *have* + a past participle in response to the following stated situations and questions.

EXAMPLES: a. I have a little bit of a hangover.
                <u>You might have drunk too much last night.</u>
           b. They haven't received the letter yet.
                <u>I might not have remembered to put a stamp on it.</u>

1. I have a little bit of a fever, and I've been sneezing a lot for the past hour.

   _____

2. He wasn't at work yesterday.
   <u>He might have been sick work yesterday.</u>

3. They left the theater in the middle of the movie.
   <u>They might not have left the theater in the middle of the mo</u>

4. I don't know why, but their company went out of business.

   _____

5. Jack and his wife have recently gotten a divorce.

   _____

6. She didn't speak to me when I saw her on the street yesterday.
   <u>She might have been angry at me.</u>

7. My parents didn't like that movie.
   <u>They might not have liked another movie.</u>

8. I don't know why, but my boss was very tired a couple of days ago.
   <u>He might have worked a lot.</u>

9. It's hard for me to believe, but our teacher was late yesterday.

   _____

10. For some reason, they didn't take a vacation last year.

   _____

11. S/he quit his/her job. Why?

   _____

12. He didn't like his course in chemistry last semester. Why?

   _____

13. S/he dropped out of school. Why? (**Reminder:** *To drop out of school* means *to quit school.*)

   _____

3.14

PAST FORMS WITH *COULD*

Reminder: *Could,* the other form of *can,* is combined with a base form: (a) to show ability and possibility in past time: *No one **could guess** the riddle during the contest last night; Our daughter **could speak** well before she was three;* (b) to make polite requests in present time: ***Could** I please **leave** the room?* (c) to show slight probability (like *may/might*) in present time: *She **could be** sick today, but I don't think so. Could + not + a* base form is used to show impossibility in present time: *He **couldn't know** much about China; he's never been there.*

1. *Could + have +* a past participle is used to express slight probability (conjecture) in past time: *He **could have been** wrong in his decision, but I doubt it; Possibly, the doctors **could have done** more for the patient, but no one in the hospital thinks so.*

	Singular		Plural	
First person	I		we	
Second person	you	could have gone	you	could have gone
Third person	he		they	
	she			
	it			

2. *Could've* (sounds like *could-of*), the contraction of *could have,* occurs in spoken informal usage: *He **could've committed** the crime, but the police don't think so; Perhaps, they **could've reached** the top of the mountain.*
   Note: Like *should've* and *might've, could've* is not written unless dialogue is being quoted.

3. *Could have +* a past participle is also used to express past opportunity not realized: *We **could have gone** (we were able to go) to the mountains, but we stayed home instead; I **could've had** the job (they offered it to me), but I didn't accept their offer.*

4. *Could not + have +* a past participle does not mean slight probability; it means impossibility: *You **could not have received** a letter from that company; they've been out of business for years.*

I			we		
you	could not have gone		you	could not have gone	
he			they		
she					
it					

5. *Couldn't have* (sounds like *couldn't-of*), the contraction of *could not have,* occurs in informal usage: *Impossible! Hitler **couldn't have been** sane at the end.*

6. In *yes-no* and information questions with *could have*, the subject of a sentence usually occurs after *could:* **Could I** have made a mistake? Where **could they** have gone? How **could Sarah** have made such a foolish error?

7. However, when an information word(s) is the subject of a sentence, the usual question form does not occur: **What** could have happened to our guests? **Who** could have taken my wallet?

8. In *yes-no* answers, *have* may follow the modal: *Could she have done such a terrible thing? Yes, she could (have); No, she couldn't (have).*

Practice reading the following sentences aloud.

1. She could have (*could-of*) gone to the party, but she was tired.
2. Impossible! My boss couldn't have (*couldn't-of*) done that.
3. You might not have (*might-not-of*) had the right map.
4. You should have (*should-of*) gotten to class on time.
5. They really ought to have (*ought-to-of*) taken the test.
6. You might not have (*might-not-of*) used the right ingredients.
7. I may have (*may-of*) made a mistake, but I don't know.
8. You may not have (*may-not-of*) understood my question.
9. You shouldn't have (*shouldn't of*) done that.
10. You ought not to have (*ought-not-to-of*) used that method.
11. What could I have (*could-I-of*) done wrong?
12. What road should we have (*should-we-of*) taken?
13. Might the teacher have (*might-the teacher-of*) made a mistake?
14. Should I have (*should-I-of*) put more salt in the stew?
15. Why shouldn't I have (*shouldn't-I-of*) told the neighbors?
16. Where could the children have (*could-the children-of*) gone?
17. What time should the movie have (*should-the-movie-of*) begun?
18. Why couldn't you have (*couldn't-you-of*) tried harder?
19. How should I have (*should-I-of*) written that letter?
20. What might have (*might-of*) happened to them?

13   *13*

3.15

GRAMMAR EXERCISE   Name _____ Date _____

Focus: Slight Probability and Conjecture with *Could*

Fill in the blanks with appropriate affirmative verb phrases containing *could* + *have* + a past participle. Practice using the contraction *could've*.

EXAMPLES: a. (send) Why didn't they get the letter? I <u>could have sent</u> it to the wrong address, but I don't think so.

b. (use) Why are these dishes still dirty? I <u>could have used</u> the wrong kind of soap when I washed them, but I don't think so.

1. (forget) Why hasn't he shown up yet? He <u>could have forgotten</u> our appointment, but I doubt it because he always remembers.

2. (take) Why are we lost? We <u>could have taken</u> the wrong road at the intersection, but I read the map very carefully.

3. (be) Why didn't she say hello to me? She <u>could have been</u> angry at me, but I can't believe it—she's one of my best friends.

4. (steal) Where's my watch? Someone in the office <u>could have stolen</u> it, but I can't believe that.

5. (get) Why isn't our car working right? We <u>could have gotten</u> the wrong kind of gas at our last stop, but I don't think so.

6. (buy) These new shoes aren't very comfortable. I <u>could have bought</u> the wrong size, but I don't think so.

7. (miss) Why haven't they come yet? Well, they <u>could have missed</u> the bus, or they might have forgotten the date. Who knows?
   Note: The verb phrases in the remaining sentences of this exercise express <u>past opportunity</u> <u>not realized</u>.

8. (go) We <u>could have gone</u> to Europe on our vacation last year, but we didn't want to. We went to Japan instead. —упекаю—

9. (take) I <u>could have taken</u> another course in Spanish, but I didn't care to. I took a course in French instead.

10. (marry) She <u>could have married</u> the richest man in town, but she preferred to marry the man she loved instead.

11. (be) He <u>could have been</u> the president, but he wasn't interested.

12. (have) They <u>could have had</u> children, but they chose not to.

13. (stop) He <u>could have stoped</u> smoking, but he didn't try to.

14. (buy) We <u>could have bought</u> an expensive car, but we bought a cheap one instead.

15. (marry) He <u>could have married</u> the most beautiful and successful woman in town, but he married the woman he loved instead.

16. (become) She <u>could have become</u> a successful businesswoman, but she became an artist instead.

17. (stay) I <u>could have stayed</u> up late last night, but I went to bed instead.

3.16

GRAMMAR EXERCISE   Name _____ Date _____

        Focus: Impossibility with *Could Not*

Fill in the blanks with appropriate negative verb phrases containing *could + not + have* + a past participle. Practice using contractions.

EXAMPLES: a. Impossible! Einstein <u>couldn't have made</u> a mistake.

           b. Thank you so much. I <u>couldn't have made</u> the right decision without your help and guidance.

1. Impossible! The thieves _____ the bank through those doors. They are almost three inches of solid steel.

2. No, I'm afraid you're wrong. Dick _____ at the last meeting because I saw him in the park at the time.

3. He _____ that crime. He was in the hospital when it took place.

4. It was a wonderful movie. It _____ better.

5. It was a terrible meal. It _____ worse.

6. We _____ this exercise at the beginning of the course.

7. When we saw our son/daughter receive the prize for the best student in the graduating class,

we _____ happier.

8. Their child _____ this beautiful letter; she's only eleven. They must have done it for her.

9. I'm sorry, but I'm afraid you're wrong. That writer _____ this book. He'd already been dead for thirty years when the book was published, and the book is about current events.

10. Impossible! That student _____ on the final examination because s/he's too honest.

11. Impossible! I _____ such a foolish thing; I wasn't there.

12. It's hard to believe. S/he _____ drunk at that party because s/he never drinks.

13. Impossible! You _____ to him on the phone; he doesn't have one.

14. I'm sorry, but you _____ me at that party because I wasn't there.

15. No! S/he _____ that money from the company; I know s/he would never do such a thing.

16. I _____ that race, no matter how hard I tried; the competition was too good.

3.17

WRITING EXERCISE   Name _____ Date _____

> Focus: Asking Questions with *Could*

Make (aloud and/or in writing) appropriate *yes-no* questions with *could* + subject + *have* + a past participle and any other necessary words in response to the following stated situations and questions.

EXAMPLES: a. He didn't say hello when I saw him on the street. <u>Could he have been angry at me?</u>
           b. The teacher hasn't come yet. <u>Could she have missed her train?</u>

1. This soup is a little bland.

    Could it have

2. He didn't say much when I made the suggestion.

    Could he have said much ?

3. She's always here, but for some reason she wasn't here yesterday.

    Could she have

4. This steak is a little tough, isn't it?

    _____

5. Our car isn't working right.

    Could it have worked right.

6. The patient didn't feel well yesterday.

    Could he have felt well ?

7. I sent them a letter a week ago, but they haven't gotten it yet.

    Could I have

8. When I got back to my apartment, the door was open.

    _____

9. Why hasn't she come yet? I've been waiting here for an hour.

    _____

10. Most of my house plants died.

    _____

11. Don/Jill was in a very quiet mood all day long yesterday.

    _____

12. These new shoes are a little tight/loose.

    _____

13. My stomach is a little upset.

    _____

14. Why haven't our guests come yet? They should have been here two hours ago.

    _____

3.18

PAST FORMS WITH *MUST*

> **Reminder:** *Must* may be used to express necessity in present time only: *We **must protect** our freedom at all costs.* We must use *had to,* the past form of the idiom *have to,* for necessity in past time: *I myself **had to tell** my parents the bad news about my sister.*

1. To show strong probability (deduction) in past time, *must* combined with *have* and a past participle occurs in a verb phrase: *Building a pyramid **must have been** a long and hard job; When Neil Armstrong first stepped on the moon, he **must have been** thrilled.*

		Singular		Plural
First person	I		we	
Second person	you	} must have gone	you	} must have gone
Third person	he		they	
	she			
	it			

2. *Must've* (sounds like *must-of*), the contraction of *must have,* occurs in spoken informal usage: *What a mess the kitchen is in! The children **must've had** some kind of cooking project.*
   Note: Like *should've, might've,* and *could've, must've* is not written unless dialogue is being quoted.

3. *Not* follows *must* in negative verb phrases: *Che Guevara **must not have had** accurate information when he decided to start a revolution in Bolivia; Before the Cuban Revolution, the rich **must not have understood** the problems of the poor.*

4. *Mustn't,* the contraction of *must not,* occurs in informal usage: *They **mustn't have practiced** much before the game; they didn't score one point.*
   Pronunciation Note: *Mustn't have* sounds like *mustn't-of.*
   Reminder: No question forms occur when we use *must* for strong probability (deduction).

Practice reading the following sentences aloud.

1. It must have (*must-of*) been terrible to fight in the war.
2. You mustn't have (*mustn't-of*) had the right formula in the experiment.
3. Life for the rich before the revolution must have been wonderful.
4. He mustn't have done enough homework for the course.
5. You must have said the wrong thing to her.
6. The judge mustn't have made the right decision.
7. The general mustn't have listened to his advisers.
8. The last exercise must have been difficult for some of the students.

11

3.19

GRAMMAR EXERCISE   Name _____ Date _____

Focus: Strong Probability (Deduction) with *Must*

Fill in the blanks with *must* + *have* + a past participle.

EXAMPLES: a. (work) You <u>must have worked</u> very hard on that project. It's excellent!
b. (be) The Pilgrims <u>must have been</u> thrilled when their ship, the *Mayflower,* first landed in the New World.

1. (take) We're lost! We _must have taken_ a wrong turn at the last intersection. (be) Our map _must have been_ wrong.

2. (say) Everyone in the other room is laughing. Someone _must have said_ something funny.

3. (have) They _must have had_ a good time on their vacation in Europe; they're still talking about it. (spend) They _must have spent_ a great deal of money.

4. (do) My boss is angry at me. I _must have done_ something wrong.

5. (cook) This meat is tough. I _____ it too long.

6. (buy) This shirt doesn't fit. I _____ the wrong size.

7. (study) She got a high grade. She _____ hard.

8. (send) They never got the letter. I _____ it to the wrong address. (get) It _____ lost.

9. (be) Visiting your friend at the hospital _____ a depressing experience. (appreciate) He _____ your visit. (enjoy) He _____ it.

10. (happen) Why is she crying? Something terrible _____ to her. (get) She _____ some bad news.

11. (go) All the lights in our neighbors' house are off. They _____ to bed.

12. (cost) Look at her beautiful coat. It _____ a lot.

13. (give) Their little boy is very spoiled. They _____ him too much when he was younger.

14. (say) She seems angry at me. I _____ something wrong.

15. (be) You were in the battle zone, weren't you? It _____ terrible. (be) You _____ afraid for your life.

16. (make) It was a very difficult exam. I _____ quite a few mistakes. (fail) I _____ it.

17. (be) Did you go to the Mardi Gras in Rio? It _____ an exciting experience. (have) You _____ a good time.

18. (have) Did you graduate from Harvard University? You _____ a wonderful educational experience.

Strong Probability (Deduction) with *Must*   **83**

3.20

Name _____ Date _____

        Focus: Strong Probability (Deduction) with *Must*   ✓

Fill in the blanks with *must* + *not* + *have* + a past participle. **Pronunciation Reminder:** *Mustn't have* sounds like *mustn't-of.*

EXAMPLES: a. (choose) I gave her a blue sweater for her birthday, but she didn't seem to like it. I <u>mustn't have chosen</u> the right color.

          b. (pick) I <u>mustn't have picked out</u> (chosen) the right thing.

1. (have) They never talk about their vacation in Mexico. They _____ a good time. (be) It _____ the right place for them.

2. (feed) The dog still acts hungry. I _____ her enough.

3. (study) It's one of the easiest courses at school, but she got a bad grade. She _____ _____ hard enough.

4. (put) I got the letter back from the post office. I _____ enough stamps on it.

5. (like) I haven't received an answer from my girlfriend yet, and it's been two months. She _____ it. (say) I _____ the right thing. (explain) I _____ myself clearly.

6. (put) This soup tastes bland. The cook _____ any salt in it. (have) He _____ the right recipe.

7. (fix) My TV still doesn't work right. The TV man _____ it right. (have) He _____ the right parts.

8. (use) The cake was terrible. I _____ the right ingredients.

9. (have) I wasn't able to find their house. I _____ the right directions.

10. (pay) Their house isn't very nice. They _____ much money for it. (look) They _____ for it for very long.

11. (cook) This meat is very tough. I _____ it at the right temperature. (have) I _____ the right directions. (be) The recipe _____ _____ right.

12. (sleep) Our boss looks very tired today. He _____ well last night.

13. (enjoy) He doesn't want to talk about the party last night. He _____ himself. (have) He _____ a good time. (be) His girlfriend _____ _____ there.

14. (use) These photographs are very poor. I _____ the right exposure.

3.21

WRITING EXERCISE　　　　　　　　Name _____ Date _____

Focus: Strong Probability (Deduction) with *Must*

Compose (aloud and/or in writing) appropriate statements containing verb phrases with *must* (+ *not*) + *have* + a past participle in response to the following stated situations. **Pronunciation Reminder:** *Must have* sounds like *must-of*, and *mustn't have* sounds like *mustn't-of*.

EXAMPLES:　a.　When they returned from their vacation, they looked very refreshed.
　　　　　　　　　They must have had a good time while they were away.
　　　　　　　b.　When I first met my new neighbor, he said he was George Washington.
　　　　　　　　　He must have been crazy, or drunk.

1. Thousands of people bought tickets for that show.

　　_____

2. They didn't want to talk about the party.

　　_____

3. We wanted to take a drive to Smithtown, but we ended up in Bordentown instead.

　　_____

　　(*To end up in a place* can mean *to arrive at a place by accident or surprise: Columbus wanted to get to India, but he ended up in America instead.*)

4. He wanted to get a job in an office, but he ended up in a factory instead.

　　_____

5. The bride/groom was crying and standing alone at the altar.

　　_____

6. I asked for a steak at the restaurant, but I ended up with (finally got) chicken.

　　_____

7. That politician wanted to make a lot of money, but he ended up in jail instead.

　　_____

8. The aristocrats had everything before the revolution took place.

　　_____

9. I wanted to get to the east side of town, but I ended up on the west side.

　　_____

10. He wanted to have everything, but he ended up with nothing.

　　_____

11. He had a good time at the party, but he ended up with a hangover.

　　_____

12. We took our last winter vacation in Moscow in February.

　　_____

13. A friend of mine spent a whole summer in the Sahara desert.

　　_____

PAST CONTINUOUS FORMS WITH MODALS

1. Modal auxiliaries may also occur in verb phrases combined with *have* (as a second auxiliary), *been* (as a third auxiliary), and a present participle (as a main verb). This kind of verb phrase is used to emphasize the duration of an event in past time: *I should have been thinking more carefully while I was taking the test, but I was tired; A lot of thoughts must have been running through Marie Antoinette's mind as she was waiting for her execution at the guillotine.*

I
you   should
he   ought to
she   may   have been going
it   might
we   could
you   must
they

2. Negative verb phrases are formed by placing *not* after the modal: *It **must not** have been raining very much before we arrived in Turkey because the countryside was dry. The kids **shouldn't** have been playing around while the teacher was out of the room.*
Note: *Not* is inserted between *ought* and *to* in a negative verb phrase: *They **ought not to** have been insulting the King.*
Reminder: Negative verb phrases containing *ought to* rarely occur in American English.

I
you   should
he   ought
she   may   not (to) have been going
it   might
we   could
you   must
they

3. *Yes-no* and information questions are formed by placing the subject of a sentence after the modal: ***Should we** have been using that technique during the experiment? What **could I** have been thinking about when I made that stupid mistake?*

4. In *yes-no* answers, a modal + *have* follows the subject of the answer. *Been* can also be used, but its use is optional: *Could they have been making a mistake? Yes, they could have (been); No, they couldn't have (been); Should they have been finishing the job by that time? Yes, they should have (been); No, they shouldn't have (been).*

3.23

GRAMMAR EXERCISE

Name _____ Date _____

Focus: *Should* and *Ought to*

Fill in the blanks with appropriate verb phrases containing *should* (*not*), (*ought* [*not*] *to*) + *have* + *been* + a present participle. When a negative verb phrase is appropriate, remember that *ought not to* seldom occurs in American English.

EXAMPLES: a. When I got home, the children were all watching TV. They <u>should have been doing</u> their homework.

           b. When my boss came back into the office, I <u>shouldn't have been reading</u> the newspaper.

1. When I made that unkind remark to my mother, I _____ more thoughtfully.

2. When Mr. Smith attended his father's funeral, he _____ more appropriate clothes than he was.

3. When I was at the beach last Sunday, I _____ more suntan lotion; I got a very bad sunburn.

4. I _____ through that town so fast in my car. The police stopped me and gave me a ticket.

5. While the speaker was delivering the speech, she _____ her hands so much; it was distracting and spoiled the total effect of the presentation.

6. I _____ a calculator while I was doing my income tax return; I made quite a few mistakes.

7. He _____ more about his family when he decided to put all his money into that foolish business speculation.

8. I _____ my homework in such poor light. It made my eyes very tired.

9. Unfortunately, he doesn't have any money now. He _____ more about his future when he was younger and able to work hard.

11. At work the other day, all of us _____ at the water cooler when the boss came into the office.

12. They _____ more food during the party the other night; everyone was hungry.

13. He _____ about his wife behind her back while she was out of the room. No one liked it.

3.24

GRAMMAR EXERCISE   Name _____ Date _____

Focus: *May/Might*

Fill in the blanks with appropriate verb phrases containing *may* (*might*) (+ *not*) + *have* + *been* + a present participle.

EXAMPLES: a. Why were all of the students confused during the last exercise? They <u>may not have been</u> <u>following</u> the directions correctly.
            b. Jill sounded a little angry when I called her last night. She <u>might have been sleeping</u>.

1. Why didn't Mary want to go to the dance with me?

    She _____ for a better invitation.

2. Why didn't he want to talk when I called?

    He _____ something more important.

3. Why was he so nervous and upset when I saw him last?

    He _____ problems at work or at home.

4. Why did your boss want to go home early?

    He _____ well.

5. Why did they want to transfer their daughter to another school?

    She _____ well at the school she was in.

6. Why did his father have to go to a lawyer?

    He _____ trouble with the government.

7. Why couldn't she come to work yesterday?

    Her child _____ well.

8. Why didn't they sell their car to me when I offered my price?

    They _____ for a better offer.

9. The little boy didn't want to show me his hands.

    He _____ something in them.

10. Why didn't they want to talk about their children?

    They _____ some kind of problem with them.

11. Why did he lose his job?

    He _____ his work well.

12. Why wasn't he hitting any homeruns at the last game?

    He _____ well that day. Who knows?

13. Why was that woman in such a hurry?

    She _____ to an important meeting.

14. Why didn't John/Mary want to go out with me last night?

    S/he _____ with her parents.

3.25

GRAMMAR EXERCISE   Name _____ Date _____

Focus: *Must*

Fill in the blanks with appropriate verb phrases containing *must* (+ *not*) + *have* + *been* + a present participle.

EXAMPLES: a. When we got out of the movies, the streets were all wet. It <u>must have been raining</u> while we were in the theater.
  b. He's a good student, but he got a bad grade in the course. He <u>must not have been thinking</u> while he was taking the final exam.

1. When they got married, the two of them _____ about their futures.

2. When I got home last night, my neighbor's house was all dark. They _____

    _____, or they might've been out.

3. Look at all these mistakes! The student _____ his dictionary while he was writing this composition.

4. Mary sounded angry when I called her around 11:30 last night. She _____ .

5. Bill _____ on the phone in the other room because I could hear only his voice. He might've been talking to himself, but I doubt it.

6. When I began this course, I _____ a lot more mistakes than I am now. Don't you think so?

7. He speaks English very well, doesn't he? Yes, he _____ it for a long time before he came to the United States.

8. Why did you do that? You _____ your head when you made that foolish mistake.

9. My boss _____ well yesterday because he went home a few hours earlier than he usually does.

10. The patient _____ clearly when she decided to commit suicide.

11. Raymond _____ hard from the beginning to the end of the course because he got the highest mark in the class.

12. The guests _____ a good time at the party because they all went home early.

13. The pianist played very well at the concert last night, didn't she? Yes, she _____

    _____ a long time before she finally decided to perform in public.

3.26

GRAMMAR EXERCISE   Name _____ Date _____

Focus: *Could*

Fill in the blanks with appropriate affirmative verb phrases containing *could* + *have* + *been* + a present participle.

EXAMPLES: a. A few of the students <u>could have been cheating</u> during the examination, but the teacher doubts it.
b. Why were our neighbors so noisy last night? They <u>could have been having</u> a party, but I don't think so.

1. My boss isn't satisfied with the project I've just finished. Possibly, I _____

    _____ the wrong approach while I was doing the job, but I don't think so. (Use *taking*.)

2. Why did you waste your time at the library yesterday? You _____
    your homework while you were there.

3. When he was younger and in better health than he is now, he _____
    a lot more money, but he wanted to have a good time instead.

4. We shouldn't have gone to that awful party last night; we _____
    a good time at home instead.

5. No, I think you're wrong. That fellow _____ good luck during
    that card game, but he couldn't have been cheating because he isn't smart enough to cheat.

6. Why didn't you take that job? You _____ for one of the most
    important firms in the United States.

7. Why didn't you study German while you were in Germany? You _____

    _____ a second language while you were living there.

8. Jane seemed very excited yesterday. She _____ for a call from
    her brother in Australia, but I'm not sure.

9. A few of the students _____ trouble with the material during the
    first part of the course, but they're not now.

10. The people in the last government _____ more for the poor, but
    they were only interested in their pockets.

11. I _____ at the university last semester, but I wanted to take some
    time off. (*To take time off* means *to take a vacation from one's usual routine.*)

3.27

WRITING EXERCISE   Name _____ Date _____

Focus: Reviewing Past Forms of Modals

Compose (aloud and/or in writing) appropriate statements in response to the following stated situations and questions. Use the modals given in parentheses.

EXAMPLES: a. When I last saw John, he was wearing a black arm band.
          (must) <u>Someone in his family must have died.</u>
      b. She took woolen clothes when she went to Florida on her trip.
          (should) <u>She should have taken cotton clothes.</u>

1. The teacher was angry at all of the students, and s/he's never gotten angry before.

(must) _____

2. Timmy got a spanking when his father came home.

(must) _____

3. When I asked her the question, she slapped my face.

(must) _____

4. During the break in my English class, some of the students were speaking Spanish and French.

(should) _____

5. He put all his money into one business and lost it all.

(should) _____

6. She's a very good student, but she didn't get a good grade in the course.

(must) _____

7. The dishes weren't clean after I washed them.

(might) _____

8. He misspelled a lot of words while he was writing the composition.

(should) _____

9. That young boy doesn't have any money, but he suddenly has a beautiful new bicycle.

(might) _____

10. Dick and Janet are not speaking to each other.

(must) _____

11. Why is my boss angry at me?

(could) _____

12. Why didn't they accept the invitation to my picnic?

(may) _____

13. When my boss got to work yesterday, I was reading the newspaper.

(should) _____

3.28

USED TO + A BASE FORM

Note: In the remainder of this chapter, we will discuss certain expressions and idioms that are closely related to modal auxiliaries in that they give special meanings to the base forms they precede.

1. *Used to* + a base form is used for (a) a condition that once existed but which no longer does: *People **used to believe** the world was flat* (we now know it is round); *London **used to be** the largest city in the world* (Tokyo is now the largest); and (b) a past custom (habitual activity) that occurred with regularity in past time but now no longer does: *When I was a child, I **used to ride** my bike to school every day; When I got home, I **used to feed** the chickens before I did my homework; I **used to do** these things every day.*
   Pronunciation Note: *Used* (before *to*) sounds like *use* (pronounced as a noun.)

2. Sometimes, *used to* is used for a condition that existed in past time and still does: *When I was a child, I used to ride a bicycle to school, and I still do; I used to study hard, and I still do.*

3. *Any more* and *any longer* are adverbial expressions frequently found in sentences containing *used to* (most often in negative *but* clauses): *Women used to wear hats a lot, but they don't **any more**; He used to teach at a university, but he doesn't **any longer**.*

4. Negative statements with *used to* are seldom used, but they occur in sentences like: *I **didn't use to like** Chinese food, but now I do; I **didn't use to appreciate** classical music, but now I do.*

5. As in negative statements, *used to* becomes a base form in questions: *Did you **use to** play with dolls when you were a little girl? What time did you **use to** get up every morning while you were at school?* However, the idiom does not change in form when the information word is the subject: *When you were a baby, **who used to** take care of you when your parents were not at home?*

6. Students sometimes confuse *used to* with the adverb *usually*. *Used to* refers only to a habitual activity in past time, while *usually* may refer to a habitual activity in past *or* present time. Compare:

Correct	Wrong
I used to go to school every day when I was little.	*I used to go to school every day now.*
I usually eat my native food now.	*I used to eat my native food now.*

Note: The idiom *be used to,* which has a completely different meaning from *used to,* will be discussed in the chapter on gerunds.

3.29

Focus: Past Custom with *Used to* + a Base Form

Supply appropriate base forms in the blanks.

EXAMPLES: a. Before Columbus discovered America, people used to believe that the world was flat.

        b. When I was a child on a ranch in the Far West, my grandmother used to tell me stories about cowboys and Indians.

1. When he was much younger, he used to _____ in God, but now he doesn't.

2. While I was working at a bank, before I became an English teacher, I used to _____ a calculator all day long.

3. When I was in the mountains on my vacation, I used to _____ long hikes through the forests.

4. Because Mary had a lot of sun in her old apartment, she used to _____ a lot of house plants.

5. He used to _____ a lot of baseball when he was younger, and he still does.

6. My grandfather used to _____ a lot of chess, but now he's completely satisfied with checkers.

7. When I was little, my parents used to _____ stories to me before I went to sleep.

8. A horse used to _____ an important means of transportation.

9. While s/he was studying to be a doctor, s/he used to _____ hours and hours at the library.

10. When I was younger, I used to _____ nervous in a social situation, but when I meet people now, I'm more confident of myself.

11. When they were in China on their vacation, they used to _____ rice every day.

12. That actress used to _____ in a lot of movies, but now she's retired. She used to _____ in comedies.

13. When I was a child in the western part of the United States, a lot of cowboys used to _____ for my father on our ranch.

14. While we were living in Mexico, we used to _____ all our food at open markets.

15. When I was on my two-month vacation in Acapulco, I used to _____ swimming three or four times a day.

16. When our daughter was a little girl, she used to _____ house. (*To play house* means *to pretend to have a house.*)

17. When I was a child, I used to _____ a lot of candy, and I still do.

3.30

Focus: *Used to* + a Base Form in Main Clauses

Complete the following sentences with appropriate main clauses containing verb phrases with *used to* + a base form.

EXAMPLES: a. When I was on my vacation in Hawaii, I used to eat pineapple for breakfast every morning.
b. When I spent that summer in France, I used to drink wine with all of my meals except breakfast.

1. When I was a child, _____
_____.

2. While he was playing with the New York Yankees, _____
_____.

(The New York Yankees is a famous baseball team in the United States.)

3. When my grandfather/grandmother was still alive, _____
_____.

4. When I was in high school, _____
_____.

5. When I was in elementary school, _____
_____.

6. When I was on my last vacation (in the mountains/at the beach/in Europe/in the Orient), _____.

7. When my mother/father was a child, _____
_____.

8. When I first started to speak English, _____
_____.

9. When I first started this course, _____
_____.

10. When Bob was working for the government, _____
_____.

11. While we were living in New York/London/Paris/Tokyo/Rio, _____
_____.

12. While Mary was still working at the United Nations in New York, _____
_____.

13. When our son was still at the university, _____
_____.

14. When my teacher was younger, _____
_____.

WOULD LIKE

1. *Would* (another form of *will*) + *like* is a polite synonym for *want*: **I would like** (*want*) *an ice cream cone, please;* **I would like** (*want*) *another cocktail, please.*

2. We usually contract *would* and subject pronouns when we speak: **I'd** (*I would*) *like a new car for Christmas;* **She'd** (*she would*) *like to take a trip around the world.*

3. *Not* is inserted between *would* and *like* in negative verb phrases: **I would not like** (*do not want*) *an argument, please.*

4. *Wouldn't,* the contraction of *would not,* occurs in informal usage: **I wouldn't** *like another cocktail, would you?*

	Singular		Plural	
First person	I		we	
Second person	you	would (not) like	you	would (not) like
Third person	he		they	
	she			
	it			

5. In questions, a subject is inserted between *would* and *like:* **Would you like** *some advice? What kind of house* **would you like?** *Would* follows subjects in *yes-no* answers: *Yes,* **I would;** *No,* **I wouldn't.**

6. *Wouldn't* precedes a subject in negative questions: **Wouldn't you** *like another piece of cake? Why* **wouldn't you** *like it?*
   Pronunciation Note: (a) *Would* sounds like *wood;* (b) *would you* sounds like *would-jew;* (c) *wouldn't you* sounds like *wouldn't-chew.*

7. *Would like* most often is accompanied by an infinitive (never a base form): **We'd like to take** *a break now;* **Would you like to have** *another Coke?* **Wouldn't you like to go** *for a walk?*

8. Do not confuse *like* (enjoy) with *would like* (want); for example, *I* **like** (*enjoy*) *wine with my meals; I'd* **like** (*want*) *another glass of wine.*

9. Also, be careful not to confuse the contractions *'d* (*would*) with *'d* (*had*). When *'d* is followed by *like* (or another base form), it is the contraction of a subject pronoun and *would:* **I'd** (*would*) *like to go home.* When *'d* is followed by a past participle (or *better*), it is a contraction of a subject pronoun and *had:* **She'd** (*had*) *gone by that time;* **You'd** (*had*) *better be good.*

3.32

GRAMMAR EXERCISE   Name _____ Date _____

Focus: *Would like* + an Infinitive

Supply appropriate infinitives in the blanks. Practice questions and answers.

EXAMPLES: a. You'd like <u>to have</u> another piece of cake, wouldn't you?
              b. I wouldn't like <u>to be</u> in the President's shoes during this crisis. (*To be in someone's shoes* is a figurative expression meaning *to be in someone's position.*)

1. She'd like _____ another course, but she won't be able to.

2. You'd like _____ a different kind of job, wouldn't you?

3. My brother would like _____ to the game, but I wouldn't.

4. Thank you, but I wouldn't like _____ another drink.

5. Would you like _____ dinner now?

6. Would you like _____ to the movies or stay home? It's up to you. (*It's up to you* means *it's your decision.*)

7. Would you like _____ with me? It's a beautiful record.

8. Would you like _____ care of my cat while I'm away on a business trip?

9. Would you like _____ over to my house tonight for a card game. (*To come [go] over to a place* means *to visit a place.*)

10. Would you like _____ over to the park and fly our kites?

11. He wouldn't like _____ a long trip around the world, but she'd like to.

12. Would you like _____ over to my house tonight for dinner?

13. What would you like _____?

14. Wouldn't you like _____ in Paris? I'm surprised.

15. Would you like _____ my wife/husband?

16. Would you like _____ a break now?

17. Wouldn't you like _____ in an Italian restaurant tonight?

18. Why wouldn't you like _____ in the United States for the rest of your life?

19. Would you like _____ in your native country for good? (*For good* means *forever.*)

Now complete the sentences.

20. I wouldn't like_____.

21. Where would you like _____?

22. What kind of [supply noun] _____ would you like_____?

23. What would you like _____?

24. I'd/you'd/she'd/we'd like _____.

3.33

GRAMMAR EXERCISE   Name _____ Date _____

> Focus: *Would Rather* + a Base Form

1. *Would rather* + a base form shows preference: ***I'd rather be*** (*prefer to be*) *a lawyer than a doctor;* ***I'd rather live*** (*prefer to live*) *in a warm climate than a cold climate.*

2. In statements, *than* is inserted between the two choices: *I'd rather be happy **than** rich.* In questions, we may replace *than* with *or: Would you rather go (do you prefer to go) to Europe on a ship **or** a plane? What is your choice? What would you rather be, a painter **or** a writer? What is your preference?*
   Remember: (a) *Would like* means *want.* (b) *Would rather* means *preference.*

Make statements and questions. Use the words given in the parentheses as cues. Pronunciation Reminder: *Would you* sounds like *would-jew.*

EXAMPLES: a. (double bed/single bed) I'd rather sleep on a double bed.
            b. (Europe/the Orient) Would you rather go to the Orient or Europe?

1. (small school/large school) _____

2. (single/married) _____

3. (doctor/lawyer) _____

4. (apartment/house) _____

5. (love/money) _____

6. (French/German) _____

7. (wine/beer) _____

8. (Russia/China) _____

9. (an American/a European car) _____

10. (a movie/play) _____

11. (a new radio/a new color TV) _____

12. (a French restaurant/a Chinese restaurant) _____

13. (Latin America/North America) _____

14. (an architect/a lawyer) _____

15. (a hot dog/a hamburger) _____

16. (Coca-Cola/Pepsi-Cola) _____

17. (a Chevrolet/a Ford) _____

18. (the country/the city) _____

19. (the President/the Queen) _____

HAD BETTER + A BASE FORM

1. Like the modal *should, had better* + a base form expresses advisability. Even though *had better* is a past form, the idiom never refers to past time; it may refer only to the present or the future. Subject pronouns and *had* almost always occur as contractions: ***You'd*** *better take care of that problem;* ***I'd*** *better get to the bank before it closes.*

2. *Not* is inserted between *better* and the base form in a negative verb phrase: *I'd* ***better not take*** *a long coffee break, or my boss might get angry; You'd* ***better not reveal*** *this information to the police.*

	Singular		Plural	
First person	I	⎫	we	⎫
Second person	you	⎬ 'd better (not) go	you	⎬ 'd better (not) go
Third person	he	⎭	they	⎭
	she			
	it			

Note: *Had better* is rather informal in tone.

3. *Had better* shows a stronger sense of advisability than *should.* There is the implication (suggestion) that we may have to face an undesirable result if we do not follow the advice; it is a kind of warning: *You'd better go to the dentist,* ***or you might lose your teeth;*** *You'd better pay your taxes,* ***or the government will be looking for you.***

4. *Had better* is quite often used in the main clause of a complex sentence followed by a subordinate clause introduced by *or else* (otherwise): *You'd better stop smoking,* ***or else*** *you might develop a serious lung condition; He'd better pay more attention to his wife,* ***or else*** *she will leave him.*

5. Questions do not occur with *had better* except for negative *yes-no* questions when we want to emphasize the advisability (warning): ***Hadn't he better speak*** *to his lawyer about the problem?* (It sounds serious.) ***Hadn't you better sit down*** *before you fall down?* (You look sick.)
   Pronunciation Note: *Hadn't you* sounds like *hadn't-chew.*
   Note: *Had best,* particularly in British English, sometimes occurs: *We'd best not say anything about this problem to the teacher.*

3.35

GRAMMAR EXERCISE   Name _____ Date _____

Focus: *Had Better* + a Base Form

Supply appropriate base forms in the blanks.

EXAMPLES: a. Listen, children! You'd better <u>be</u> good, or Santa Claus won't bring you any presents for Christmas.
  b. I'd better <u>take</u> a couple more aspirins, or this headache won't go away.

1. I'd better not _____ late again tomorrow, or my boss might get angry.

2. You'd better _____ something about the problem before it gets worse. You'd better not _____ another day.

3. You'd better not _____ this secret, or I'll get angry.

4. I'd better not _____ another cocktail, or I'll get drunk.

5. You'd better _____ all of your taxes; otherwise, you might get into trouble with the government.

6. I'd better _____ care of this letter right away, or else I might have a problem with my boss.

7. You'd better _____ to the dentist immediately, or else you might lose that tooth.

8. Listen, children! You'd better _____ good, or else your father might give you all a spanking when he gets home from work.

9. Be careful! You'd better not _____ the street against the red light.

10. They'd better _____ me to their party; otherwise, I won't invite them to mine.

11. We'd better _____ our homework, or the teacher will be disappointed. We'd better _____ up all the new words.

12. Sh! We'd better _____ talking about that now. Someone's listening in on our conversation. (*To listen in on a conversation* means *to listen to a conversation but not to participate* [often secretly]: *Government spies are listening in on my phone conversations.*)

13. You'd better not _____ me on my home phone. Someone has been listening in on my calls.

14. You'd better _____ careful with that cat, Betsy; she might scratch you.

15. You'd better not _____ so much candy, or else you might have trouble with your teeth.

16. You'd better _____ that ice cream in the freezer, or else it will melt.

WRITING EXERCISE   Name _____ Date _____

Focus: *Had Better* + a Base Form

Compose (aloud and/or in writing) appropriate statements containing verb phrases with *had better* + a base form in response to the following stated situations. **Reminder:** This form does not occur in formal usage.

EXAMPLES: a. One of my teeth is bothering me. You'd better go to the dentist, or you might lose it.
b. It's my father's birthday next week. You'd better send him a birthday card, or he'll be disappointed.

1. We're going to take a hike up to the top of the mountain.

    _____

2. I've just bought a pound of ice cream.

    _____

3. We're going to take a trip through the Sahara Desert.

    _____

4. He's got a problem with the teacher.

    _____

5. This fish looks a little old, doesn't it?

    _____

6. That water looks polluted, doesn't it?

    _____

7. I'm going to write a letter to the President.

    _____

8. Someone is listening in on our conversation. I can hear a buzzing on our line.

    _____

9. We're going to take a trip to Russia in February.

    _____

10. My plane is going to take off at exactly 10:00 A.M.

    _____

11. We're going to go to Florida on our vacation.

    _____

12. My lawyer is a little crooked. (*Crooked* can mean *not honest.*)

    _____

13. She's had a terrible headache for almost three weeks.

    _____

14. I've been standing on my feet for at least twelve hours.

    _____

3.37

HAVE GOT TO + A BASE FORM

1. *Have got to* + a base form is used to express a strong sense of necessity: *I've got to* (*must*) *go for a physical examination right away; You've got to* (*must*) *listen to your conscience.*

2. *Have got to* shows a stronger sense of necessity than the modal *must* and the idiom *have to.* Like *had better, have got to* means we will suffer some kind of undesirable result if we do not follow a certain course of action: *I've got to go to the bank,* **or else I won't have any money.**

3. *Have* occurs as an *-s* form in the third person singular: *The patient* **has** *got to have an operation immediately, or else she will die.*

4. Subject pronouns and *have* (*has*) usually occur as contractions; however, we use noncontracted forms for emphasis: *You* **have got** *to be good, Tim.*

	Singular		Plural	
First person	I	} 've (have) got to go	we	} 've (have) got to go
Second person	you		you	
Third person	he		they	
	she	} 's (has) got to go		
	it			

Note: The past participle *gotten* never occurs in this form.

5. Negatives do not occur with *have got to.* To express <u>lack</u> of necessity, we use *have to: I do not have to go; He does not have to take another course.*

6. Probably, questions with *have got to* are more frequently heard in British English. A North American speaker is more likely to use the idiom *have to* + a base form in a question: *Do you have to go? What time do you have to go?*
   Note: Subjects follow *have* or *has* in questions and *yes-no* answers: **Have you** *got to go?* **Yes, I have; No, I haven't; What time** **have you** *got to get up in the morning?*
   Note 2: Try not to confuse *have got to* (to show necessity) with *have got* (to show possession); for example, *I've got to* (*must*) *go to my lawyer; I've got* (*have*) *a secret.*
   Special Note: Questions like *Do you got to go?* and *What time do you got to go?* are sometimes heard, but these forms are nonstandard and do not occur among educated people.
   Pronunciation Note: When one is speaking very quickly, *got to* sounds like *gotta;* for example, *I've "gotta" do a lot of homework tonight.*

3.38

Focus: *Have Got To* + a Base Form

Supply appropriate base forms in the blanks.

EXAMPLES: a.   You've just got to <u>see</u> that movie; it's wonderful.
               Note: *Just* is frequently used to intensify *got* in a verb phrase.
          b.   She's got to <u>do</u> something about that problem, or else she'll get into trouble.

1.   I've got to _____ to work on time tomorrow.

2.   I've got to _____ another course in English before I can enter the university. I've got to _____ my best.

3.   I've just got to _____ a job before the end of the month; I haven't got any money.

4.   Their son is blind and they've got to _____ him to a special school. He's got a lot of intelligence, so he should do well.

5.   Hurry up! I've got to _____ back to my office before my boss does; I haven't got time to go shopping.

6.   Even though I promised not to, I've just got to _____ you this secret.

7.   I can't have lunch with you because I've got to _____ to the dentist; I've got a problem with one of my teeth.

8.   After I finish my chemistry homework, I've got to _____ my algebra homework; I haven't got time to fool around.

9.   The patient has got a problem with his stomach, and he's got to _____ an operation as soon as possible.

10.   I've written a lot of checks recently, so I've just got to _____ to the bank and _____ some money right away.

11.   You've just got to _____ your best in the final exam.

12.   I've got to _____ care of this problem before I leave the office; I haven't got time to eat lunch.

13.   You've just got to _____ to your parents in this matter; they know best. You haven't got the experience that they have.

14.   I've got to _____ a few important calls before I leave for the meeting; I haven't got time to waste.

15.   I've got to _____ a lie about that incident; I don't want anyone to know about it.

16.   I've got to _____ rid of the cockroaches in my kitchen. (*To get rid of* is an idiom that means *to eliminate* or *to exterminate*.)

17.   We've just got to _____ a break soon.

3.39

Focus: *Have Got To* + a Base Form

Compose (aloud and/or in writing) appropriate statements containing verb phrases with *have got to* + a base form in response to the following stated situations. **Reminder:** This form does not occur in formal usage.

EXAMPLES: a. John has got a lot of homework to do. What does he have to do?
<u>He's got to stay home and finish it.</u>
b. His mother has been very sick lately.
<u>She's got to enter the hospital for a serious operation.</u>

1. There are a lot of cockroaches in our kitchen.

_____

2. My car isn't working right.

_____

3. I haven't bought a Christmas present for my mother yet.

_____ *I have got to buy* _____

4. There isn't any food in the refrigerator for dinner.

_____

5. I've got a problem with my boss at work.

_____

6. It's going to be the best game of the season.

_____

7. You're not going to tell anyone this secret, are you?

_____

8. They've had their car for almost fifteen years.

_____

9. There are a lot of mosquitoes in the house. Where did they come from?

_____

10. It's three o'clock in the morning, and the guests are still here.

_____

11. He doesn't like his job because he doesn't get along with his boss.

_____

12. We don't have any milk and the stores are all closed.

_____

13. Everyone in the class is tired.

_____

google

ADVERBIAL CLAUSES

4

4.1

SUBORDINATE CLAUSES

Note: A COMPLEX SENTENCE consists of a main (independent) clause and one or more subordinate (dependent) clauses. There are three types of subordinate clauses: (a) ADVERBIAL CLAUSE: *I laughed **because it was funny*** (*because it was funny* modifies the verb *laughed*); (b) ADJECTIVE CLAUSE: *He **who laughs last** laughs best* (*who laughs last* modifies the pronoun *he*); and (c) NOUN CLAUSE: *Do you know **who laughed the most?*** (*who laughed the most* is the direct object of the verb *know*).

Although we have discussed adverbial clauses at some length in Book 1 of this work, it will be helpful to refresh our memories by briefly reviewing the function and use of some of the adverbial clauses and their positions in a sentence.

1. A TIME CLAUSE, which may tell when or how long, is a subordinate adverbial clause introduced by such subordinate conjunctions as *when, while,* and *until: It was thrilling **when the sun rose over the mountains;** We were walking on the beach **while the sun was setting over the Pacific;** We will not surrender to the enemy **until our last soldier falls.***

2. A CLAUSE OF REASON, introduced by the subordinate conjunction *because,* tells why and gives a reason for a situation that is expressed in the main clause of a sentence: *He was angry **because his boss had insulted him;** I couldn't buy anything **because I'd run out of cash.***

3. A CLAUSE OF CONCESSION, introduced by the subordinate conjunctions *although* and *even though,* is also called a CLAUSE OF CONTRAST because it draws a strong contrast between the two events expressed in the main and subordinate clauses: ***Although she didn't love him,** she still married him; **Even though they had fought with great bravery,** the Indians finally had to surrender to the Union Army.*

4. Adverbial clauses occur in the three basic positions in a complex sentence: (a) initial position: ***Because I was tired,** I went to bed earlier than usual;* (b) mid-position: *Because it was very hot, **when we went to the beach** we took a lot of beer;* and (c) final position: *We were nervous **because there was a telegram waiting for us at home.***
   Pronunciation Reminder: When an adverbial clause occurs in initial position, a comma usually follows: *Because the male lion has a lazy nature, the female must do all the hunting.* However, if the adverbial clause is short, the comma may be omitted because there is little loss of clarity: *Because he's rich he's selfish; When it's hot I perspire.*

5. *Since* is sometimes used as a subordinate conjunction to introduce a clause of reason, and the clause is usually in initial position: ***Since the patient has a high fever,** he must stay in bed.*
   Reminder: A *because* clause is usually in final position: *Grandmother is lonely **because most of her old friends have died.***
   Note: A clause of reason introduced by *since* is not used as frequently as a *because* clause.

22 afaua

4.2

SENTENCE COMPLETION   Name _____ Date _____

Focus: Reviewing Time Clauses

Complete the following time clauses. Use a variety of tenses and modal auxiliaries. **Reminder:** The simple present tense after subordinate conjunctions means future time.

EXAMPLES: a. I'd never studied English before when I started this course.
b. She won't find a good job until she speaks and writes English well.

1. S/he should have studied more before _____

_____.

2. They're going to get married as soon as _____

_____.

3. S/he hasn't been a happy person since _____

_____.

4. I wasn't thinking about anything in particular when _____

_____.

5. S/he's not going to get married until _____

_____.

6. I was thinking about a lot of things as _____

_____.

(*As* is sometimes used as a synonym for *when* or *while*.)

7. John and Mary won't be happy till _____

_____.

(*Till* has the same meaning as *until;* however, it most often occurs in speaking.)

8. You may use my dictionary as long as_____

_____.

(*As long as* means *during the time that: He'll be happy as long as he has money.*)

9. He will keep his job as long as_____

_____.

10. You may keep my car for yourself and your family as long as _____

_____.

11. I was thinking about this class as _____

_____.

12. S/he will stay at the university until _____

_____.

13. S/he will stay at the beach till_____

_____.

4.3

SENTENCE COMPLETION

Focus: Reviewing Clauses of Reason with *Because*

On a separate piece of paper, complete the following sentences with appropriate clauses of reason introduced by *because*.

EXAMPLES: a. We didn't go shopping *because it was raining*.
   b. She was disappointed *because she hadn't received the first prize*.

1. We left the party early/late . . .
2. S/he was crying/laughing/screaming . . .
3. I was angry/tired/happy/unhappy/excited . . .
4. I haven't got any money left in my wallet . . .
5. I was annoyed with myself/my roommate/my wife/my husband . . .
6. S/he was put in jail . . .
7. I had a feeling of great satisfaction/disappointment . . .
8. They don't want to go to Europe this summer . . .
9. I was in a good/terrific/bad/terrible mood . . .
10. S/he's worried/upset . . .
11. I don't have to do anything about this problem . . .
12. The party was/wasn't a success . . .
13. S/he couldn't play in the last game . . .
14. I'd rather stay home tonight . . .
15. I'd better not say anything about this matter . . .
16. S/he can't take a taxi home . . .

4.4

SENTENCE COMPLETION

Focus: Clauses of Reason with *Since*

Complete the following sentences with appropriate main clauses. **Reminder:** A *since* clause expressing reason usually occurs in the initial position of a sentence.

EXAMPLES: a. Since I didn't have much money with me, *I couldn't go out to dinner with my friends*.
   b. Since our little boy is so little, *he can't walk across the street alone*.

1. Since s/he doesn't speak English very well, . . .
2. Since my girlfriend/boyfriend isn't going to be at the party, . . .
3. Since my lawyer won't take care of the problem, . . .
4. Since there is little money in my bank account, . . .
5. Since her husband has just recently died, . . .
6. Since it's so beautiful/awful today, . . .
7. Since s/he speaks English like a native, . . .
8. Since I have a slight fever, . . .
9. Since I feel very well, . . .
10. Since I did my homework last night, . . .

4.5

RESULT CLAUSES

1. A RESULT CLAUSE is another type of adverbial clause; it is used to show the result of another clause: *Grandfather is so old* (situation) *that it's hard for him to walk without a cane* (result).

2. The subordinate conjunction *so that* is used in a sentence containing a result clause; however it is "split" in a variety of ways: (a) split by adjective (+ prepositional phrase): *She was so angry (at me) that she slapped my face;* (b) split by adjective + noun (+ prepositional phrase): *He has so much money (in the bank) that he doesn't have to work.*
Note: The adjectives *much, little,* and *few* frequently occur in this pattern; (c) split by adverb (+ prepositional phrase): *She was playing so well (in the game) that everyone was surprised.*

3. In informal usage, *that* is omitted and replaced by a comma in writing and a pause in speech: *She is so beautiful,* (pause) *I can't believe it; He threw the ball so fast, the other player fumbled; He had so much love for his country, he gave his life in the war.*

4.6

SENTENCE COMPLETION

Focus: *So* + Adjective (+ Prepositional Phrase) + *That*

On a separate piece of paper, complete the following sentences with appropriate clauses of result.

EXAMPLES: a. I'm so hungry *that I could eat a whole chicken.*
b. The children are so tired, *they must go to bed right away.*
Reminder: When *that* is omitted, we replace it with a comma.

1. I was so angry at my boss . . .
2. This package is so heavy . . .
3. The movie was so bad/sad , , ,
4. This coffee is so hot/bitter . . .
5. My dictionary is so old . . .
6. My feet are so tired . . .
7. Her English is so good/bad . . .
8. My grandmother is so old . . .
9. I was so nervous/anxious . . .
10. This food is so bad/good . . .
11. S/he is so heavy . . .
12. Today is so hot/cold . . .
13. The last course was so easy/difficult/boring/interesting . . .
14. The program was so funny . . .
15. The explanation was so good . . .
16. S/he ate so much/little . . .
17. My eyes are so tired . . .
18. Last night was so rainy . . .
19. I'm so busy . . .
20. I'm so restless . . .
21. The patient is so sick/well . . .
22. This exercise is so easy . . .
23. I'm so thirsty/hungry . . .

4.7

SENTENCE COMPLETION

Focus: *So* + Adjective + Noun (+ Prepositional Phrase) + *That*

On a separate piece of paper, complete the following sentences with appropriate clauses of result.

EXAMPLES: a. I ate so much food at dinner *that I got a stomach ache.*
b. I had so many letters on my desk, *I couldn't read them all.*
Reminder: When *that* is omitted, we replace it with a comma.

1. We've studied so many things in the course . . .
2. S/he has so many problems with his/her boss . . .
3. There were so many exercises in the last homework assignment . . .
4. S/he made so many mistakes in the final examination . . .
5. S/he drank so many cocktails . . .
6. Our club sold so few tickets to the dance . . .
7. There was so much food on my plate . . .
8. S/he makes so little money with the company . . .
9. There were so many people at the parade . . .
(Use the words *police* and *count* in this sentence.)
10. I put so many things in my suitcase . . .
(Use *anything else* in this sentence.)
11. There were so many people at the reception for the Queen . . .
12. There was so little/much food in the refrigerator . . .
13. They had so many problems with their child . . .
14. My company lost so much money with that new product . . .

4.8

SENTENCE COMPLETION

Focus: *So* + Adverb (+ Prepositional Phrase) + *That*

Complete the following sentences with appropriate clauses of result.

EXAMPLES: a. The little boy ate so fast *that he got sick.*
b. The thief ran so fast, *the police couldn't catch him.*

1. During the class, the questions were coming so quickly . . .
2. Time goes so fast/slowly for me . . .
3. The teacher explained the procedure so well/poorly to the class . . .
4. S/he was speaking so softly/loudly . . .
5. The pitcher was pitching the balls so quickly . . .
6. S/he was acting so foolishly at the party . . .
7. While I was coming to school, it was raining so hard . . .
8. You treated me so kindly when I had a problem . . .
9. The soprano was singing so badly/beautifully at the concert . . .
10. The team was playing so poorly/well during the game . . .
11. The pianist had performed so beautifully/extraordinarily well . . .
12. This exercise has gone by so quickly . . .

4.9

PURPOSE CLAUSES WITH SO THAT

1. *So that* is also used to introduce a PURPOSE CLAUSE. Like a clause of reason introduced by *because,* a purpose clause may answer a *why* question; (*Why did you go to the store?*) *I went to the store **so that I could buy some sugar;** (**Why** did you take a taxi to work?) I took a taxi to work **so that I wouldn't be late.***

2. In informal usage, particularly in speaking, *that* is omitted: *Let's hurry up so we won't be late; You must be nice to people so they will be nice to you; I want to take a nap so I won't be tired later.*
   Special Punctuation Note: No comma, with or without *that,* is used in this pattern.

3. Almost always, the modals *may, can,* and *will* (and their past forms) are the verb forms used in purpose clauses introduced by *so that: They want to go to London so that they **may see** the Queen; The doctor gave the patient penicillin so that the infection **might go** away; We want to buy a car so that we **can drive** out to California; We bought bicycles so that we **could go** for rides in Central Park; We're going to hire a good orchestra so that the party **will be** a great success; I took an umbrella with me so that I **wouldn't get** wet.*
   Note: When *that* is omitted, it is sometimes difficult to tell whether *so* is a coordinate or subordinate conjunction. A good rule to follow is: when *so* cannot be used with *that,* it is a coordinate conjunction like *and* and *but;* for example, in *I was tired, so I went to bed, so* is a coordinate conjunction and the sentence is compound, not complex; we cannot use *that.* Also note that we use a comma in this case.
   Reminder: A compound sentence consists of two main clauses joined together by a coordinate conjunction: *The actor wasn't very good, **but** the actress was wonderful; The food at dinner was excellent, **and** the wine was superb; The weather wasn't very nice, **so** we stayed inside.* A complex sentence consists of a main clause and a subordinate clause introduced by a subordinate conjunction: *I was tired **because** I hadn't slept well; I studied hard **so that** I would get a good grade.*

4.10

SENTENCE COMPLETION

Focus: So (That) Introducing Purpose Clauses

On a separate piece of paper, complete the following sentences with purpose clauses introduced by so (that). Use only the modals can (could), will (would), and may (might) + appropriate base forms. **Reminder:** No comma precedes a purpose clause.

EXAMPLES: a. We want to rent a car this weekend *so that we can go out of town.*

              b. We took the train to California *so that we could see the sights.*

              c. I took a taxi to work *so I wouldn't be late.*

1. S/he wants to enter a language institute . . .
2. We rented a car last weekend . . .
3. You'd better put the fish in the refrigerator . . .
4. Let's hurry up . . .
5. I have to get to work on time tomorrow . . .
6. I must be nice to my boss . . .
7. I must go to the bank right away and get some money . . .
8. We're going to have twelve people for dinner, but I've bought food for fifteen . . .
9. When we went on our trip to the desert, we put an extra can of water in our car trunk . . .
10. I'm going to take a special course in writing . . .
11. I want to find a part-time job . . .
12. I left my house a little early yesterday morning . . .
13. We must take very good care of these plants . . .
14. She put the ice cream in the freezer . . .
15. I have to leave work a little early today . . .
16. I want to buy a tape recorder . . .
17. I want to buy a telescope . . .

Now complete the sentences with appropriate main clauses.

EXAMPLES: d. *I went to the library* so that I could check out a few books.

              e. *We want to take a camera with us* so we can take pictures of the game.

18. . . . so that I may visit the Vatican in Rome.
19. . . . so I could get rid of the cockroaches in the kitchen.
20. . . . so that she will get better.
21. . . . so that I wouldn't catch a cold.
22. . . . so I won't be late to the meeting.
23. . . . so that we may buy a larger house.
24. . . . so that my English will improve.
25. . . . so I can smoke a cigarette.

4.11

EXPRESSING PURPOSE WITH *IN ORDER* + INFINITIVE

1. *In order* + an infinitive phrase is also used to show purpose: *He's studying at night school in order to improve his English; I went to the store in order to buy some sugar.*

2. *In order* can be omitted and an infinitive phrase itself can show purpose: *She went on a diet (in order) to lose weight; The doctor gave the patient penicillin (in order) to cure the infection.*

3. The preposition *for* + a noun may be used to show purpose in a prepositional phrase: *I went to the store for some sugar; She's at the university for a medical degree.*
   Note: Do not confuse a *for* phrase with an infinitive phrase: *I went to the store for* (not *for to buy*) *some sugar; We must eat to live* (not *for to live*).

4. *What . . . for* is a separable colloquial expression meaning *why.* It is used informally to ask information questions that require an answer either with a *for* phrase or with *in order* plus an infinitive phrase. *What* is placed at the beginning of a question, and *for* is placed at the end: ***What** did you go to the store **for?** . . . for some sugar; . . . (in order) to get some sugar; **What** did you speak to your lawyer **for?** . . . for some advice; . . . (in order) to get some advice.*

4.12

SENTENCE COMPLETION   Name _____ Date _____

Focus: *In Order* + Infinitive Phrase

Complete the following sentences with (*in order* +) infinitive phrase. **Reminder:** *In order* is optional.

EXAMPLES: a. I have to get a part time job in order to make some extra money.
              b. I've got to go to the store to get some bread.

1. I've just got to get to the bank before it closes _____.

2. I bought a tape recorder/a telescope/a calculator/a tool box _____

    _____.

3. I want to stop in Arizona on my way to Los Angeles _____.

4. You should live with an English-speaking roommate _____.

5. I've got to go to the immigration authorities _____.

6. You've got to have a lot of money/time/ambition _____.

7. You've got to have a passport/visa_____.

8. A doctor must have a car _____.

9. When you go on a trip, it's nice to go by car_____.

10. We must take a taxi _____.

4.12 (*Continued*)

11. I've got to take an aspirin _____.

12. I must speak and write English well _____.

13. You must be able to speak more than one language_____.

14. You've got to get a prescription from your doctor _____.

15. A salesperson must have a phone _____.

4.13

SENTENCE COMPLETION

Focus: *For* Phrases vs. Infinitive Phrases

Read the following sentences aloud, completing each with a *for* phrase and then with an infinitive phrase. Practice *what . . . for* questions.

EXAMPLES: a. I went to the drugstore (*for some shampoo*) *to get some shampoo. What did you go to the store for?*

b. Grandpa has gone to bed (*for his afternoon nap*) *to take his afternoon nap. What has Grandpa gone to bed for?*

1. I had to go to the bookstore . . .
2. We stopped at the gas station . . .
3. I had to look in my dictionary . . .
4. I went to the stationery shop . . .
5. He went to the butcher shop . . .
6. I have to go to the bank . . .
7. Unfortunately, I'm going to have to speak to my lawyer . . .
8. I went to the barber/hairdresser . . .
9. I phoned the operator . . .
10. I went to the doctor/dentist . . .
11. She has to go to the post office . . .
12. He has just entered the hospital . . .
13. I really should go to the store . . .
14. I went to the best department store in town . . .
15. I'm going to speak to that policeman . . .
16. He's working at a part-time job . . .
17. I have to go to the kitchen/the attic/the basement . . .
18. They've gone to the mountains/the beach/the desert . . .
19. I've got to go to the florist . . .
20. They've gone to the police . . .

4.14

RESULT CLAUSES WITH *SUCH . . . THAT*

1. *Such . . . that* is also used in complex sentences containing result clauses: *It was such a hot day* (situation) *that we stayed at the beach all day* (result).

2. Like *so that, such that* is "split" in a variety of ways: (a) split by *a (an)* + adjective + singular countable noun (+ prepositional phrase): *It was such **a big steak** (on my plate) that I couldn't eat it all;* (b) split by adjective + plural countable noun (+ prepositional phrase): *They have such **wonderful parties** (at their house) that I always enjoy going;* (c) split by adjective + uncountable noun (+ prepositional phrase): *This is such **expensive perfume** that I can't afford to buy it.*

3. In informal usage, *that* is omitted and replaced by a comma in writing and by a pause in speech: *She was such a beautiful woman, I couldn't believe my eyes; It was such a terrible story, I couldn't believe my ears.*

4.15

SENTENCE COMPLETION   Name _____ Date _____

Focus: *Such + A (An) + Adjective + Singular Countable Noun + That*

Complete the following sentences with appropriate clauses of result.

EXAMPLES: a. There was such a good movie on TV that I stayed up late last night.
              b. She was such a brilliant scientist, she won the Nobel Prize.

1. It was such a beautiful/rainy/windy day _____.

2. He was such an unhappy man _____.

3. It was such a difficult problem (use *solve*) _____.

4. It was such a terrible dilemma (use *resolve*) _____.

5. We saw such a funny show _____.

6. This victory is such a great moment (use *celebrate*)_____.

7. I have such an old dictionary_____.

8. It was such a hot/cold day/night _____.

9. My company made such a big mistake _____.

10. It was such a long and boring book/movie _____.

11. S/he made such a foolish remark at the meeting _____.

12. It was such a crowded/exciting party _____.

13. S/he is such an egotistical person _____.

14. We have such an old house/car/TV _____.

15. Her grandfather is such an old man _____.

16. I had such a bad headache _____.

17. It was such a difficult/an easy exercise _____.

18. We have such a small/large apartment/house_____.

4.16

SENTENCE COMPLETION

Focus: *Such* + *A (An)* + Adjective + Singular Countable Noun + *That*

Complete the following sentences with appropriate main clauses.

EXAMPLES: a. *It was such a crowded reception* that we had to stand up.
b. *He made such an expensive mistake* that the company fired him.

1. . . . that we took a long hike through the forest.
2. . . . that she became one of the most famous actresses in the world.
3. . . . that I bought it as soon as I saw it at the store.
4. . . . that I had to use several extra blankets on the bed.
5. . . . that I couldn't afford to buy it.
6. . . . that nobody likes him/her.
7. . . . that we were the last guests to leave.
8. . . . that he became a famous singer at the Metropolitan Opera.
9. . . . that I couldn't understand any of it.
10. . . . that I had to go to my lawyer/doctor/teacher/priest/minister.
11. . . . that the store couldn't have given it away. (*To give something away* can mean *to give something to someone without charging money.*)
12. . . . that I didn't have enough money to pay the bill in cash.
13. . . . that I didn't get a very good grade.
14. . . . that I'm going to give it away.
15. . . . that I was crying/laughing from the beginning to the end.

4.17

SENTENCE COMPLETION

Focus: *Such* + Adjective + Plural Countable Noun (+ Prepositional Phrase) + *That*

Complete the following sentences with appropriate clauses of result.

EXAMPLES: a. These are such delicious oysters, *I'm going to have some more*.
b. These are such old chairs *that we're going to give them away*.

1. These are such old-looking fish . . .
2. I was having such terrible problems with my boss/my secretary . . .
3. They are such wonderful/terrible people . . .
4. Grandmother has such poor eyes/teeth . . .
5. I've been having such terrible nightmares . . .
6. My company produces such wonderful products . . .
7. S/he was receiving such terrible phone calls from a stranger . . .
8. S/he was making such foolish remarks . . .
9. My dictionary has such poor definitions . . .
10. They always have such interesting/boring meetings . . .
11. He has such wonderful ideas for the future of his company . . .
12. That movie has received such wonderful reviews in the newspapers . . .
13. These are such difficult/easy exercises . . .

4.18

SENTENCE COMPLETION

Focus: *Such* + Adjective + Uncountable Noun (+ *Prepositional Phrase*) + *That*

On a separate piece of paper, complete the following sentences with appropriate clauses of result.

EXAMPLES: a. This is such good coffee, *I'm going to have another cup.*
                b. I feel such great happiness *that I must tell you about it.*

  1. This is such delicious water/chocolate/fruit . . .
  2. We had such wonderful weather during our vacation . . .
  3. That is such expensive meat . . .
  4. They had such wonderful wine at the dinner party . . .
  5. The speaker spoke with such wonderful clarity . . .
  6. S/he always offers such good advice . . .
  7. Juliet felt such great love for Romeo . . .
  8. The patient is suffering from such terrible depression . . .
  9. My boss spoke with such great anger . . .
10. This city has such terrible pollution . . .

4.19

SENTENCE COMPLETION

Focus: *Such That* in Clauses of Reason Introduced by *Because*

Complete the following sentences with *because* clauses, following the pattern given in the examples.

EXAMPLES: a. We didn't enjoy our vacation in Chicago *because we had such a noisy hotel room that we couldn't sleep.*
                b. I didn't go shopping *because it was such a rainy day that I couldn't go out.*

  1. We had a good time on our vacation at the beach/in the mountains . . .
  2. We didn't go to the movies last night . . .
  3. S/he became the president . . .
  4. I threw that dictionary away . . .
  5. S/he became a famous athlete/author . . .
  6. I failed/passed that course . . .
  7. I feel very tired today . . .
  8. I don't want to eat a very big dinner . . .
  9. We didn't enjoy ourselves at the party . . .
10. That restaurant is making a lot of money . . .
11. I didn't go to work/school yesterday . . .
12. I'm going to throw these shoes away . . .
13. I'm going to give this chair away . . .

4.20

BUT CLAUSES OF UNEXPECTED RESULT

1. *But* clauses, which are used to show positive-negative relationships (e.g., *I was tired, but she wasn't*), are called CLAUSES OF UNEXPECTED RESULT because the result is unexpected or not logical according to the situation in the other clause. Compare:

Expected Result	Unexpected Result
I was tired, so I went to bed.	*I was tired, but I didn't go to bed.*
We won the game, so we celebrated with a night-long party.	*They won the game, but everyone on the team was crying.*
She used the best ingredients, so the cake was delicious.	*She used the best ingredients, but the cake was horrible.*

   Reminder: Try not to confuse a result clause introduced by *so* with a purpose clause introduced by *so (that)*: (result) *I was tired, so I went to bed;* (purpose) *I went to bed early so (that) I would be fresh the next morning for the job interview.*

2. The adverb *still* is frequently used in a *but* clause of unexpected result. It usually precedes verb phrases; however, it can follow modals: *He studies very hard, but he **still doesn't get** good grades; My horse is very old, but she **can still run** fast.*

3. *Still* has two meanings: (1) nevertheless (*It's warm out, but it's still raining—It's raining despite the fact that it's warm*); (2) continuance (*It's warm out, but it's still raining—It rained before, and it hasn't stopped*).

4. *Still* usually follows the verb *be: The patient is getting better, but he is **still** a little sick; It wasn't a very nice day, but the kids were **still** playing outside.*

5. However, for emphasis, *still* is sometimes put before the verb *be: You must respect your parents; They might sometimes be wrong, but they **still** are your parents; It's almost the end of December, but it **still** is warm.*

6. *Anyway (anyhow)*, in informal usage, is used in *but* clauses of unexpected result: *The doctors did everything possible, but the patient died **anyway** (anyhow); I was extremely tired, but I went out **anyway** (anyhow). Anyway* appears at the end of a clause.

7. Even though the pattern is redundant, and it is not considered good usage, *still* and *anyway* may occur together in the same *but* clause: *I didn't take my medicine, but I **still** feel well **anyway** (anyhow).*
   Punctuation Note: A comma usually precedes a *but* clause.

4.21

SENTENCE COMPLETION

Focus: *Still* in *But* Clauses of Unexpected Result

On a separate piece of paper, complete the following sentences with *but* clauses containing *still*.

EXAMPLES: a. My gas gauge says empty, *but the engine is still running*.
             b. He studies very hard, *but he still doesn't get good grades*.

1. S/he never studies, . . .
2. S/he's eighty-five years old, . . .
3. The government collects a lot of taxes, . . .
4. I drank three glasses of water, . . .
5. S/he's a good-looking person, . . .
6. I took three aspirins, . . .
7. I apologized to him, . . .
8. His explanation was good, . . .
9. They are very much in love, . . .
10. They have everything they need, . . .
11. I often/never read the Bible, . . .
12. The patient has left the hospital, . . .
13. I ate a whole chicken, . . .
14. I'm not tired, . . .
15. I'm feeling better, . . .
16. He's been living in England for ten years, . . .
17. S/he never eats candy, . . .
18. S/he's a nice person, . . .
19. It is bad for me, . . .
20. I don't have money, . . .
21. S/he's only twelve, . . .
22. I fixed my watch, . . .
23. He doesn't like her, . . .

4.22

SENTENCE COMPLETION

Focus: *Still* or *Anyway/Anyhow* in *But* Clauses of Unexpected Result

Complete the following sentences with appropriate *but* clauses.

EXAMPLES: a. Life isn't easy, *but I still have a good time*.
             b. The other team wasn't any good, *but they won anyway*.

1. I was very careful when I wrote the letter, . . .
2. I didn't have a fever, . . .
3. The weather was terrible during our whole vacation, . . .
4. The reception on our TV wasn't very good, . . .
5. I tried to take good care of my house plants, . . .
6. There wasn't any hot water, . . .
7. His pronunciation is/isn't good, . . .
8. I was angry at my girlfriend/boyfriend, . . .
9. I felt/didn't feel well, . . .
10. The food and drinks weren't very good at the party, . . .
11. I tried to be very diplomatic with him during our conversation, . . .
12. I liked/didn't like the actor in the movie, . . .
13. I didn't want to go to school/work yesterday, . . .
14. I don't have an appetite, . . .
15. This was/wasn't an easy exercise, . . .

4.23

CLAUSES OF CONCESSION (CONTRAST)

1. The subordinate conjunctions *although, though,* and *even though* have the same meaning and are used to introduce subordinate adverbial clauses of concession, which are always accompanied by main clauses of unexpected result: *Although he is the King of the jungle, the male lion is very lazy.*

2. *Though* and *even though* are less formal than *although,* and *even though* expresses the strongest sense of concession of the three conjunctions. *Though* and *although* clauses usually occur in the initial position of a sentence: *Though the days on the desert were hot,* the nights were cold; *Although Napoleon had the largest army the world had ever seen,* he suffered a bitter defeat at Waterloo.

3. *Even though* occurs more frequently in final position than either *though* or *although:* The catcher fumbled the ball *even though the pitcher hadn't thrown it very fast;* He made the most points in the game *even though he had played the worst of all the players on the team.*

4. In informal usage, the adverbs *still* and *anyway* may be used in the main clause of a sentence containing a subordinate concessive clause: *Though we were having a good time, we still wanted to go home; Even though I wasn't tired, I went to bed early anyway.*

5. The concessive prepositions *despite* and *in spite of* may be combined with a noun: *We went to the game despite the cold weather* (even though the weather was cold); *We went shopping for Christmas presents in spite of the rain* (even though it was raining).

6. *Despite* and *in spite of* combined with *the fact (that)* may be used as subordinate conjunctions to introduce concessive clauses: *Despite the fact (that) a lot of ants invaded our picnic, we still had a good time; In spite of the fact (that) she's never studied Chinese, she speaks it quite well.*

   Punctuation Reminder: When an adverbial clause is in initial position, a comma usually follows the clause: *Although Hitler was a brilliant leader, he led the German people to disaster.*

4.24

SENTENCE COMPLETION   Name _____ Date _____

Focus: Main Clauses of Unexpected Result

Complete the following sentences with appropriate main clauses of unexpected result. Use the simple past tense only. **Reminder:** The past perfect tense is used for an event that preceded another event in the past.

EXAMPLES: a. Even though I'd slept a lot, I was still tired.
           b. Even though the operation had been a success, the patient died.

1. Even though s/he hadn't studied much, _____.

2. Even though s/he'd apologized to me, _____.

3. Even though I'd been cleaning my apartment all day, _____.

4. Even though I'd drunk a lot of beer and wine, _____.

5. Even though s/he'd made a promise, _____.

6. Even though we had had no rain for a month, _____.

4.24 (Continued)

7. Even though they'd been practicing a lot, _____.

8. Even though the general had carefully planned the attack, _____.

9. Even though s/he'd taken three aspirins, _____.

10. Even though Columbus had made a fantastic discovery, _____.

11. Even though s/he'd worked very hard for the company, _____.

12. Even though s/he'd received a lot of presents, _____.

4.25

SENTENCE COMPLETION

   Focus: Clauses of Concession with *Even Though*

Complete the following sentences with *even though* clauses.

EXAMPLES: a. Napoleon died a lonely and unhappy man <u>even though he had once been the most famous</u> man in the world.
   b. They're not happy <u>even though they have everything they need.</u>

1. They're very stingy (selfish) people _____.

2. I still understand everything in the course _____.

3. S/he goes/doesn't go to church _____.

4. S/he's always talking about science _____.

5. My favorite team won/lost the last game _____.

6. S/he speaks/doesn't speak French well _____.

7. We went/didn't go on a picnic _____.

8. His company is/isn't going to fire him _____.

9. I'm (not) going to apologize to him _____.

10. S/he's (not) going to take another course in English _____.

11. They are very good friends _____.

12. We're (not) very happy with our apartment _____.

13. I'll help you with this problem _____.

14. We did/didn't do well in this exercise _____.

4.26

SENTENCE COMPLETION

Focus: Clauses of Concession with *Even Though/Though/Although*

Complete the following sentences with clauses of unexpected result. Write the exercise on a separate piece of paper; use commas when appropriate.

EXAMPLES: a. Though they tried very hard, *they couldn't beat the other team.*
            b. *We went skiing* even though there wasn't much snow.

1. Even though I hadn't studied much during the course . . .
2. . . . even though he wasn't feeling well.
3. Though he doesn't make much money . . .
4. . . . even though I work like a horse.
5. Although he had made an important scientific discovery . . .
6. . . . even though she's a little heavy.
7. Although she's never studied German . . .
8. . . . even though I work for a good company.
9. Though it's almost the end of April/December . . .
10. . . . even though she's a beautiful actress.
11. Although we are making many advances in industrial development . . .
12. . . . even though they had fought bravely.
13. Though I've already eaten a lot . . .
14. . . . even though I'm afraid.

4.27

SENTENCE COMPLETION

Focus: *Despite* and *Despite the Fact* (*That*)

Complete the following sentences with clauses of unexpected result.

EXAMPLES: a. Despite my bad cold, *I'm still going to go swimming.*
            b. Despite the fact that I don't make much money, *I like my job.*

1. Despite all of the heat, ants, and mosquitoes, . . .
2. Despite the fact that there was a transportation strike, . . .
3. Despite the rain/wind/snow, . . .
4. Despite the fact that she has very poor pronunciation, . . .
5. Despite his/her selfishness, . . .
6. Despite the fact that she hadn't done any homework for the course, . . .
7. Despite the fact that I hadn't slept well the night before, . . .
8. Despite the fact that it hadn't rained for more than a month, . . .
9. Despite the fact that they hadn't practiced at all, . . .
10. Despite the poor weather conditions, . . .
11. Despite my anger, . . .
12. Despite the crowded conditions of the city, . . .
13. Despite his superior intelligence, . . .

4.28

ADVERBIAL *THAT* CLAUSES AFTER ADJECTIVES OF FEELING AND EMOTION

1. An adverbial clause introduced by the subordinate conjunction *that* may follow a main clause which contains a form of the verb *be* and an adjective expressing feeling or emotion: *He's sorry **that he's made so many mistakes in his life**; The people of the world were shocked **that the United States had dropped an atomic bomb on Japan.***

2. A *that* clause after adjectives expressing feeling and emotion can be similar in meaning to a *because* clause: *Everyone was sad that (because) the vacation was coming to an end soon; He is excited that (because) he's finally found the woman of his dreams.*

3. Adverbial *that* clauses tell *why: (Why are you so excited?) I'm excited that I'm graduating from the university soon; (Why are you surprised?) I'm surprised that my girlfriend hasn't remembered my birthday.*

4. We use *that* clauses after main clauses that contain the following adjectives (a partial list):

afraid	conscious	furious	jealous	sorry
angry	content	glad	positive	sure
(un)certain	envious	(un)happy	proud	
confident	fearful	hopeful	sad	

5. Adverbial *that* clauses also follow main clauses that contain the following *-ed* participial adjectives (a partial list):

amazed	contented	irritated	shocked	troubled
annoyed	depressed	perplexed	startled	worried
ashamed	disappointed	pleased	stunned	
astonished	disgusted	relieved	surprised	
concerned	impressed	satisfied	thrilled	

6. In informal usage, *that* is omitted: *I'm thrilled (that) our team has won the game; We're happy (that) you've finally found a job.* However, *that* is not usually omitted when the adverbial clause follows an *-ed* participial adjective. *The doctor is pleased **that the patient's** condition has improved.*

4.29

Focus: Adverbial *That* Clauses

Complete the following sentences with *that* clauses. Do not omit *that* when it follows *-ed* adjectives. Use a variety of tenses and modals.

EXAMPLES: a. I'm afraid that I might have made a lot of mistakes on the exam.
b. I was surprised that my mother had forgotten my birthday.
c. He's very happy he doesn't have to work tomorrow.

1. When I got to the party, I was disappointed/glad _____.

2. At the graduation ceremonies, we were very proud_____.

3. I was surprised/shocked/stunned _____.

4. I'm terribly sorry_____.

5. The General/Admiral/Queen is worried _____.

6. The people of the nation are afraid/worried/fearful _____.

7. When the operation was over, the surgeon was afraid _____.

8. After the wedding, everyone in the family was relieved _____.

9. The little boy/girl was ashamed _____.

10. All of my friends are glad/happy/excited/thrilled _____.

11. All of us in the office are upset/angry/furious_____.

12. Poor Frank/Nora is extremely depressed _____.

13. When the course was over, a few students were disappointed_____.

14. My boss is very pleased _____.

15. When Adam and Eve left the Garden of Eden, they were ashamed _____.

16. When I read the story in the newspaper, I was shocked _____.

17. The door was open when I got home, but I was sure _____.

18. After the game, we were all thrilled/disappointed _____.

19. When I introduced him to Barbara, he was jealous_____.

20. Bill and Cora haven't been getting along for years. I'm surprised _____.

21. What wonderful news! I'm so proud _____.

22. When I walked out of the job interview, I was afraid _____.
(Use the expression *to make a good impression* in this sentence.)

23. The other day my boss/teacher/wife was very annoyed _____.

24. No, I think I'm right. I'm sure/certain/confident _____.

25. At the end of the war, Bill's parents were relieved _____.

26. I'm impressed _____.

27. Before my grandfather died, he was satisfied _____.

28. After I'd spoken to the police, I was afraid _____.

4.30

FUTURE-POSSIBLE REAL CONDITIONS

1. A future-possible conditional statement consists of a conditional (subordinate) clause that is introduced by the subordinate conjunction *if* and a result (main) clause. Most often, a base form or an *-s* form occurs in the *if* clause, and the future tense occurs in the result clause: *If he realizes his goal* (condition), *he will be a very happy man* (result); *If you follow the directions carefully* (condition), *your project will be a success* (result).
   Note: The simple present tense after *if* means future time.

2. A conditional (*if*) clause may occur in the initial or final position: ***If it's a nice day tomorrow, we'll have our lunch in the garden,*** or *We'll have lunch in the garden **if it's a nice day tomorrow.***
   Punctuation Reminder: When a subordinate adverbial clause (e.g., an *if* clause) occurs in initial position, a comma usually separates it from the main clause: *If a message comes for you, I'll call you immediately.*

4.31

GRAMMAR EXERCISE   Name _____ Date _____

Focus: Future-Possible Real Conditions

Supply a base form or an -s form in the *if* clause and a verb in the future tense in the result clause.

EXAMPLES: a. If I <u>have</u> enough time tomorrow. I <u>will go</u> shopping.
    b. If she <u>breaks</u> her promise to marry John, he <u>will be</u> unhappy.

1. If they __*help*__ us with our problem, we __*will help*__ them with theirs.

2. If everyone __*arrives*__ to work on time, our boss __*will be*__ surprised.

3. If I __*make*__ the same mistake again, my boss __*will be*__ angry at me

4. If our team __*wins*__ the game, all of us __*will be*__ surprised.

5. If it __*is a*__ nice next Sunday, we __*will go*__ on a hike.

6. If you __*stop*__ smoking, you __*will feel*__ much better.

7. If we __*take*__ a taxi to work, we __*will arrive*__ there faster.

8. If my girlfriend __*forget*__ my birthday, I __*will be*__ disappointed.

9. If the world __*stops*__ tomorrow, it __*will be*__ a surprise to everyone.

10. If it __*rains*__ tomorrow, I __*will take*__ my umbrella to work.

11. If I __*make*__ any trouble with the government, I __*will reported*__ to my lawyer immediately.

12. We __*will buy*__ a new car if we __*get*__ enough money in the bank.

13. Our teacher __*will get*__ angry if everyone __*come*__ late to class.

14. I __*will call*__ the police immediately if somebody __*broke*__ my house.

15. I __*will be*__ very happy if I __*win*__ the lottery.

4.31 (*Continued*)

16. The teacher _will be_ disappointed if nobody _does_ his/her homework.

17. I _will drink_ white wine if I _eat_ fish for dinner tonight.

18. She _will goes_ to the party if she _find_ someone to go with.

19. I _will wear_ my heavy coat if it _is_ cold tomorrow morning.

20. He _will be_ a very worried man if he _looses_ his job.

21. The patient _will be_ better if she _takes_ this medicine.

22. I _will late_ to school late if I _miss_ the bus.

Now fill in the blanks with base forms only.

23. If you don't _put_ any salt in the soup, it won't _be_ good.

24. If you don't _wather_ your house plants, they will _dead._.

25. If my company doesn't _get_ new management, it will _be_ out of business.

26. If I don't _get_ a letter from my parents soon, I will _be_ worried. If I don't _get_ any letters, I won't _write_ any.

27. If you don't _keep_ my secret, I won't _keep_ yours.

28. I won't _go_ to the party if you don't _invate_ me.

29. If the government doesn't _do_ something about the problem in that part of the country, there will _be_ trouble.

30. If you don't _stop_ eating candy, you won't _loose_ any weight.

Now complete the sentences with your own words. Use commas when appropriate.

31. If I lose my job/girlfriend/boyfriend . . .
32. If I run out of money/gas/food . . .
33. I will be surprised/disappointed/amazed . . .
34. He won't go on a vacation/to the beach . . .
35. If you don't take your medicine . . .
36. I will call my lawyer/the police/my teacher . . .
37. If it rains/doesn't rain tomorrow . . .
38. She will be disappointed . . .
39. I will/won't get angry . . .
40. . . . if she doesn't have any money.
41. . . . he won't be able to go to school.
42. . . . s/he will get a divorce.
43. . . . if s/he says no.
44. . . . s/he won't get a good grade.
45. . . . if I am ever rich.
46. . . . s/he will end up in jail.
47. . . . if s/he inherits a lot of money.
48. . . . we will run out of gas.
49. . . . if we don't take a break.

4.32

OTHER FORMS IN FUTURE-POSSIBLE REAL CONDITIONS

1. To emphasize the continuing nature (duration) of a possible event in future time, we use the present continuous tense in an *if* clause: **If it's raining tomorrow,** I'll take my umbrella; **If it's snowing tomorrow,** the children won't be able to go to school.
   Remember: A verb in the present continuous tense or the simple present tense after *if* means future time.

2. Besides the future tense with *will*, we may also use *be going to* + a base form or the present continuous tense in a result clause: *If we're not busy tomorrow,* we**'re going to take** (*will take*) *a long walk in the park; If we go to the beach tomorrow,* we**'re taking** (*will take*) *a picnic lunch.*

3. The imperative mood is sometimes used in a result clause: *If it gets too warm, please turn down the heat; If the dog starts barking, take it out for a walk.*

4.33

GRAMMAR EXERCISE   Name _____ Date _____

Focus: The Present Continuous Tense in *If* and Result Clauses

Supply appropriate present participles in the blanks.

EXAMPLES: a. If the wind isn't <u>blowing</u>, we won't be able to go sailing.
            b. If it's <u>raining</u> tomorrow, we'll have the party inside.

1. If the patient is _____ better on Friday, she's going to leave the hospital.

2. We're _____ to the beach tomorrow if the sun is _____.

3. We're _____ to the movies tonight if our TV isn't _____.

4. If the children aren't _____ when I get home late tonight, I'm going to get angry.

5. If I'm not _____ well tomorrow, I'm not _____ to work.

6. If she's _____ when you call her up, she'll get angry.

7. We'll win the game tomorrow if our star player is _____.

8. If he isn't _____ at the university by the end of the year, he's going to be very disappointed.

9. If the wind is _____ hard tomorrow, I'll wear a hat.

10. If the doctor isn't _____ in surgery this afternoon, she will be in her office.

11. If my favorite dancer isn't _____ in the next program, I'm _____ home.

12. If any of the students are _____ during the next exam, the teacher will be surprised.

4.34

Focus: The Imperative Mood in Result Clauses

Reminder: The subject in the imperative mood is not mentioned but is understood: (*You*) *please close the door*. The understood subject in the imperative mood is always second person singular or plural.

Supply appropriate base forms in the blanks.

EXAMPLES: a. If the radio is too loud, please <u>tell</u> me.
           b. If you leave the house, please don't <u>forget</u> to lock the door.

1. Children, if it's raining tomorrow, don't _____ to school.

2. If you play the radio after midnight, please _____ it low.

3. Son, if you take the car out tonight, don't _____ fast.

4. If you go to Italy next summer, _____ sure to go to Florence.

5. If you don't know a word, _____ it up in your dictionary.

6. If you run out of money, _____ sure to tell me.

7. If you have trouble with the police, _____ to your lawyer.

8. If you get sick, don't _____ afraid to go to the doctor.

9. If your team loses the game, don't _____ about it.

4.35

SENTENCE COMPLETION

Focus: Reviewing *If* and Result Clauses

Complete the following sentences with appropriate clauses. Use commas when appropriate.

EXAMPLES: a. If I have a toothache, *I'll go to the dentist immediately*.
           b. The fish is going to spoil *if you don't put it in the refrigerator*.

1. If I lose my hair/job/money . . .
2. If an earthquake/hurricane/war comes . . .
3. I will get very angry . . .
4. My mother and father will be very disappointed . . .
5. The ice cream will melt . . .
6. [supply name] _____ will be very disappointed . . .
7. His/her mother and father will be very happy/unhappy . . .
8. If you have a problem/headache/toothache/sore throat . . .
9. If the government doesn't do something about [make up something] . . .
10. The patient will die/live . . .
11. I will/won't be sorry . . .
12. [supply name] _____ will get angry at me . . .
13. I will get angry at [supply name] _____ . . .
14. Dad is going to get angry at Billy/Betsy . . .
15. Please open/close the window . . .

4.36

MODALS AND IDIOMS IN CONDITIONAL AND RESULT CLAUSES

1. Modal auxiliaries may occur in result clauses: *If my car is working tomorrow, I **can take** you to work; If I'm not tired tomorrow night, I **may go** out with my girlfriend; You **must enter** the hospital if your doctor orders it; If you have a problem with that job, you **should speak** to your boss about it, but it's up to you.*

2. *Can* sometimes occurs in *if* clauses: *If you **can come** with me to the party, I'll have a much better time; If I **can help** you with the project tomorrow, I'll be glad to do so.*

3. *Must* also sometimes occurs in *if* clauses: *If you **must go** to a doctor, please go to a good one; If you **must go** out today, be sure to wear a warm coat.*

4. We often use the idioms *have to* (*have got to*) and *be able to* in *if* clauses: *If I **have to go** to my lawyer about this problem, it will cost me a lot; If we**'re able to take** care of this matter for you, we'll be glad to do so.*

5. We may use the above idioms in both *if* and result clauses. However, the idiom *had better* may occur only in result clauses: *If you have any trouble with your car, you**'d better take** it to the garage.*

6. Like all other adverbial clauses, *if* clauses do not change in form in *yes-no* and information questions: ***If I tell you a secret,** will you reveal it to anyone? What will you do **if you get sick?***

4.37

GRAMMAR EXERCISE   Name _____ Date _____

Focus: Modals, Idioms, and Questions in Future-Possible Real Conditions

Supply appropriate base forms or -s forms in the blanks.

EXAMPLES: a. If you don't <u>deal</u> with this problem soon, you might <u>get</u> into trouble. (*To deal with* means *to take care of.*)

b. If we <u>run</u> out of gas, we'll have to <u>sleep</u> in the car overnight. (*Overnight* means *all night long.*)

1. If I _____ to Moscow in February, what kind of clothes should I _____? Must I _____ a visa if I _____?

2. She has to _____ to work soon if her husband doesn't _____ a job.

3. If you can't _____ rid of the cockroaches yourself, you should _____ a professional exterminator.

4. You ought to _____ your best suit if you _____ to the party.

5. What cities should she _____ if she _____ to Brazil?

6. Can I _____ a few dollars from you if I _____ out of money?

7. If the weather _____ nice on Sunday, we may _____ to the beach.

8. If the car doesn't _____ better by Friday, I'd better _____ it to the garage.

9. If there _____ another war, will anyone _____ nuclear weapons?

4.37 (Continued)

10. You might _____ lost if you don't _____ a compass on your hike.

11. If inflation _____ worse, what will _____ to our money?

12. What places should I _____ if I _____ to South America next summer? What kind of clothes should I _____ if I _____?

Now complete the sentences with appropriate clauses. Use commas or question marks when appropriate.

13. You'd better go to your doctor/lawyer/teacher _____.

14. What will your parents do _____.

15. If there is another world war _____.

16. I might go to the police_____.

17. You'd better not say much _____.

18. S/he won't be able to go on a vacation _____.

19. If it's warm/cold/rainy tomorrow _____.

20. If they don't fix our car by tomorrow _____.

21. What will you do about this problem _____.

22. How will you feel _____.

23. What will you do _____.

24. What will happen _____.

25. Whom should I call _____.

26. If you can't get rid of the cockroaches _____.

27. If my/your wife/husband doesn't come home soon _____.

28. How will s/he feel _____.

29. What should I do _____.

30. You ought to go to a lawyer/priest/psychiatrist _____.

31. If I don't have to go to school/work tomorrow _____.

Special Note: You may have noticed that we have not been using *will* in *if* clauses in these exercises. Only rarely is *will* used in an *if* clause; its use is very formal: *If you will submit the application in duplicate, it will be greatly appreciated.* Such formality is not appropriate in our everyday conversation.

Reminder: A verb in the simple present tense or the present continuous tense after *if* means future time.

4.38

PRESENT-UNREAL CONDITIONS

1. A present-unreal conditional statement consists of a conditional clause introduced by the subordinate conjunction *if* and a result clause. A past form is most often used in the *if* clause to mean present time, and *would*, the other form of *will*, plus a base form occurs in the result clause: *If I **spoke** English well, I **would get** a better job; If I **knew** the secret to success, I **would be** a millionaire.*

2. A present-unreal conditional (*if*) clause expresses a situation that is contrary to fact or reality—in other words, unreal. Compare:

Reality	Condition
I don't speak English well.	*If I **spoke** English well, I'd be in the university now.*
She doesn't have a car.	*If she **had a car**, she'd drive to work every day.*
He has a lot of money.	*If he **didn't have any money**, he would borrow some from the bank.*
I have a bad cold.	*If I **didn't have a bad cold**, I would go to the beach today.*

3. The result clause in a present-unreal conditional statement shows a hypothetical result. It draws a conclusion based on the condition expressed in the conditional clause. Compare:

Condition	Hypothetical Result
If he won a lot of money,	*he wouldn't quit his job.*
If I knew that woman,	*I would ask her to go out.*

4. *Not* is inserted between *would* and a base form to make a negative verb phrase: *If I spoke English well, I **would not be** here. Wouldn't,* the contraction of *would not,* occurs in informal usage: *If he had a lot of money, he **wouldn't work**.*

5. The verb *be* has a special (subjunctive) form in a present-unreal conditional clause; *were* is used in all persons: *If I **were** a millionaire, I'd take it easy for the rest of my life.*

Singular		Plural	
if	I you he she it $\Big\}$ **were**	if	we you they $\Big\}$ **were**

   Note: *Was* is sometimes heard and seen in *if* clauses in present-unreal conditions: *If I was that guy, I'd keep my mouth shut;* however, its use is nonstandard, and it does not occur in educated speech and writing.

6. The *if* clause may occur in the initial or final position of a sentence: *If I **were** you, I would be more careful with my money,* or *I'd be more careful with my money **if I were you**.* When an adverbial clause occurs in the initial position, a comma separates it from the main clause.

4.38 (Continued)

Note: A present-unreal condition is traditionally called a SUBJUNCTIVE form.

Special Reminder: A verb in the present or present continuous tense after *if* means future time, and a past form after *if* means present time. Compare:

Future Time	Present Time
If I **have** enough money next summer, I'll go to Europe.	If I **had** enough money now, I would go to Europe.
If I'**m** sick, I'll go home.	If I **were** sick, I would go home.

4.39

GRAMMAR EXERCISE Name _____ Date _____

Focus: Present-Unreal Conditions

Supply an appropriate past form in the *if* clause, and *would* + a base form in the result clause. Do not use any negative forms.

EXAMPLES: a. Fortunately, I'm not sick.
If I <u>were</u> sick, I <u>would go</u> to the doctor.
b. She has no car.
If she <u>had</u> a car, she'd <u>spend</u> her weekends out of town.

1. I don't have a headache.
If I ___had___ a headache, I ___would take___ an aspirin.

2. Alaska has a very cold climate.
If Alaska ___had___ a warmer climate, I ___would go___ there.

3. He doesn't speak English very well.
If he ___spoke___ English better, he ___would attend___ the university.

4. I realize I'm not you.
If I ___were___ you, I ___would___ speak to my lawyer about this.

5. I'm not the President.
If I ___were___ the President, I ___would do___ things differently.

6. It's very cold today.
If it ___were___ warmer, we ___would go___ to the beach.

7. I don't have any free time.
If I ___had___ more free time, I ___would look___ for a better job.

8. I'm not a rich person.
If I ___were___ a rich person, I ___would spend___ my money to help people.

9. I don't understand your question.
If I ___understood___ your question, I ___would be___ able to answer you.

10. I don't have enough money.
If I ___had___ enough money, I ___would live___ in the best part of town.

4.39 *(Continued)*

11. New York is a very crowded city.

    We _would live_ in New York if it _were_ less crowded.

12. Our apartment isn't very large.

    We _would be_ much happier if our apartment _were_ larger.

13. We do not have peace in the world.

    All of us _would be_ happier if we _had_ peace in the world.

14. People are sometimes selfish.

    The world _would be_ a better place if people _were_ less selfish.

15. I'm not as rich as Rockefeller.

    I _would have_ a completely different kind of life if I _were_ as rich as Rockefeller.

16. This is not the correct formula.

    I _would be_ able to do the experiment if this _were_ the correct formula.

17. I don't have very much money in the bank.

    I _would take_ a trip around the world if I _had_ a lot of money.

18. He doesn't study hard enough in his courses.

    He _would get_ better grades if he _studied_ harder.

19. I'm not that woman.

    I _would use_ less perfume if I _were_ that woman.

20. I don't have a university education.

    I _would be_ able to get a better job if I _had_ a university education.

Now use negative or affirmative forms.

EXAMPLES: c. I don't speak English well.
    If I spoke English well, I wouldn't be here.

   d. It's very cold today.
    If it weren't so cold, we would have lunch in the garden.

21. Fortunately, her little girl isn't sick today.

    If her little girl _were_ sick, she _wouldn't be_ here.

22. Cigarette smoking is dangerous to your health.

    If I _were_ you, I _wouldn't smoke_.

23. He has a lot of money.

    If he _didn't have_ any money, he _would go_ to the bank.

24. We have a very nice car.

    If we _didn't have_ a car, we _wouldn't be_ able to drive to the country every weekend.

25. The patient is very old.

    If the patient _weren't_ so old, the surgeon _would operate_ on her.

26. She is extremely tired.

    If she _____ so tired, she _____ out to dinner.

27. I have a lot of wonderful friends.

    If I _didn't have_ any friends, I _would be_ a very unhappy person.

28. We all have a tongue.

    If we _____ a tongue, we _____ able to speak.

29. We all have a brain.

    If we _____ a brain, we _____ able to think.

30. I have a very good calculator.

    If I _____ a calculator, I _____ in a bad situation.

31. Both of us are extremely tired.

    If we _____ so tired, we _____ to come to your party.

32. He has a phone.

    He _____ able to call his customers if _____ a phone.

33. Many of the students in my class are helped financially by their parents.

    They _____ here if they _____ their help.

34. My company's president is very bad.

    We _____ in such trouble if we _____ a better president.

35. I'm very hungry.

    I _____ in such a bad mood if I _____ so hungry.

Now complete the sentences with appropriate clauses. Use commas when necessary.

36. If I didn't have any money_____.

37. I would be a much happier person _____.

38. If I were a man/woman_____.

39. I would be very happy/unhappy _____.

40. If I were the richest man/woman in the world_____.

41. I would get a better job _____.

42. If I felt sick/tired _____.

43. The world would be a better place _____.

44. If I had more free time _____.

45. I would do things differently_____.

46. If I were younger/older than I am _____.

47. If I didn't have so much homework tonight _____.

48. If I were the King of the Jungle_____.

4.40

OTHER FORMS IN PRESENT-UNREAL CONDITIONS

1. Continuous forms may occur in both the *if* and result clauses in the present-unreal: *If I were rich, I **would be living** in the largest house in town; If it **were raining** now, I wouldn't go out.*

2. The idiom *have to* may occur in both *if* and result clauses to mean necessity: *If I **had to go** to the dentist today, I'd probably be in a bad mood; If I **didn't have to work** today, I'd go for a drive with my friends; If I had a lot of money, I wouldn't **have to work**; If it were raining, I **would have to take** an umbrella.*

3. The modal *could* + a base form sometimes occurs in an *if* clause to express ability or possibility: *If you **could lift** that piano by yourself, I would be very surprised; If I **could afford** to buy a new car, I would buy a European one.*

4. *Could* (and *might* for possibility) also occurs in place of *would* in result clauses to express ability or possibility: *If this package were smaller, I **could carry** it home; If he studied harder, he **could be** the best student in the class; If I had enough money in the bank, I **might buy** a house, but I don't know.*

5. As in future-possible real conditions, the *if* clause in a present-unreal conditional statement does not change its form in *yes-no* and information questions: *If you had a lot of money, would you travel a lot? What would you do if you had a lot of money?*

4.41

GRAMMAR EXERCISE   Name _____ Date _____

Focus: Mixed Forms in Present-Unreal Conditions

Supply appropriate base forms in the blanks.

EXAMPLES: a. If I could <u>speak</u> English well, I wouldn't <u>be</u> here.
   b. If our teacher could <u>work</u> miracles, we would <u>be speaking</u> like native speakers. (*To work miracles* means *to perform miracles.*)

1. I would have to _____ artificial light for my house plants if I didn't _____ good sunlight.

2. What would you _____ if you were the richest person in the world?

3. If we had a car, we could _____ out of town for the weekend.

4. If I could _____ miracles, I would _____ millions.

5. If I had a lot of money, I might _____ a trip around the world.

6. I'd _____ the children of the poor if I were rich, wouldn't you?

7. Where would you _____ if you had an unrestricted choice?

8. If you had the power of the President, what would you _____?

9. If I had more time on my hands, I'd _____ glad to help you. (*To have time on one's hands* means *to have free time.*)

10. He would _____ at the university if he didn't have to _____.

11. If you were I (*me* in informal usage), what would you _____?

12. If I were she (*her* in informal usage), I wouldn't _____ about people behind their backs.

13. If I were he (*him* in informal usage), I wouldn't _____ so stingy.

14. I'm sorry, I could _____ you if I had more free time.
    Note: A frequent response to a question like *Can you help/tell/show me?* is *No, I'm sorry, I would if I could, but I can't.* A common response to a *would you like to* question—*Would you like to help/show/tell me?* is: *I would if I could, but I can't.*

15. What would you _____ if you didn't have to _____?

16. If I could afford to _____ a trip around the world, I would _____ you to go with me. Would you go?
    Note: Frequently, particularly when we speak, we omit the *if* clause because it is understood: *Would you go out tonight (if you didn't have so much homework)?*

Now complete the sentences with appropriate clauses. Use commas or question marks when appropriate.

17. If I could work miracles _____

18. If I could be invisible _____

19. If I didn't have to work _____

20. I wouldn't give homework _____

21. I would have to go to my doctor/lawyer _____

22. If it were raining now _____

23. If I were heavy _____

24. What would you do _____

25. Where would you have to go _____

26. Where would you live _____

27. If you were I _____

28. If I could speak English well _____

29. If I lost my hair/teeth/job _____

30. I would have to go back to my native country _____

31. I would have to go to the bank/store/drugstore _____

32. I would have to go to bed _____

33. I would have to take a bus to school/work _____

4.42

PAST-UNREAL CONDITIONS

1. A past-unreal conditional statement consists of an *if* clause that contains a verb in the past perfect tense, and a result clause containing *would have* (as auxiliaries) plus a past participle as a main verb: *If I **had been** Columbus, I **would have stayed** home.*

2. *Would've* (sounds like *would-of*), the contraction of *would have,* and *wouldn't have* (sounds like *wouldn't-of*), the contraction of *would not have,* occur in spoken informal usage: *If you'd drunk less coffee last night, you **would've** slept better; If I'd had my umbrella yesterday, I **wouldn't have** gotten so wet.*
   Note: Like *should've, might've, could've,* and *must've, would've* is not written unless dialogue is being quoted.
   Reminder: *'d* followed by a past participle (*'d gone*) is a contraction of *had;* *'d* followed by a base form (*'d have*) is a contraction of *would.*

3. A past-unreal conditional clause expresses a situation in past time that was contrary to fact or reality, in other words, unreal. Compare:

Reality	Condition
I wasn't tired last night.	*If I **had been** tired last night, I would have gone to bed earlier.*
He didn't vote in that election.	*If he **had voted** in that election, he wouldn't have voted for Nixon.*

4. Result clauses in past-unreal conditional statements show a hypothetical conclusion based on the condition expressed in the conditional (*if*) clause. Compare:

Condition	Result
If I had been Napoleon,	*I wouldn't have gone to Waterloo.*
If I had been Julius Caesar,	*I would have listened to the fortune teller.*
If I had been President Truman,	*I wouldn't have dropped an atomic bomb on Japan.*

5. When an *if* clause occurs in the initial position of a sentence, a comma usually follows: *If John F. Kennedy had lived, he would have been a great president.* No comma occurs when an *if* clause appears in the final position: *He would have been a great president if he hadn't been assassinated in Dallas.*

4.43

Focus: Past-Unreal Conditions

Supply an appropriate verb phrase in the past perfect tense in the *if* (conditional) clause, and *would have* plus an appropriate past participle in the result clause. Do not use any negative forms.

EXAMPLES: a. He didn't do much homework in the last course.
             If he <u>had done</u> more homework, he <u>would have gotten</u> a good grade.
         b. We had very little money last summer.
             If we<u>'d had</u> more money, we <u>would have gone</u> to Europe.

1. Yesterday was very cold.

   If it _____ warmer, we _____ swimming.

2. I used very little tomato sauce in the spaghetti.

   If I _____ more tomato sauce, it _____ better.

3. I didn't have a headache last night.

   If I _____ a headache, I _____ an aspirin.

4. They didn't get married because they weren't in love.

   If they _____ in love, they _____ married.

5. I didn't have my car yesterday because my wife was using it.

   If I _____ my car, I _____ a long drive in the country.

6. The party was boring.

   If they _____ a dance band, it _____ more fun.

Now use negative forms as well.

EXAMPLES: a. I was sick yesterday.
             If I <u>hadn't been</u> sick yesterday, I <u>wouldn't have gone</u> to the doctor.
         d. I ate those bad shrimp.
             If I <u>hadn't eaten</u> those bad shrimp, I <u>wouldn't have gotten</u> such a bad stomach ache.

7. I was tired last night, so I didn't go out.

   If I _____ tired last night, I _____ out.

8. Our neighbors' house burned down because nobody called the fire department.

   If somebody _____ the fire department, their house _____ down.

9. Cleopatra killed herself.

   If I _____ Cleopatra, I _____ myself.

10. You didn't use a dictionary when you wrote your composition.

    If you _____ one, you _____ so many mistakes.

11. He didn't study very much.

    If he _____ more, he _____ such a bad grade.

Name _____ Date _____

12. I didn't put any wine in the stew; it tasted very bland.

    The stew _____ better if I _____ some wine in it.

13. She was very sick, so she didn't come to school.

    She _____ to school if she _____ so sick.

14. Adam and Eve ate the forbidden fruit.

    I _____ the forbidden fruit if I _____ they.

15. I didn't forget to send my mother a birthday card.

    My mother _____ disappointed if I _____ to send her a birthday card.

16. You didn't take care of that problem soon enough.

    If you _____ care of it sooner, you _____ into such trouble.

17. Napoleon went to Waterloo.

    I _____ to Waterloo if I _____ Napoleon.

18. I got up very late yesterday morning.

    If I _____ up earlier, I _____ late to work.

19. I cooked the chicken for twenty minutes.

    It _____ better if I _____ it longer.

20. I didn't take very good care of my house plants.

    If I _____ better care of them, they _____ .

21. I drank a lot of coffee last night.

    If I _____ so much coffee last night, I _____ such a sleepless night.

22. We didn't stop at the last gas station.

    If we _____ at the last gas station, we _____ lost.

23. We got lost on our hike in the forest.

    We _____ lost if we _____ a compass.

24. I didn't go to the dentist.

    If I _____ to the dentist, I _____ that tooth.

25. There was a lot of talk but no action in the movie.

    If there _____ less talk and more action, I _____ the movie more.

26. It was raining all the time during our vacation in Italy.

    We _____ ourselves more if we _____ better weather.

27. We didn't do this exercise at the beginning of the course.

    If we _____ it at the beginning of the course, we _____ able to do it.

28. We didn't have a map with us.

    If we _____ one, we _____ lost.

4.44

OTHER FORMS IN PAST-UNREAL CONDITIONS

1. We use *could have* + a past participle in a result clause to express: (a) ability: *If the package hadn't been so heavy, I **could have carried** it home;* (b) possibility: *If we had had more money last summer, we **could have gone** to Europe;* and (c) impossibility: *If I had been Cain, I **couldn't have killed** my brother.*

2. We use *might have* + a past participle to show possibility: *If I had called her up after midnight, she **might have been** asleep; If I had told our secret to anyone, she **might have gotten** angry.*

3. Continuous forms occasionally occur in both conditional and result clauses: *If it **had been raining** yesterday, I would have taken my umbrella; If I had called them up at six oclock, they **might have been sleeping**.*

4.45

GRAMMAR EXERCISE   Name _____ Date _____

Focus: *Could* and *Might*

Supply appropriate past participles in the blanks.

EXAMPLES: a. If we had <u>used</u> a different method, we might have had better results.
b. If our car had been working, we could have <u>gone</u> for a drive.

1. If my company had _____ more money on product development, it might not have _____ out of business.

2. If we'd _____ more money, we could have _____ in a better restaurant.

3. If the United States hadn't _____ the Second World War, Germany might have _____. Who knows?

4. If Bobby Kennedy had _____, he might have _____ President.

5. If the patient had _____ an operation, he might not have _____.

6. If the weather had _____ nicer, we might have _____ to the beach, but I don't really think so.

7. If John F. Kennedy hadn't _____, he might have _____ one of the greatest presidents in the history of the United States.

8. If I hadn't _____ a dictionary, I couldn't have _____ such a good composition.

9. If yesterday had _____ Sunday, I couldn't have _____ to the bank.

Now complete the sentence with appropriate result clauses.

10. If yesterday had been Sunday, _____.

11. If I had had a lot of money last summer, _____.

12. If my boss had been out of the office yesterday, _____.

13. If my TV set hadn't been working, _____.

14. If it had been raining yesterday, _____.

4.46

Focus: *Could Have* in *If* Clauses

Could have + a past participle sometimes makes an appearance in past-unreal conditions (*if* clauses). *Could have* following *if* means *had been able to; could not have* means *had not been able to: If I could have helped (had been able to help) you with your project, I would have been glad to do so; If I couldn't have gone (hadn't been able to go), I would have been very disappointed.*

Supply appropriate past participles in the blanks.

EXAMPLES: a. If I could have gone to the mountains yesterday, I would have taken my children with me. I would have taken a map, too.
   b. If I could have gone to the party, I would certainly have gone.

1. If I couldn't have _____ at your party, I would have _____ sorry.

2. If I could have _____ a new car last year, I wouldn't have _____ an American one.

3. If I could have _____ a vacation last year, I might have _____ to Japan.

4. If we could have _____ it, we would have _____ a larger house.

5. If we could have _____ to the meeting, we would have _____.
   Note: This sentence could be shortened to, *If we could have, we would have.* Remember these short responses: *If I could, I would, but I can't* (for present time); *If I could have, I would have, but I couldn't* (for past time).

4.47

QUESTIONS WITH PAST-UNREAL CONDITIONS

1. In *yes-no* and information questions, the subject of a result clause is inserted between *would* (or *could* or *might*) and *have*: **Would you have** gone to the moon if you could have? **What would you have done if you had been Romeo?**
   Reminder: When an information word is the subject of a sentence, the usual question form is not used: **What would have happened if the Soviet Union had dropped an atomic bomb on the United States?**

2. *Would* and *have* occur together (usually in a contracted form) in *yes* answers: *Would you have done that? Yes, I would have;* In *no* answers, *have* follows *wouldn't: Would you have married her? No, I wouldn't (couldn't) have.*
   Reminder: *Wouldn't (couldn't) have* sounds like *wouldn't-(couldn't-)of.*

4.48

Focus: Questions with Past-Unreal Conditions

Supply appropriate past participles in the blanks.

EXAMPLES: a. If you had <u>married</u> the wrong person, what would you have <u>done</u>? Would you have <u>gotten</u> a divorce?
Pronunciation Note: (*What*) *would you have* sounds like (*what*) *would-jew-of* when we are speaking quickly.
b. What might have <u>happened</u> if you had <u>cheated</u> on the examination?

1. What would you have _____ if you had _____ into trouble with your boss?

2. If you had _____ out of money on your vacation, what would you have _____? Would you have _____ your parents?

3. What would you have _____ with you if you had _____ to the Sahara/Florida/the beach/the store?

4. What would you have _____ with you if you had _____ on a hike in the mountains?

5. Who would you have _____ to if you had _____ a problem with one of your neighbors? Would you have _____ the police?

6. What would you have _____ if someone had _____ your apartment?

Now complete the following questions. Use commas when appropriate; do not forget question marks.

7. What would have happened _____

8. If you could have taken a vacation _____

9. What would you have done_____

10. How would you have felt _____

11. If it had been a nice/cold day_____

12. What might have happened _____

13. Where would you have gone _____

4.49

SENTENCE COMPLETION

Focus: Past-Unreal Conditions

Complete the following sentences with appropriate *if* or result clauses. Use commas when appropriate.

EXAMPLES: a. If we had tried this exercise at the beginning of the course, *we couldn't have done it*.
b. I would have been disappointed *if I had gotten a bad grade*.

4.49 (*Continued*)

1. If I had been Napoleon/Stalin/Cain/Romeo/King Henry VIII/Harry Truman/Jimmy Carter/Richard Nixon/Patricia Hearst/Fidel Castro/Adam and Eve/Marilyn Monroe/Elizabeth Taylor/the President . . .
2. If I had lost my hair/teeth/money/girlfriend/boyfriend/wife/husband/job/school materials . . .
3. If it had been windy/rainy/hot/cold yesterday . . .
4. If the patient had/hadn't had the operation . . .
5. I might have gone to the police/Central Intelligence Agency (CIA)/Federal Bureau of Investigation (FBI) . . .
6. I would have gone to the Internal Revenue Service (IRS) . . .
   Note: The IRS collects taxes.
7. I wouldn't have gone to school/work/the party . . .
8. I couldn't have come to the last class . . .
9. I might not have gone home last night . . .
10. I would have gotten angry . . .

4.50

GRAMMAR EXERCISE   Name _____ Date _____

Focus: Reviewing Future-Possible and Unreal Conditions

Memorize: 1. In a future-possible conditional clause, the present (continuous) tense following *if* means future possibility.
2. In a present-unreal conditional clause, a past form following *if* means present unreality.
3. In a past-unreal conditional clause, a verb in the past perfect tense following *if* means past unreality.

Memorize: 1. *If I have time tomorrow, I will go to the park.*
2. *If I had time today, I would go to the park.*
3. *If I had had time yesterday, I would have gone to the park.*

Memorize: In a present-unreal conditional clause, the verb *be* takes the special (subjunctive) form *were* in all persons.

$$
\text{If}\ \left. \begin{array}{l} \text{I} \\ \text{you} \\ \text{he} \\ \text{she} \\ \text{it} \\ \text{we} \\ \text{you} \\ \text{they} \end{array} \right\}\ \text{were} \ldots
$$

In the blanks, supply appropriate forms of the base forms given in parentheses.

EXAMPLES: a. (be/go) If it is a nice day tomorrow, we won't go to work.
           b. (be/share) If I were a rich man, I would share my wealth.

1. (make/get) If I _____ a mistake yesterday, my boss _____ mad at me.

2. (rain/walk) If it _____ tomorrow, I _____ to work.

3. (have/be) If I _____ the time now, I _____ glad to help you.

4. (go/be) I _____ to work today if I _____ sick.

5. (put/spoil) If you _____ the fish in the refrigerator last night, it _____.

6. (do/get) If I _____ more homework last semester, I _____ a better grade in the course.

Now complete the sentences with appropriate clauses. Use commas when appropriate.

7. I will go/would go/would have gone to [supply place] . . .
8. If I am/were/had been [complete *if* clause] . . .
9. If I eat/ate/had eaten . . .
10. If I have/had/had had . . .
11. If I drink/drank/had drunk . . .
12. I will make/would make/would have made . . .
13. If he studies/studied/had studied harder . . .
14. If I don't have/didn't have/hadn't had . . .

4.51

PRESENT RESULT CLAUSES FOLLOWING PAST-UNREAL *IF* CLAUSES

A present result clause containing *would* (*could* or *might*) + a base form may be combined with a past-unreal conditional (*if*) clause. In this kind of sentence, the event or nonevent in the *if* clause is the reason for the situation that is stated in the result clause.

Past-Unreal Condition	Present Result
*If I **had studied** English when I was younger,*	*I **wouldn't be** in this class.*
*If the South **had won** the Civil War,*	*the United States **might be** a divided nation today.*
*If my father **had never met** my mother,*	*I **wouldn't be** here today.*
*If we **had brought** a map with us,*	*we **wouldn't be** lost now.*
*If I **hadn't stayed** at the beach for so long,*	*I **wouldn't have** such a bad sunburn now.*
*If they **hadn't wasted** their money,*	*they **would be** wealthy today.*

4.52

Focus: Present Result Following Past-Unreal Conditions in *If* Clauses

Supply appropriate verb phrases in the past perfect tense in the *if* clauses of the following sentences.

EXAMPLES: a. If I had studied English when I was younger, I wouldn't be sitting in this classroom today.
b. If I <u>hadn't drunk</u> so much last night, I wouldn't have such a bad hangover now.

1. If he _____ the crime, he wouldn't be in jail now.

2. If I _____ a little something to eat before I came to class, I wouldn't be so hungry now.

3. If I _____ longer last night, I wouldn't be so tired now.

4. If she _____ her husband, she wouldn't be such a happy woman.

5. If he _____ many hours each day, he wouldn't be a famous violinist today.

6. If you _____ your medicine, you wouldn't be feeling better now.

7. If he _____ so hard for so many years, he wouldn't have such a successful business.

8. If she _____ more about the future when she was younger, she wouldn't be in such a bad financial situation now.

9. If we _____ left instead of right at the last intersection, we wouldn't be lost now.

10. If the patient _____ the operation, she might not be alive today.

11. If Germany _____ the Second World War, it (she) wouldn't be a divided nation today.

12. If she _____ good care of her health, she wouldn't be feeling so well now.

13. If I _____ my homework last night, I could go to the game this afternoon, but I didn't do it, so I can't go.

14. If he _____ to me, I wouldn't be angry at him now.

15. If you _____ to work today on time, your boss wouldn't be so annoyed.

16. If I _____ those mushrooms last night at dinner, I wouldn't have such a stomach ache now.

17. If he _____ out of town, he would be at her birthday party.

4.53

UNLESS

1. *Unless* may replace *if* to introduce clauses in future-possible real conditions and present- and past-unreal conditions. *Unless* means *if not: He won't go to the dance unless his wife goes* (*if his wife does **not** go*).

2. Verbal phrases in *unless* clauses have the same form as those in *if* clauses; however, a negative verb phrase usually expresses an affirmative condition, and an affirmative verb phrase usually expresses a negative condition.

    (a) Future-possible real conditions: *We will go to the beach tomorrow **unless it rains** (if it doesn't rain); You will get a good grade in the course **unless you don't do your homework** (if you do your homework).*

    (b) Present-unreal condition: *They couldn't afford to live in such a beautiful apartment **unless they were rich** (if they weren't rich); I wouldn't want to ask that boy to go to the dance with me **unless I knew him** (if I didn't know him).*

    (c) Past-unreal condition: *I would have quit my job **unless I had gotten a raise** (if I hadn't gotten a raise); I would have gone to the meeting **unless I hadn't felt well** (if I had felt well).*

3. Most often, however, *unless* introduces conditional clauses containing affirmative verb phrases, and the result clause in the same sentence contains a negative verb phrase: *We **won't be able to reach** the top of the mountain unless the weather **changes**; That teacher **wouldn't be** absent from school unless he **were** sick; They **couldn't have afforded** a vacation in Europe last summer unless they **had borrowed** money from the bank.*

4.54

GRAMMAR EXERCISE   Name _____ Date _____

Focus: *Unless* Clauses in Future-Possible Real Conditions

Supply appropriate base forms or -s forms in the *unless* clauses.

EXAMPLES: a. Listen Bobby! You won't feel better unless you <u>take</u> this medicine.
            b. I won't tell you my secret unless you <u>promise</u> to keep it a secret.

1. Bob won't get a promotion in that company unless he _____ harder.

2. We'll drive all the way to California unless our car _____ down. (For a machine *to break down* means *to stop working properly.*)

3. Your party next Saturday night won't be a success unless you _____ interesting people.

4. John won't go to the party unless he _____ an invitation.

5. We'll give the party in the garden next Sunday afternoon unless it _____.

6. We'll go to the beach tomorrow unless the weather _____.

7. He won't go to the game unless his girlfriend _____ with him.

4.54 (Continued)

Name _____ Date _____

8. The patient won't get better unless he _____ an operation.

9. They won't call off the game unless it _____. (*To call off* means *to cancel*.)

10. She won't marry her boyfriend unless he _____ off his beard.

11. I'm afraid that he won't be able to find a good job unless his English _____.

12. I won't quit my present job unless I _____ a better one.

13. I'm not going to do anything about that problem unless it _____ worse than it already is.

14. I won't stay with my company unless they _____ me a raise.

15. I won't tell you my secret unless you _____ me yours.

16. They won't put off the meeting unless the boss _____ sick. (*To put off* means *to postpone*.)

17. Conditions will not get better in the country unless the government _____ new social programs.

18. The patient won't be able to leave the hospital unless her condition _____.

19. S/he won't be a happy person unless s/he _____ romance.

20. This soup won't taste any good unless you _____ some salt in it.

21. We won't get lost on our hike unless we _____ the compass.

22. The children won't play outside today unless the rain _____.

23. There won't be a class tomorrow unless the teacher _____ better.

24. I won't be late tonight unless I _____ my train.

25. We won't do another exercise unless we _____ time.

26. My car won't run properly unless I _____ a new battery.

27. He won't begin work on his new book unless he _____ a contract.

4.55

SENTENCE COMPLETION   Name _____ Date _____

Focus: Present-Unreal and Past-Unreal Conditions in *Unless* Clauses

Complete the following sentences with appropriate present-unreal and past-unreal conditional clauses introduced by *unless*.

EXAMPLES: a. They couldn't afford to live in such a beautiful house <u>unless they were very rich</u>.
b. I wouldn't have taken a taxi to work yesterday <u>unless it had been raining</u>.

1. Our little boy wouldn't have gotten a spanking_____
_____.

2. I couldn't afford to live in Paris_____.

3. He wouldn't be in the hospital _____.

4. I wouldn't have gone to the party last night _____
_____.

5. She wouldn't marry a man_____.

6. He wouldn't marry a woman _____.

7. We couldn't have gone to Europe last summer _____
_____.

8. They wouldn't have met each other _____.

9. You couldn't find a good job in Paris _____
_____.

10. I wouldn't have been able to solve that problem _____
_____.

11. I wouldn't have taken that medicine_____.

12. They wouldn't buy that house _____.

13. It would be difficult to find a job in Tokyo _____
_____.

14. We would have given the reception in the garden _____
_____.

15. I wouldn't have gotten a good grade in that course _____
_____.

16. That person wouldn't be the president of the company _____
_____.

17. He wouldn't have asked me that favor _____.

4.56

GENERALIZATIONS WITH REAL CONDITIONS

1. Real conditions are used to show a generalization about events that sometimes take place in present time. When this occurs *if* has the meaning of *when* (it does not mean a condition), and the simple present tense means present time (not future time) in both the *if* and result clauses: *If (when) he **has** money, he usually **spends** it right away; If (when) our baby **cries**, it usually means **she's** hungry; If (when) I **have** a legal problem, I always **go** to my lawyer.*

2. Real conditions are also used for a generalization about an event that took place in past time with some kind of regularity. When this occurs, the past tense is used in both *if* and result clauses: *During our vacation, if (when) the weather **wasn't** nice, we **stayed** inside and **played** cards; If (when) it **was** cold, we **didn't go** swimming.*

3. *Used to* + a base form is also used in the result clause in such sentences: *When I was a boy, if (when) the weather was nice, I **used to go** (went) swimming; If (when) I was sick, I **used to stay** (stayed) home from school.*

4. Besides *used to* and the past tense, we may use *would* + a base form for past custom in the result clause: *When I was a young boy, if my father was busy, I **would go** (used to go, went) out to the fields to get the cows; If my mother was busy, I **would take** (used to take, took) care of my baby sister; If I didn't have homework, I **would help** (used to help, helped) my father milk the cows; If my father didn't want to give me money, I **would go** (used to go, went) to my grandmother.*

5. When used for past custom, *would* and *used to* are not always interchangeable (particularly with the verb *be*). In this particular use, *would* is never used for a general situation that once existed but no longer does; for example, *His father used to (never would) be an engineer, but now he's a businessman; I used to (never would) like country music, but now I don't; That actress used to (never would) appear in movies, but now she's retired from the screen.*

4.57

SENTENCE COMPLETION   Name _____ Date _____

Focus: Generalizations with Real Conditions

Complete the following sentences with appropriate *if* or result clauses. Use the present tense only. For variety, sometimes use frequency adverbs like *usually*, *generally*, and *always* in the result clauses. **Reminder:** When making a generalization with real conditions, *if* means *when*.

EXAMPLES: a. If the weather is nice, we usually have breakfast in the garden.
              b. I usually go to bed early if I have an early appointment the next morning.

1. If I have too much to drink at a party, _____.

2. If I get tired in the afternoon, _____.

3. I usually take very few clothes _____.

4. If I don't know a word, _____.

5. If my boss has a legal problem, _____.

6. If our little girl doesn't feel well, _____.

7. I usually take a long drive in my car _____.

8. We never go to the beach _____.

9. If I eat Chinese food at a restaurant, _____.

10. If I have a toothache, _____.

11. If my boss doesn't have any cash to pay for something, _____

    _____.

12. If the weather is very hot/cold, _____.

13. If I am in a bad mood, _____.

14. If our little boy is naughty, _____.

15. If I serve chicken to my guests, _____.

16. If my grandfather is tired after lunch, _____.

17. If a friend of mine is in trouble, _____.

18. If it's raining, _____.

19. If my mother is using my father's car, _____.

20. If my father/mother gets angry, _____.

21. If my dog and my cat are in the same room together, _____

    _____.

22. If I have a problem, _____.

4.58

Name _____ Date _____

Focus: Past Custom with *Would* + a Base Form

Complete the following sentences with appropriate main clauses with verb phrases containing *would* (+ *not*) + a base form to express past custom. **Reminder:** When making a generalization with real conditions, *if* means *when*.

EXAMPLES: a. (when I was a little boy) If I didn't feel well, I would stay home from school.
               b. (during our vacation) If the weather was cold, we wouldn't go swimming.

1. (when I was at the university) If I did my homework, _____.

   If I didn't do my homework, _____.

2. (when I was a little boy at the dinner table) If my father didn't say a prayer before dinner, _____.

3. (while I was living in Switzerland) If the weather was nice, _____

   _____.

4. (during our vacation) If it was raining, _____.

5. (before penicillin) If a patient had an extremely serious infection, _____

   _____.

6. (before the age of the airplane) If my grandfather wanted to go to Europe, _____

   _____.

7. (before I was sixteen) If I had an invitation to a party, _____

   _____.

8. (when I was a baseball player) If I had an injury, _____.

9. (before Columbus discovered America) If you said the world was round, _____

   _____.

10. (while I was in China on my vacation) If the waiter didn't offer me a fork and knife at a restaurant, _____.

11. (when I was a child) If I didn't have any money, _____.

12. (when I was very small) If my mother wasn't home, _____.

13. (when I had a car) If it wasn't working, _____.

14. (when our daughter was a little girl) If she didn't have her doll with her, _____

   _____.

15. (when I had a bike) If the weather was nice, _____.

NOUN CLAUSES

5

5.1

DIRECT AND INDIRECT OBJECTS

Reminder: A noun that is the DIRECT OBJECT of a verb usually tells <u>what</u>: *I gave the teacher an apple* (**What** *did you give the teacher?*); a noun that is the INDIRECT OBJECT of a verb usually tells <u>to</u> or <u>for whom</u>: *I gave **the teacher** an apple* (**To whom** *did you give an apple?*); *The policeman drew **me** a map* (**For whom** *did the policeman draw a map?*).

The prepositions *to* and *for* are used only when a direct object follows the verb: *He owes **the bank** a great deal of money* (= *He owes a great deal of money **to the bank***); *Shah Jehan built **his wife** the Taj Mahal* (= *Shah Jehan built the Taj Mahal **for his wife***).

1. A NOUN CLAUSE — which, like all clauses, always contains a verb and its subject — can occupy the same position in a sentence as a noun, and function in the same way; for example, a noun clause may be used as the direct object of certain verbs: *The President has told **the nation** (indirect object) **that there will be peace** (direct object).

2. Noun clauses are derived from statements, questions, requests, and exclamations. A noun clause that is derived from a statement is introduced by the subordinate conjunction *that*: (*The earth is round*) *Everyone knows **that the earth is round;*** (*Time has gone fast*) *It's hard to believe **that time has gone so fast.***

3. *That* is omitted in informal usage: *She claims (that) she's the best student in the class; They've suddenly announced (that) they're going to get married.*
Reminder: *That* clauses which follow adjectives of emotion and feeling have been classified as adverbial clauses in this textbook: *We were all thrilled (why?) that man had finally landed on the moon.*

4. An indirect object may precede a noun clause that is a direct object: *Please tell me* (indirect object) *that you love me* (direct object); or the noun clause may immediately follow the verb: *Please say that you love me.*

5. Noun clauses introduced by *that* may occur as direct objects of verbs called VERBS OF INDIRECT SPEECH. Some verbs of indirect speech are:

admit	complain	hint	remark	swear
announce	confess	mention	report	whisper
boast	declare	proclaim	say	
claim	explain	relate	state	

6. These verbs may be followed by *to* + an indirect object + a *that* clause, or they may be immediately followed by a *that* clause: *She has said (to everyone) that she's just gotten engaged; He's always hinting (to Maria) that he wants to go out with her; She has carefully explained (to her son) that he must not cheat at school.*
Note: *To* or *for* may precede an indirect object only if a noun clause follows.

7. The verbs of indirect speech such as (dis)agree, argue, forecast, maintain, and predict are not followed by a to phrase: *The radio predicts that it will rain; The fortune teller has forecast that I will have good luck; The student maintains that he didn't cheat on the examination.*

8. The following verbs of indirect speech are always followed by an indirect object without to:

assure	inform	persuade	remind	tell
convince	notify	promise	teach	warn

For example, *My doctor has assured **me** that my health is good; He has finally persuaded **her** that she should be his wife; Jesus taught **us** that we should love our neighbors as we love ourselves; She warned **the children** not to play in the street.*

9. Although the verb *tell* usually requires an indirect object without to, *tell* also occurs in certain idioms, with or without an indirect object—for example, (a) tell a story: *Please tell (me) the story of Cinderella, Mommy;* (b) tell a secret: *Please don't tell (anyone) this secret;* (c) tell the truth: *Do you swear to tell (us) the whole truth and nothing but the truth?* (d) tell a lie: *People who tell (other people) lies often lie to themselves;* (e) tell a fortune: *Can you tell (me) my fortune?* (f) tell the time: *Can your little boy tell (people) the time?*

10. *Say* and *tell* can be confusing to students. *Say* is never followed by an indirect object without to. Compare:

Wrong	Correct
*She said **me** that she was sick.*	*She said **to me** that she was sick.*
*I am saying **you** that I love you.*	*I am saying **to you** that I love you.*

Except for the certain idioms that we have already discussed, *tell* is never followed by an indirect object with to. Compare:

Wrong	Correct
*I told **to her** that I was sick.*	*I told **her** that I was sick.*
*He is telling **to us** that he needs our help.*	*He is telling **us** that he needs our help.*

11. Even though a to phrase may follow the verb *say*, the phrase is most often omitted because the indirect object is understood or not necessary: *Columbus said that the earth is round; My doctor is always saying that I must stop smoking.*

12. Speakers new to the language sometimes confuse the verbs *speak* and *talk* with *say* and *tell*. *Speak* can mean *to greet: I spoke to him when I saw him in the hall; Speak* is also used in reference to such formal situations as: *The President spoke (discussed) with his cabinet about the situation in the Middle East; The professor spoke (gave a lecture) about the evolution of man.* And *speak* is always used with the names of languages: *A friend of mine speaks English, French, and Spanish all fluently.*

13. *Talk* is used when we are referring to a conversation between two or more people: *He often talks to his neighbor over the backyard fence; Everyone was talking about me when I came into the room. Talk* is rarely followed by a direct object except in a few idioms: *Let's talk business; They are talking treason.*

5.2

SENTENCE COMPLETION

Focus: Indirect Objects with *To*

On a separate piece of paper, complete the following sentences with appropriate noun clauses.

EXAMPLES: a. The prophet has proclaimed to the world *that the end is coming*.
            b. She has finally confessed to John *she is in love with him*.

1. S/he's always saying to everyone . . .
2. The thief has admitted to the police . . .
3. My lawyer/doctor/teacher/dentist has carefully explained to me . . .
4. I'm always saying to myself . . .
5. She finally announced to her parents . . .
6. I must confess to my doctor/lawyer/priest/myself . . .
7. S/he's always boasting to everyone at the office . . .
8. I've complained to my landlord/landlady many times
9. The government has just reported to the press . . .
10. My boss has hinted to me . . .
11. Yesterday s/he mentioned to me . . .
12. The President has just announced to the nation . . .

5.3

SENTENCE COMPLETION

Focus: Indirect Objects without *To*

Complete the following sentences with appropriate noun clauses.

EXAMPLES: a. One of the Ten Commandments tells us *that we must not kill*.
            b. My secretary has just reminded me *I have an appointment*.

1. That sign warns drivers/pedestrians/smokers . . .
2. One of the Ten Commandments tells us . . .
3. Please promise me . . .
4. I've been trying to convince my girlfriend/boyfriend . . .
5. The doctors have assured the patient . . .
6. The Internal Revenue Service has notified me . . .
7. This experience has taught me . . .
8. The author of this book has convinced me . . .
9. The label on this bottle of medicine warns you . . .
10. His/her parents have warned him/her . . .
11. Never tell anyone . . .
12. My doctor/dentist/lawyer/teacher assures me . . .
13. The expression on your face tells me . . .
14. I have just informed my boss/landlord/secretary . . .

5.3 *(Continued)*

Now supply your own indirect objects.

EXAMPLES: c. I'm always telling *myself that I shouldn't smoke, but I do anyway*.
             d. The bank has notified *us there is no money left in our account*.

15. I have told . . .
16. I'm trying to convince/persuade . . .
17. Are you going to tell . . .
18. S/he is always telling . . .

5.4

SENTENCE COMPLETION

       Focus: No Indirect Object

On a separate piece of paper, complete the following sentences with appropriate noun clauses. Do not use any indirect objects in this exercise.

EXAMPLES: a. The *Times of India* reports *that a few skirmishes have taken place at one of the country's northern borders*.
             b. The prophet predicts *the world will come to an end in the year 2000*.

1. All of the newspapers in town say . . .
2. The thief denies/admits . . .
3. The Associated Press/Reuters/Tass reports . . .
4. This contract/the Bible/the Koran states . . .
5. The mayor of the city claims . . .
6. One of our spies in the enemy camp relates . . .
7. The Pope has proclaimed . . .
8. I swear on the Bible . . .
9. *The New York Times/Le Figaro/Le Monde/Excelsior/La Prensa/Pravda/The Times* (of London) has recently reported . . .
10. The principal/headmaster/headmistress has announced . . .
11. This thesis argues . . .
12. The patient is always complaining . . .
13. I think you are wrong. I don't agree . . .
14. The statistics in this report forecast . . .
15. One of the students in the class admits . . .
16. Doctor! One of our patients is saying . . .
17. The American/Russian/Cuban Ambassador claims . . .
18. The Internal Revenue Service (IRS) claims . . .
19. One of the Ten Commandments states . . .
20. A spokesman for the government admits/denies . . .
21. A great prophet has recently predicted . . .

5.5

VERBS OF MENTAL ACTIVITY

Noun clauses introduced by *that* are also used as direct objects of verbs which are called VERBS OF MENTAL ACTIVITY: *I know (that) all of us will have a great deal of success in our lives; Columbus wanted to prove (that) the earth is round.* Following are some verbs of mental activity.

assume	decide	forget	know	realize	understand
believe	discover	guess	learn	recall	
calculate	doubt	hear	notice	regret	
(don't) care	dream	hope	pretend	remember	
conclude	feel	imagine	prove	reveal	
consider	find out	indicate	question	think	

5.6

SENTENCE COMPLETION

Focus: Noun Clauses Following Verbs of Mental Activity

On a separate piece of paper, complete the following sentences with appropriate noun clauses.

EXAMPLES:
- a. Many people believe *that God exists.*
- b. We all know *no one is perfect.*
- c. I've never questioned *that my parents love me.*

1. I have just decided . . .
2. I sometimes dream . . .
3. I think/know/realize/feel . . .
4. Because I've studied hard in this course, I imagine/guess . . .
5. Catholics/Protestants/Jews believe . . .
6. I doubt . . .
7. Our little boy/girl is always pretending . . .
8. Everyone in the nation regrets . . .
9. The police have recently found out (discovered) . . .
10. Your parents should understand . . .
11. Ted and Anna have finally decided . . .
12. I have recently heard/noticed/learned . . .
13. Children often pretend . . .
14. I'm sorry, I realize . . .
15. I have always believed . . .
16. Because of the poor acting/music/direction, I feel . . .
17. Many people hope . . .
18. According to my figures, I calculate . . .
19. This student's composition indicates/shows . . .
20. Please don't forget . . .
21. Many of the students assume . . .

5.7

VERB AGREEMENT/THE RULE OF SEQUENCE OF TENSES

1. The RULE OF SEQUENCE OF TENSES states that a verb in a subordinate clause must agree with the verb in the main clause of a complex sentence. It is necessary to follow the rule in a sentence containing a noun clause when the main verb is in past form.

2. Study how the following changes are made when noun clauses are derived from direct statements and the main verb is in its past form.

    (a) The present tense is changed to the past tense:
    *She said, "I go to school." She said that she **went** to school.*

    (b) The present continuous tense is changed to the past continuous tense:
    *She said, "I am going to school." She said that she **was going** to school.*

    (c) The past tense is changed to the past perfect tense:
    *She said, "I went to school." She said that she **had gone** to school.*

    (d) The past continuous tense is changed to the past perfect continuous tense:
    *She said, "I was going to school." She said that she **had been going** to school.*

    (e) The present perfect (continuous) tense is changed to the past perfect (continuous) tense:
    *She said, "I have gone." She said that she **had gone**.*
    *She said, "I have been going." She said that she **had been going**."*

3. Also, when following the rule of sequence of tenses, past forms of modal auxiliaries are used so that they will agree with the past form of the main verb.

    (a) *Can* is changed to *could:*
    *She said, "I can go." She said that she **could** go.*

    (b) *May* is changed to *might.*
    *She said, "I may go." She said that she **might** go.*

    (c) *Must* is changed to *had to.*
    *She said, "I must go." She said that she **had to** go.*

    (d) *Will* is changed to *would.*
    *She said, "I will go." She said that she **would** go.*

4. We do not follow the rule of sequence of tenses when the main verb is in its present form: *She says she goes to school; She says she has gone to school; She says she will go to school.*

5.8

DIRECT AND INDIRECT SPEECH

1. DIRECT SPEECH is a speaker's exact words. In direct speech, QUOTATION MARKS (") are used in the written language: *He said, "I am not hungry because I had a big lunch." They said, "We will get married soon."*

2. INDIRECT SPEECH (reported speech) is the restatement of the speaker's original words. Grammatically, the quoted material, often introduced by *that,* is a noun clause. Quotation marks are not used, and pronouns are usually transformed from one person to another. Most often, so that the restatement may remain logical, verbs in the noun clause are changed into past forms in accordance with the rule of sequence of tenses. Compare:

   (a) He said, *"I am living with my parents."*
       He said that he was living with his parents."

   (b) She said, *"I don't like to live by myself."*
       She said that she didn't like to live by herself.

   (c) He said, *"I like your blouse."*
       He told me that he liked my blouse.

   (d) They said, *"We want to bring our children with us to your party."*
       They told me that they wanted to bring their children with them to my party.

3. In less formal usage, the rule of sequence of tenses is often not observed, particularly when the event expressed by the main verb occurs shortly after the event expressed by the verb in the noun clause: *She just told me* (only a few minutes ago) *that she is in love with me; John is on the phone now; he said that he will be here in about half an hour.*

4. Also, the rule of sequence of tenses is not observed if we are expressing a universal truth or discussing a customary event: *The priest loudly proclaimed that God is a supreme being; The young boy correctly said that H_2O is the formula for water; I told the little girl that the sun always sets in the west, but she didn't believe me.*

5. Frequently, when we are following the rule, there may be more than one tense change in a single sentence: *He said, "I can't go to the game because I didn't do my homework."* (*He said that he couldn't go to the game because he hadn't done his homework.*)

5.9

SENTENCE COMPLETION
Name _____ Date _____

Focus: Following the Rule of Sequence of Tenses

Transform the following direct statements in quotation marks into appropriate noun clauses so that you may complete the following indirect statements. Follow the rule of sequence of tenses and transform the pronouns where necessary.

EXAMPLES: a. "I don't understand your explanation." I told him that I didn't understand his explanation."
             b. "I spoke to your lawyer about my problem." Mary told me she had spoken to my lawyer about her problem.

1. "My problem is similar to yours." John told me _____.

2. "I don't enjoy living by myself." Barbara said _____.

5.9 (Continued)

3. "I'll be very glad to help you." Mrs. Johnson told me _____.

4. "I have committed a mortal sin." Mary confessed to the priest _____

_____.

5. "I didn't steal any money from you." John swore on the Bible _____

_____.

6. "I am the best student in my class." Bill boasted _____.

7. "I will kill you with my knife." The thief threatened _____.

8. "I'm looking forward to taking my vacation." Anna said _____.
   (*To look forward to* means *to anticipate with pleasure.*)

9. "I don't look forward to going to the dentist." He complained _____

_____.

10. "I didn't enjoy myself at the game." Wanda said _____.

11. "I can't take the examination for my chemistry class because I didn't study for it." Jack told

    me _____.

12. "I bought a new car for myself." My teacher told me _____.

13. "We're having such a terrible problem with our neighbor that we must go to the police."

    They angrily told me _____.

14. "I must tell you a secret about your boss." She whispered to me _____

_____.

15. "I have a hangover because I drank too much." Dick said _____

_____.

16. "I myself am responsible for all my company's money." Mary said _____

_____.

17. "I'm not going to my girlfriend's party because she didn't invite me." Richard told me

_____.

18. "We must take our son to the hospital because he's become so sick that he can't eat." Our

    neighbors told us _____.

19. "There may be a new war in the Far East." The radio said _____

_____.

20. "I'm angry because my lawyer didn't take care of it." Bill said _____

_____.

21. "I will have to take care of it myself." He then said _____

_____.

22. "My husband and I are going to get a divorce." Grace said _____

_____.

5.10

NEAR PAST VERSUS DISTANT PAST IN INDIRECT SPEECH

1. In indirect speech, particularly when a statement is made about the DISTANT PAST, the various words and expressions of time, place, and modification used in direct speech must be changed so that they logically agree with the rule of sequence of tenses. Compare:

Direct Speech	Indirect Speech
*She said, "I'm going to be **here tomorrow**."*	*She said that she was going to be **there the following day**.*

2. However, when we make a statement about an event that has taken place in the NEAR PAST, a change does not necessarily have to be made because confusion is less likely to occur. Compare:

Near Past	Distant Past
*When I spoke to her **this morning**, she told me that she was going to see me **tomorrow**.*	*When I spoke to her **a couple of weeks ago**, she told me that she was going to see me **the following day**.*

3. So we can see that when we make an indirect statement about an event in the Distant Past, some necessary changes must logically be made. Most of the usual changes to be made are:

   (a) *ago* to *before/earlier*
   (b) *now* to *then*
   (c) *here* to *there*
   (d) *this/these* to *that/those*
   (e) *today/tonight* to *that day/that night*
   (f) *yesterday* to *the day before/the previous day*
   (g) *tomorrow* to *the following day* (formal)/*the next day* (informal)
   (h) *last week/last month/last year* to *the week/month/year before*
   (i) *tomorrow morning/afternoon/evening/night* to *the following (the next) morning/afternoon/evening/night*
   (j) *at this time* to *at that time*

5.11

SENTENCE COMPLETION

Focus: Indirect Statements about Events in the Distant Past

Transform the following direct statements in quotation marks into appropriate noun clauses in order to complete the following indirect statement. Observe the rule of sequence of tenses, transform pronouns, and change the italicized word or words in the direct statements accordingly.

EXAMPLES:
    a. "I don't feel well because I didn't take my medicine *this morning*." A couple of weeks ago, he told me *that he didn't feel well because he hadn't taken his medicine that morning*.

    b. "I'll return *this* book to you *tomorrow*." He promised me four months ago *he would return that book to me the following day*.

1. "I'll be working on *this* project until *next month*." Some time ago, Mary told me . . .
2. "I'll enter the university *next year*." Around 1973, she told me . . .
3. "I'll return your call before the end of *today*." At the end of our phone conversation a couple of weeks ago, she promised me . . .
4. "I have just heard some gossip about you *this morning*." When I saw her at the spring meeting, she told me . . .
5. "I went to the doctor *a couple of days ago* for a physical." When I saw Dick last, he told me . . .
6. "The world will end *next year*." In 1972 the prophet predicted . . .
7. "We will deliver your new refrigerator by the end of *this week*." The letter from the store promised us . . .
8. "*This* problem is mine." Bill told me . . .
9. "I just got a new job *yesterday*." When I saw her on the street a couple of months ago, Angela told me . . .
10. "It will stop raining *tomorrow*." Before the flood last spring, the weatherman on TV wrongly predicted . . .
11. "You will have more fun *today* than you had *yesterday*." The next day at breakfast, they promised me . . .
12. "*Now* is not a good time for me to tell you the story." When I saw him in the hall the other day, he told me . . .
13. "I'm not hungry because I had lunch only *a couple of hours ago*." I offered Mary something to eat, but she said . . .
14. "It's been raining since early *last night*." When I last spoke to my mother on the phone, she complained . . .
15. "We're discussing many serious problems at *this time*." While I was in Europe on a business trip, my boss wired me . . .
16. "We're having a lot of serious social and economic problems *here*." While I was visiting South Africa, many people told me . . .
17. "*Now* is the time to attack our enemy." While he was talking to his staff, the General suddenly declared . . .
18. "I'm sorry I can't speak to you *now* because I'm having dinner with my family." When I called him on the phone, Robert told me . . .
19. "You can't do the more difficult exercises *now*." At the beginning of the course, the teacher told us . . .

5.12

NOUN CLAUSES DERIVED FROM *YES-NO* QUESTIONS

1. In a noun clause derived from a *yes-no* question, the introductory word *whether* (or *if*) introduces the clause: *I don't know **whether** (if) the weather will change.*
   Note: *Whether* and *weather* have almost the same pronunciation.

2. When a noun clause is derived from a *yes-no* question, the quotation marks and the question mark are dropped because the sentence is no longer a question.

Original Question	Derivation
She's asking me, "Will you be here?"	*She's asking me if I will be here.*

3. *Whether* is used in more formal usage: *I don't know **whether** the ambassador has arrived yet;* and *if* occurs in informal usage: *I asked him **if** he was going to play in the next game.*

4. *Ask* is always followed by an indirect object <u>without</u> *to*: *The children are asking me if they can go to the movies; Please ask them if they can help us.*

5. If a main verb is in its past form, the rule of sequence of tenses must be observed when a noun clause is derived from a *yes-no* question: *My lawyer **asked** me whether I **had sent** the correct form to the government; I **asked** her if she **could go** out with me.*

6. The introductory word *whether* suggests a choice because it introduces a clause derived from a *yes-no* question. When a negative choice might be expected with *whether,* the words *or not* are added: *No one knows **whether or not** they will get a raise; The doctor doesn't know **whether or not** the patient will live.*

7. For emphasis, *or not* occurs at the end of a noun clause if the clause is short: *She doesn't know **whether** she should marry him **or not**; Tell me **whether** you want to hear this secret **or not**.*

8. *Or not* occurs with *if* in only very informal usage: *We didn't know **if** we would win the game **or not**.*

5.13

SENTENCE COMPLETION

Name _____ Date _____

Focus: Noun Clauses Derived from *Yes-No* Questions

Transform the following direct *yes-no* questions in quotation marks into appropriate noun clauses so that you may complete the following indirect statements. Use *whether* or *if* to introduce each clause. When it is necessary, observe the rule of sequence of tenses.

EXAMPLES: a. "Can you go to the party with me?" She asked Bill *whether he could go to the party with her.*
b. "Will the train arrive on time?" I don't know *if the train will arrive on time.*

1. "Is the president going to resign?" Everyone wants to know _____

   _____.

2. "Do you have time to help me?" Bill asked me _____.

3. "Am I doing the right thing?" I'm always asking myself _____

   _____.

5.13 (*Continued*)

4. "Did you put the right address on the envelope?" I asked him _____

   _____.

5. "Have you fixed my car yet?" I asked them _____.

6. "Is it going to rain?" I don't know _____.

7. "Will there be a war in the Middle East?" No one knows _____ _____

   _____.

8. "Did you receive a letter from your parents?" I asked Wanda _____

   _____.

9. "Do you love me?" I've asked him/her many times _____.

10. "Did you do your homework?" My teacher asked me _____.

11. "Were you born in a hospital or at home?" The doctor asked me_____

    _____.

12. "Is the meeting going to begin at the usual time?" I forgot to ask my boss _____

    _____.

13. "Are you going to get married soon?" Everyone is asking us_____

    _____.

14. "Did you steal that money?" The police asked him _____.

15. "Did you report the crime to the police?" I didn't ask Bill _____

    _____.

16. "Has the teacher come yet?" I don't know _____.

17. "Is she angry at me?" I don't care _____.

18. "Can you go to the park with us?" They asked me _____ _____.

19. "Will you be here tomorrow?" Ask them _____.

20. "Are you going to go to the party by yourself?" She asked me _____

    _____.

21. "May I borrow your car?" John asked me _____.

22. "Have you ever been in Greece?" I asked them_____.

23. "Will you help me with my project?" Barbara asked me _____

    _____.

24. "Are they going to be at the meeting?" I really don't know _____

    _____.

25. "May we bring our children with us to your party?" They asked me _____

    _____.

26. "Can you tell the time?" I asked the little girl _____

27. "Do you have my phone number?" She asked me_____.

5.14

SENTENCE COMPLETION

Focus: *Whether or Not* in Indirect Statements

Transform the following direct *yes-no* questions in quotation marks into appropriate noun clauses so that you may complete the following indirect statements. To introduce each noun clause, use *whether or not*. For practice and variety, vary the position of *or not* in the sentences. When it is appropriate, observe the rule of sequence of tenses.

EXAMPLES: a. "Can you go to the party?" I don't know *whether or not I can go to the party.*
  b. "Are you happy about her decision?" I didn't know *whether I was happy about her decision or not.*

1. "Are you going to the meeting tomorrow?" I don't know . . .
2. "Did you make the right decision?" I didn't know . . .
3. "Should you marry him/her?" I can't make up my mind . . .
4. "Did you pay your phone bill?" I couldn't remember . . .
5. "Have you gotten the job?" Tomorrow, I will find out . . .
6. "Will it rain tomorrow?" Because I'm not familiar with this part of the country, I can't say . . .
7. "Is s/he telling the truth?" Even though I had tried every means to find out, I still couldn't discover . . .
8. "Does s/he love you?" I really don't know . . .
9. "Did s/he apologize to you?" I didn't care . . .
10. "Is s/he going to leave you?" I don't know . . .
11. "Do you want to hear this secret?" Tell me . . .
12. "Will they come to the conference?" I didn't know . . .
13. "Do you need money?" Please tell me right now . . .
14. "Did you get the job?" At the interview last week, they wouldn't tell me . . .
15. "Is she serious about her proposal?" I can't make up my mind . . .
16. "Do you want to eat out?" I can't decide . . .
17. "Did they make a final decision?" The government authorities wouldn't tell me . . .
18. "Will you have trouble with the immigration authorities?" I really didn't know . . .
19. "Is the operation going to be a success?" The doctors won't say . . .
20. "Should you quit your job?" I can't decide . . .

Now make up your own noun clauses.

21. I can't make up my mind . . .
22. It's hard to decide . . .
23. My teacher wouldn't tell me . . .
24. He didn't know . . .
25. Sam and Alice could not be sure . . .

5.15

NOUN CLAUSES DERIVED FROM INFORMATION QUESTIONS

1. When a noun clause is derived from an information question, an information word (or words) introduces the clause: *No one knows exactly* ***how long the earth has existed;*** *I wonder* ***why I haven't gotten a raise.***

2. In a noun clause derived from an information question, the subject of the clause follows the information word. The subject never follows an auxiliary in a noun clause, and the auxiliary *do* is omitted. Also, quotation marks are not used and, if the clause is being used in a statement, the question mark is dropped because the clause is no longer a question. Compare:

Original Question	Derivation
She asked, "Where do you live?"	*She asked me* ***where I lived.***
She asked, "Why can't you stay?"	*She asked me* ***why I couldn't stay.***
She asked, "Where are your brother and sister?"	*She asked me* ***where my brother and sister were.***

3. If a main verb is in its past form, the rule of sequence of tenses must be observed when a noun clause is derived from an information question. Compare:

Direct	Indirect
She asked, "How many languages do you speak?"	*She **asked** me how many languages I **spoke.***
She asked, "Where did you go?"	*She **asked** me where I **had gone.***

4. When a noun clause occurs in a *yes-no* question, the form of the clause does <u>not</u> change. Compare:

Statement	Yes-No Question
I don't know ***where she lives.***	*Do you know* ***where she lives?***
I asked them ***what time they had left.***	*Did you ask them* ***what time they had left?***

5.16

SENTENCE COMPLETION   Name _____ Date _____

Focus: Noun Clauses Derived from Information Questions

Transform the following direct information questions in quotation marks into appropriate noun clauses so that you may complete the following indirect statements. When it is appropriate, observe the rule of sequence of tenses.

EXAMPLES: a. "Where are Martha and Bill?" I don't know *where Martha and Bill are.*
b. "Where are the elevators?" I asked the porter in the lobby *where the elevators were.*

1. "What time is it?" Ask that policeman _____.

2. "How much did you pay for your wallet?" I couldn't remember _____

_____.

3. "Why won't you confess your sins?" The priest asked me _____

_____.

4. "Why did you make that mistake?" My lawyer explained to me _____ _____

5. "What does this word mean?" No one knows _____.

6. "Why have you left your husband?" She doesn't want to say _____ _____

7. "What did you have for dinner last night?" The other morning, I completely forgot _____ _____.

8. "Where did he land?" Columbus didn't exactly know _____.

9. "How important was his discovery?" When the scientist died, he didn't know _____ _____.

10. "How much are these apples?" The sign doesn't say _____.

11. "What kind of coffee is this?" The label on the can doesn't say _____ _____.

12. "Who did you go with?" I didn't want to tell anyone _____.

13. "How much does this cost?" I don't know _____.

14. "Where are all of my old school friends?" I often wonder_____ _____.

15. "Why did you steal the money?" The thief wouldn't admit _____ _____.

16. "What is the formula for water?" A lot of people don't know _____ _____.

17. "Whose book is this?" I don't care_____.

18. "Why did he end up in jail?" The poor fellow couldn't understand_____ _____.

19. "How serious was her mistake?" She didn't realize _____.

20. "Why are you angry at me?" She asked me _____.

21. "Where did you put my book?" I asked him_____.

22. "Where are the children?" I don't know _____.

23. "Who took my money?" I wanted to find out _____.

24. "Why aren't you taking your medicine?" My doctor asked me_____ _____.

Now make up your own noun clauses.

25. My lawyer/teacher/doctor/dentist/boss asked me _____.

26. I asked the clerk/driver/policeman/ticket agent_____.

27. I asked the mailman/usher _____.

5.17

SENTENCE COMPLETION

Focus: *Yes-No* Questions Containing Noun Clauses

Transform the following statements and questions in quotation marks into appropriate noun clauses so that you may complete the following *yes-no* questions. When it is appropriate, observe the rule of sequence of tenses.

EXAMPLES: a. "He made a mistake." Did the General realize *that he had made a mistake?*
          b. "Do they still live in Paris?" Do you know *whether or not they still live in Paris?*

1. "How is your sister?" Do you know . . .
2. "The government has finally made a decision." Did the radio say . . .
3. "Why are you here?" Have you ever asked yourself . . .
4. "What does this word mean?" Do you know . . .
5. "She is making a mistake." Did she realize . . .
6. "What kind of tea is this?" Does the label on the box say . . .
7. "How many people are there in the world?" Do you know . . .
8. "What is your problem?" Do you yourself understand . . .
9. "Is she coming to New York soon?" Did her letter say . . .
10. "He is quitting his job." Does anyone know . . .
11. "What is your problem?" Would you please tell me . . .
12. "What time will the train leave?" Could you please tell me . . .
13. "What time is it in Bombay?" Do you know . . .
14. "I'll be waiting for you." Did she tell you on the phone . . .
15. "How much does this cost?" Could you please tell me . . .
16. "What does life mean?" Does the Bible really explain . . .
17. "Who is that person?" Did you know . . .
18. "Where is the post office?" Does anyone know . . .
19. "I've lost my job." Didn't you know . . .
20. "What is her phone number?" Would you like to know . . .
21. "Can you go to the conference?" Did you ask her . . .
22. "When will you arrive?" Did they say in their telegram . . .
23. "Has the mail come yet?" Would you happen to know . . .
      (*Would you happen to know* means *would you possibly know.*)
24. "Where are your shoes?" Don't you know . . .
25. "What kind of metal is this?" Would you happen to know . . .
26. "What is the temperature?" Would you happen to know . . .
27. "Where does he live?" Can't you find out . . .
28. "What is the meaning of this word?" Would you happen to know . . .
29. "Did you enjoy the exercise?" Our teacher asked us . . .

5.18

INFINITIVE PHRASES IN INDIRECT SPEECH

1. Sentences in the imperative mood (commands) in direct speech are changed in indirect speech to infinitive phrases which are the direct object of the main verb of a sentence. Compare:

Direct	Indirect
She said, "Be here at three o'clock."	*She told me* **to be there at three o'clock.**
She said, "Children, eat all of your food."	*She told the children* **to eat all of their food.**

Note: As in indirect statements and questions, quotation marks are not used in indirect commands.

2. In negative commands, the auxiliary *do* is dropped in indirect speech, and the adverb *not* is placed before the infinitive. Compare:

Direct	Indirect
She said, "Don't be late, John."	*She told John* **not to be late.**
She said, "Don't put any salt in my food."	*She asked me* **not to put any salt in her food.**

3. When *please* occurs in a direct command, it is omitted when the command is transformed into an infinitive phrase. Compare:

Direct	Indirect
She said, "Please sit down and rest yourself."	*She asked me* **to sit down and rest myself.**

4. Proper names that appear in direct commands frequently become indirect objects of the main verb of an indirect statement. Compare:

Direct	Indirect
She said, "Call your wife, Bob."	*She told* **Bob** *to call his wife.*
She said, "Mary, please don't reveal this secret."	*She asked* **Mary** *not to reveal the secret.*

Focus: Infinitive Phrases in Indirect Speech

Transform the following quotations in the imperative mood into appropriate infinitive phrases so that you may complete the following indirect statements and questions. Omit *please* in a phrase when it occurs. When it is appropriate, follow the rule of sequence of tenses.

EXAMPLES: a. "Please turn off the lights before you leave."
                  My boss told me <u>to turn off the lights before I left.</u>
      b. "Don't touch the painting."
                  The guard told me <u>not to touch the painting.</u>

1. "Please don't use your dictionaries while you are taking the test."

   The teacher told us_____.

2. "Don't pass through the barricades."

   The police warned us _____.

3. "Do exercises in the morning."

   The doctor told me_____.

4. "Don't smoke."

   He also told me _____.

5. "Please take care of this problem."

   I asked my lawyer _____.

6. "Do not eat the forbidden fruit."

   God told Adam and Eve_____.

7. "Speak to me before you go home."

   My boss asked me _____.

8. "Add three cups of wine to the stew."

   The recipe in my cookbook says _____.

9. "Go outside and play."

   I told the children _____.

10. "Please return the book to the right shelf."

    The librarian told me_____.

11. "Don't tease the cat."

    I told Timmy _____.

12. "Get home before midnight."

    My parents told me_____.

13. "Brush your teeth after every meal."

    My dentist told me _____.

5.20

WISH IN PRESENT TIME

1. Like the past tense after *if* in an unreal condition, the past tense in a *that* clause after *wish* expresses a wish that is contrary to fact or reality. Compare:

Reality	Wish
I don't have a lot of money.	*I wish that I **had** a lot of money.*
He has problems with his children.	*He wishes that he **didn't have** problems with his children.*

2. Like the verb *be* in *if* clauses in unreal conditions, the special (subjunctive) form *were* is used in all persons: *She foolishly wishes that she **were** a millionaire; I wish I **weren't** sick.*

3. In informal usage, *that* is omitted: *I wish (that) I had the secret to life; I wish (that) the weather were nice enough for us to go to the park today.*

4. Continuous forms may occur in *that* clauses after *wish: I wish it **weren't raining** now so that I could go out; They wish they **were living** in a better part of town.*

5. *Could* is also used in a *that* clause to express *ability* or *possibility: We wish we **could be** at your dinner tonight, but we can't; I wish I **could do** everything well.*

6. *Didn't have to* + a base form may be used in a *that* clause to express *it is not necessary: I wish I didn't have to (it weren't necessary to) work so hard.*

Reality	Wish
He has to enter the hospital.	*He wishes he **didn't have to enter** the hospital.*
I have to tell my neighbor the bad news.	*I wish I **didn't have to tell** my neighbor the bad news.*

Note: In the simple present tense, *wish* followed by an infinitive means *want: I wish (want) to speak to the person in charge. Wish* meaning *to want* is usually heard in rather formal usage.

5.21

GRAMMAR EXERCISE   Name _____ Date _____

Focus: Noun Clauses Following *Wish* for Present Time

Fill in each blank with an appropriate past form (affirmative or negative), with *could* + a base form, or with *didn't have to* + a base form.

EXAMPLES: a. (work) I wish that I <u>worked</u> for a larger company.
            b. (work) I wish that I <u>could work</u> miracles.
            c. (work) I wish I didn't <u>have to work</u> so hard at my office.

1. (be) I wish that I _____ a millionaire.

2. (tell) I wish I _____ you the secret, but I can't.

3. (have) Our little boy wishes he _____ a baby brother.

4. (know) I wish that I _____ how to swim.

5. (be) She wishes she _____ beautiful enough to be in the movies.

6. (have) I wish that I _____ this terrible headache.

7. (be) Billy wishes he _____ Santa Claus.

8. (eat) I wish I _____ fattening food, but I can't.

9. (speak) I wish I _____ English better than I do.

10. (be) She's so unhappy, she wishes that she _____ dead.

11. (go) It's such a beautiful day, I wish I _____ out, but I can't. (stay) I wish
    I _____ inside today.

12. (be) Do you ever wish you _____ somebody else?

13. (stay) I'm so tired that I wish I _____ in bed, but I can't. (go) I wish I
    _____ to work today.

14. (live) Do you wish you _____ forever?

15. (be) He wishes that his life _____ less difficult than it is.

16. (be) Oh! I wish that I _____ sick.

17. (remember) I wish that I _____ all of the irregular verbs, but I can't.
    (work) I wish my teacher _____ miracles.

18. (be) I certainly wish that I _____ in so much trouble with the government.
    (help) I wish my lawyer _____ me, but he can't. (have) I wish I _____
    _____ a better lawyer.

19. (have) My son wishes he _____ a new bicycle, a model train, and a
    chemistry set.

20. (go) I wish that I _____ to school every day.

21. (be) I wish it _____ easier to learn a second language.

22. (be) He wishes his girlfriend _____ angry at him.

23. (help) I wish I _____ the children of the poor, but I can't.

5.22

WISH IN PAST TIME

1. Like the past perfect tense in an *if* clause in a past-unreal condition, the past perfect tense in a *that* clause after *wish* expresses a wish that is contrary to fact or reality in past time. Compare:

Past Reality	Wish
It wasn't a nice day yesterday.	*I wish that it **had been** a nice day yesterday.*
I didn't have time to do my homework last night.	*I wish I **had had** time to do my homework last night.*

2. *Could have* + a past participle is used in *that* clauses after *wish* to express ability or possibility in past time.

Past Reality	Wish
I couldn't be at the parade yesterday.	*I wish I **could have been** at the parade yesterday.*
I couldn't take a nap this afternoon.	*I wish I **could have taken** a nap this afternoon.*

Note: *Couldn't have* rarely occurs in *that* clauses after *wish*.

3. Statements containing *wish* + a *that* clause referring to past time are made in response to an event or situation that takes place in either present or past time.

Situation	Wish
My feet hurt.	*I wish that I **hadn't worn** those new shoes when I went shopping.*
I can't afford to take a vacation.	*I wish I **had saved** more money last year.*
They lost the game.	*They wished they **had practiced** more.*

5.23

GRAMMAR EXERCISE

Name _____ Date _____

Focus: Noun Clauses Following *Wish* for Past Time

Fill in each blank with *had* (*hadn't*) + a past participle, or *could have* + a past participle.

EXAMPLES: a. (know) I wish I <u>had known</u> ten years ago what I know now.
  b. (put) I wish I <u>hadn't put</u> my foot in my mouth at the meeting.
  c. (go) We wish we <u>could have gone</u> to Europe last year, but we couldn't.

1. (study) I wish I _____ English when I was younger.

2. (drink) I wish I _____ so much last night; I now have a hangover.

3. (make) I wish I _____ that stupid mistake.

4. (be) I wish I _____ able to study English last semester.

5.23 (Continued)

5. (be) I wish I _____ with my family last Christmas, but I couldn't. (go) I certainly wish I _____ home.

6. (marry) He's unhappy and wishes he _____ his wife.

7. (put) This chicken is terrible. I wish I _____ so much salt on it. (follow) I wish I _____ the directions more carefully. (be) I wish I _____ less careless.

8. (bring) We're lost. I wish we _____ a map with us.

9. (eat) I've got a stomach ache. I wish I _____ so much for dinner. (be) I wish my eyes _____ bigger than my stomach. (serve) I wish they _____ me so much.

10. (win *or* lose) I wish my team _____ the last game.

11. (eat) Our little boy now wishes he _____ those green apples.

12. (help) I wish I _____ you on your last project, but I couldn't because I was too busy with my own.

13. (catch) Everyone wishes the police _____ the kidnapper.

14. (escape) We wish the murderer _____.

15. (miss) Darn it! I wish I _____ the bus.

16. (take) I wish I _____ a taxi.

Now complete the sentences.

17. My mother wishes that I_____.

18. I wish my girlfriend/boyfriend _____.

19. That politician wishes s/he _____.

20. My teacher wishes s/he _____.

21. I wish my neighbor_____.

22. I wish my boss _____.

23. Our little boy/girl wishes s/he _____.

24. My boss wishes I _____.

25. I wish _____.

5.24

WRITING EXERCISE   Name _____ Date _____

Focus: Responding to a Situation with *Wish*

Make appropriate responses to the following stated situations and remarks with sentences containing *wish* as a main verb and a *that* clause referring to past time. Use the past perfect tense only.

EXAMPLES: a. More people came to the dinner party than we had expected.
                 <u>I wish that we hadn't run out of food.</u>
             b. I wasn't feeling very well last night.
                 <u>I wish I had taken my medicine yesterday morning.</u>

1. I'm very tired/hungry/thirsty.

_____

2. My boss/girlfriend/boyfriend/neighbor is angry at me.

_____

3. The picnic wasn't much of a success.

_____

4. They are very unhappy together in their marriage.

_____

5. We didn't enjoy our last vacation in Europe.

_____

6. We ran out of gas in the middle of the desert.

_____

7. He failed the final examination.

_____

8. They're very unhappy with their new car.

_____

9. They don't like living in this city.

_____

10. All of my house plants died.

_____

11. I didn't enjoy the course in chemistry last semester.

_____

12. S/he lost her/his sweater.

_____

13. I'm afraid that I'm going to lose my job.

_____

14. My girlfriend/boyfriend hurt my feelings.

_____

5.25

ABRIDGMENT OF NOUN CLAUSES FOLLOWING *WISH* AND *HOPE*

1. Commonly, an abridgment of a *that* clause after *wish* is made in a statement which is in response to another statement made by either ourselves or another person:

   *Life is not easy. I wish **that it were.***
   *She has to work on Sundays. She wishes **she didn't.***
   *I can't help you with your problem. I wish **I could.***
   *I didn't give a very clear explanation. I wish **that I had.***
   *I couldn't get to the bank. I wish **that I could have.***
   *I can't get out of town this weekend. I wish **I could.***
   *I wasn't at the meeting. I wish **I had been.***

2. Ordinarily, we make wishes with *that* clauses that refer to present or past time: *I wish I were on the beach now; I wish that I had been born in the eighteenth century.*

   #### Hope

3. (a) Usually, we *hope* for events that may take place in the future, using a *that* clause following the verb *hope*: *I certainly hope **(that) all of your plans are realized;** The government hopes **(that) industrial and agricultural production will increase by twelve per cent next year.***

   (b) Often, we express an <u>unrealized</u> hope in past time with *would* + a base form in a *that* clause following the verb *hope*: *Napoleon hoped **that he would conquer Europe** (but he didn't); My grandfather hoped **that he would make a million dollars** (but he never did).*

   (c) When we express a hope that is related to ourselves, we may use either an infinitive phrase or a *that* clause: *I hope **to do well** in my college career,* or *I hope **that I will do well in my college career.***

   (d) When we express a hope that is <u>not</u> related to ourselves, only a *that* clause may be used: *I hope that all my classmates will do well in their future studies.*
   Note: In sentences with *hope* for the future [paragraphs (a), (c), and (d)], the present and future tenses may be used interchangeably. The present continuous tense stresses hope in the present. With certain verbs, the present tense can refer to present or future time: *I hope she is happy* could mean *now* or *sometime in the future.*

   (e) When we express a hope about the present unknown, we use one of the present tenses: *I hope my parents are having a good time in Europe; I hope I haven't made a mistake; I hope she is happy.*

   (f) When we express a hope about the past unknown, we use a past form: *I hope I didn't make a mistake.*

GRAMMAR EXERCISE   Name _____ Date _____

Focus: Abridgment of Noun Clauses Following *Wish*

Supply appropriate words in the blanks.

EXAMPLES: a. I wasn't at the last game; I wish that I <u>had been</u>.
              b. I can't work miracles; I wish I <u>could</u>.

1. She has to work very hard; she wishes that she _____.

2. I'm not a good swimmer; I wish I _____.

3. I don't make very much money in my job; I wish that I _____.

4. I can't go to the game today; I wish I _____.

5. I couldn't go out last night; I wish I _____.

6. I'm too sick to go to school today; I wish I _____.

7. He cheated on his income taxes; he wishes he _____.

8. I didn't study English when I was younger; I wish I _____.

9. Bill doesn't have a girlfriend; he wishes he _____.

10. I have to go to the dentist today; I wish that I _____.

11. I can't solve this problem without my lawyer; I wish I _____.

12. She doesn't have a typewriter; she wishes that she _____.

13. I'm not going to be able to be at the next meeting; I wish I _____.

14. We can't afford to buy a larger house; we wish we _____.

15. Mary isn't going to be at the party; I wish she _____.

16. I put too much salt in the stew; I wish I _____.

17. It's raining cats and dogs; I wish it _____.
    (*Raining cats and dogs* means *raining heavily.*)

18. Jack has to quit his job; he wishes he _____.

19. I'm not feeling well today; I wish I _____, but I'm not.

20. I have to work on Sundays; I wish I _____, but I do.

21. I can't speak French; I wish I _____, but I can't.

22. I couldn't be at the last meeting; I wish I _____.

23. He has to do the composition over; he wishes he _____, but he does.

24. I talked too much during the job interview; I wish that I _____.

25. I'm sorry, but I can't help you with this problem; I wish I _____, but I can't.

26. Time goes by so fast; I wish that it _____, but it does.

27. They have a problem with their son; they wish they _____.

28. I'm not able to find a good job; I wish that I _____.

29. I'm in trouble with my boss; I wish I _____.

5.27

GRAMMAR EXERCISE.   Name _____ Date _____

Focus: *Hope*

A Hope for the Future Related to Ourselves

Complete the following sentences with an infinitive phrase or a *that* clause, e.g., *I hope to do well (that I do well)*.

1. At the end of the course, I hope _____.

2. At the party tomorrow, I hope _____.

3. At the job interview, I hope _____.

4. At my graduation, I hope _____.

5. At the game, I hope _____.

A Hope for the Future Not Related to Ourselves

Complete the following sentences with a *that* clause containing *will* + a base form, e.g., *I hope that you will have a happy life*.

6. I hope that my teacher/parents_____.

7. I hope my neighbor/son/daughter _____.

8. I hope my girlfriend/boyfriend_____.

A Hope about the Present Unknown

Fill in the blanks with appropriate present verb forms, e.g., *I hope all my old school friends are happy*.

9. I hope everyone in this class _____ a happy life.

10. I hope the president _____ a completely honest man.

11. I hope my neighbors _____ enough money to educate their children.

12. I hope everyone in my class _____ me.

A Hope about the Past Unknown

Fill in the blanks with appropriate past forms, e.g., *I hope I made no mistakes in the exam last night*.

13. I hope I _____ the right things at yesterday's meeting.

14. She hopes she _____ well on the final examination yesterday.

15. I hope my parents _____ my explanation last night.

Unrealized Hope in the Past

Complete the following sentences with *that* clauses containing would + a base form, e.g., *Che Guevara hoped he would start a revolution in Bolivia, but he didn't*.

16. Alexander the Great hoped _____.

17. Karl Marx hoped _____.

5.27 *(Continued)*

18. The president hoped _____.

19. The mountain climbers hoped _____.

20. The Democrats/Republicans hoped _____.

21. Ponce de Leon/Magellan/Marie Antoinette/I/my parents/the people/the Americans hoped

_____.

5.28

WISHES WITH *WOULD*

1. Unlike a *that* clause containing the simple past tense or the past perfect tense following the verb *wish,* a verb phrase with *would* + a base form represents a wish that is possible to realize. Compare:

Contrary to Reality	Possible to Realize
(Mary isn't here.) *I wish she were here.*	*I wish she **would come.***
(It's raining hard.) *I wish it weren't raining.*	*I wish it **would stop** raining.*

Reminder: When referring to the future, we usually hope for an event to occur: *We all hope that there will be peace in our time.*

2. Wishes with *would* are sometimes used to make a polite request: *I wish you **would take** better care of your health; I wish you **would turn** down the radio; I wish you **would please promise** to keep this a secret.*

Past Forms of Modal Auxiliaries in *That* Clauses

3. Because past forms of modal auxiliaries like *should* and *might* are usually awkward to use in question forms, they most often occur in *that* clauses following such verbs as *think* and *feel: Do you think that I **might have made** a mistake when I decided to quit my job? Do you feel that I **should have approached** the problem in a different way?*
Reminder: *That* may be omitted in a sentence: *I wish (that) my problems would go away.*

5.29

GRAMMAR EXERCISE

Focus: Wishes with *Would*

Supply appropriate base forms in the blanks.

EXAMPLES: a. I'm a little lonely tonight. I wish somebody would call me up.
b. Darn it! I wish it would stop raining so I could go shopping.

Name _____ Date _____

1. I wish you would _____ this information a secret between us.

2. I wish those people would _____ using such dirty language.

3. You're driving so fast that I wish you'd _____ down.

4. Why is the train so late today? I wish it would _____.

5. I have a terrible cold. I wish it would _____ away.

6. I wish s/he would _____ me, but I don't think s/he will.

7. Billy, I wish you'd _____ playing with your food.

8. Nancy, I wish you'd _____ your elbows off the table.

9. What a dark and cloudy day! I wish the sun would _____ out.

10. Timmy wished it would _____ raining so he could go out and play.

11. I wish you'd _____ wishing for things you can't have.

12. I wish the government would _____ something about pollution.

13. All of the students wish the bell would _____.

14. I'm getting very impatient. I wish this meeting would _____ to an end.

5.30

SENTENCE COMPLETION

Focus: *Might Have* + Past Participle in *That* Clauses

Compose appropriate *that* clauses containing *might* (*not*) *have* + a past participle so that you may complete the following *yes-no* questions.

EXAMPLES: a. Why haven't they received the letter? Do you think *that I might have forgotten to put a stamp on it?*

b. This stew is awful! Do you think *that I might have used the wrong kind of meat?*

1. Where's my wallet? Do you think . . .
2. Why hasn't Bob gotten here yet? Is it possible . . .
3. Why did s/he go back to Europe? Do you think . . .
4. Why didn't they enjoy their vacation? Do you think . . .
5. Why did s/he leave town so suddenly? Do you think . . .
6. Why did the general make such a foolish decision? Is it possible . . .
7. Why did the teacher get angry at the student? Do you think . . .
8. Why is s/he so angry at me? Do you feel . . .
9. Why wasn't the operation a success? Do you think . . .
10. Why didn't I get a good grade in that course? Do you think . . .
11. Why do I have a stomach ache? Do you think . . .
12. Why did they buy a new house? Do you think . . .
13. Why did s/he get up and leave the room so suddenly? Do you think . . .
14. Why didn't these photographs come out better? Do you think . . .
15. Why didn't John finish the course? Do you think . . .
16. Why is everybody laughing? Do you think . . .

5.31

NOUN CLAUSES DERIVED FROM REQUESTS

1. Like noun clauses derived from statements, noun clauses derived from requests are introduced by *that*: *My lawyer urges (**that**) **I sign the contract immediately**; I suggest (**that**) **we take a little break**.*

2. Noun clauses derived from requests most frequently occur after verbs called VERBS OF URGENCY (request verbs). Some verbs of urgency are listed below:

advise	desire	propose	request	stipulate	urge
demand	insist	recommend	require	suggest	

3. The verb in a *that* clause which appears after the words in the above list is a base form: *The doctor suggested that she **enter** the hospital.*

$$\left.\begin{array}{l} \text{I} \\ \text{you} \\ \text{he} \\ \text{she} \\ \text{it} \end{array}\right\} \textbf{go} \qquad\qquad \left.\begin{array}{l} \text{we} \\ \text{you} \\ \text{they} \end{array}\right\} \textbf{go}$$

4. The verb *be* also remains a base form in all persons: *That selfish man always insists that he **be** first in line; My mother insists that I **be** home before it gets dark.*

5. The verb in a *that* clause derived from a request remains a base form regardless of the tense of the verb in the main clause: *The teacher requested that the students **do** their homework in ink; My lawyer has recommended that I **sue** the government; The committee will propose that the president of the organization **resign**.*

6. *That* clauses occasionally follow certain adjectives which are called ADJECTIVES OF URGENCY. A verb in this kind of clause takes the same form as a verb in a *that* clause following a verb of urgency: *It is **necessary** that everyone **be** at the next meeting.* Following are listed some adjectives of urgency.

advisable	better	essential	imperative	mandatory	urgent
best	desirable	good	important	necessary	vital

GRAMMAR EXERCISE   Name _____ Date _____

> Focus: *That* Clauses after Verbs of Urgency

Supply appropriate base forms in the blanks.

appear	carry	enter	give	obey	release	show	surrender
be	chew	get	keep	quit	say	stop	wear

EXAMPLES: a. In many countries, the law requires that everyone carry an identification pass at all times.

b. At the library, the guards require that all students show their identification cards.

1. My lawyer recommends that I _____ nothing to the reporters.

2. Everyone in the class has proposed to the teacher that he _____ no final examination.

3. The doctor strongly recommends that my father _____ the hospital immediately for an operation.

4. The librarian in the reading room insists that everyone _____ quiet.

5. The invitation from the White House requests that gentlemen _____ formal evening clothes to the reception.

6. Her doctor insists that she _____ smoking.

7. The invitation requests that women _____ long dresses.

8. This letter requests that I _____ at a government office for an investigation of my past taxes.

9. The rioting students and workers were demanding that the government _____ the political prisoners.

10. Our teacher always insists that we _____ on time every day.

11. S/he also insists that no one _____ gum during the class.

12. That difficult customer always insists that s/he _____ fast service, so none of the clerks likes to wait on her. (*To wait on* can mean *to serve.*)

13. He has finally proposed to her that she _____ his wife.

14. Parents have the right to demand that their children _____ them.

15. The president of the company has proposed to the board of directors that it _____ him a raise.

16. My boss has politely suggested that I _____ my job.

17. Our enemy has demanded that we _____, but we will fight until our last soldier falls.

5.33

Name _____ Date _____

Focus: *That* Clauses after Adjectives of Urgency

Supply appropriate base forms in the blanks.

| develop | enter | get | keep | renew | speak | sue |
| drink | find | have | read | resign | submit | wear |

EXAMPLES: a. While driving a car, it is absolutely essential that a driver keep his or her eyes on the road.

b. It is vital that we find a solution to the problem of pollution as soon as possible.

1. It is essential that the government _____ more effective educational programs for the poor.

2. Most people in the nation think it is best that the President _____ from office.

3. It is imperative that you _____ this material to the committee before it makes its final decision.

4. In a very hot climate, it is necessary that an individual _____ a lot of liquids.

5. It is necessary that I _____ my passport before I leave the country.

6. In the army, it is mandatory that everyone _____ his or her uniform while on duty.

7. It is important that you _____ the directions on the bottle before you take any kind of medicine.

8. It's urgent that you _____ this telegram at once.

9. I think it's advisable that he _____ to his lawyer before he makes a final decision.

10. It is mandatory by law in the United States that a man and woman _____ blood tests before they are married.

11. It is absolutely imperative that we _____ back to the shore before the hurricane comes.

12. My lawyer feels it's advisable that I _____ that company for damages.

13. My doctor feels it's urgent that I _____ the hospital at once for a complete physical examination.

14. It is extremely vital that we _____ accurate information about the enemy's position before we attack.

15. Is it really necessary that I _____ at the next meeting?

16. Is it necessary that I _____ this prescription?

17. It is very important that your boss _____ this confidential report.

-*ING* FORMS AND INFINITIVES 6

6.1

GERUNDS

1. An -*ing* form is called a GERUND when it is used in the same manner as a noun. Like nouns, a gerund may be used as the subject of a sentence: ***Swimming*** *is good for you;* ***Traveling*** *is educational.*

2. An -*ing* form is called a PRESENT PARTICIPLE when it is used as a verb: *Our children are* ***swimming*** *in the pool; His parents are* ***traveling*** *in the Far East.*

3. A gerund combined with a prepositional phrase is called a GERUND PHRASE: ***Being in Europe*** *has been a new and exciting experience for her;* ***Traveling around the world*** *would be very educational.*

4. Sometimes, usually in rather formal writing and speaking, possessive adjectives and nouns precede the gerund in a gerund phrase: ***Foo's jogging*** *keeps him in good physical shape;* ***The Ambassador's handling*** *of the situation was not acceptable to the government;* ***Her dropping out*** *of school so suddenly surprised all of her friends.*

5. Certain gerunds follow the verb *go* in idiomatic usage:

   (a) *During the winter months we often* ***go bowling.***
   (b) *I have a good idea; let's* ***go dancing*** *tonight.*
   (c) *When I was a little boy, I used to* ***go fishing*** *with my Dad.*
   (d) *My father would always* ***go golfing*** *every Saturday morning.*
   (e) *When we were in the jungle, we* ***went hunting*** *for lions.*
   (f) *Do you ever* ***go hiking*** *in the mountains during the summer?*
   (g) *Have you ever* ***gone mountain climbing*** *in Switzerland?*
   (h) *If the wind had been blowing, we would have* ***gone sailing*** *yesterday.*
   (i) *I've never liked to* ***go shopping.***
   (j) *We like to* ***go skin diving*** *when we go to Florida.*
   (k) *He never* ***goes skiing*** *because he's afraid of falling.*
   (l) *When the lake is frozen, I often* ***go skating*** *with my friends.*
   (m) *When we were in Greece on our vacation, we would* ***go swimming*** *almost every day. We'd also* ***go dancing*** *every night.*
   (n) *It's a lot of fun to* ***go window-shopping*** *during Christmas.*

GRAMMAR EXERCISE   Name _____ Date _____

Focus: Gerunds and Gerund Phrases as Subjects

Make gerunds out of the base forms in the following list and supply them in the appropriate blanks.

bark	drive	get	have	lie	sleep	swim	work
be	eat	give	jog	read	smoke	take	
cheat	fish	go	learn	ride	study	wash	

EXAMPLES: a. Being in trouble with the teacher is an uncomfortable experience.
              b. Having an operation last year saved his life.

1. Because he doesn't like to take orders, _____ in the army was a terrible experience for him.

2. _____ in this lake is forbidden.

3. Her _____ on the final examination made the teacher angry.

4. _____ in elevators is against the law.

5. _____ to the beach is relaxing and fun.

6. _____ to speak a second language well takes a long time.

7. According to the doctor, John's _____ is the cause of his coughing constantly.

8. _____ out in the rain without an umbrella is a good way to catch a cold.

9. _____ around the park two or three times a day is a good way to keep in shape.

10. _____ good health is the most important thing in life.

11. _____ care of little children is a full-time job.

12. Their _____ married surprised all of their friends.

13. _____ in the sun at the beach for long periods of time is not good for the skin.

14. _____ this blouse in hot water will ruin it.

15. _____ the newspaper every day keeps you informed.

16. _____ as a teacher can be a rewarding job.

17. _____ a party can be very expensive.

18. _____ a car without a license is against the law.

19. _____ lots of fresh fruit is very good for you.

20. _____ between the cars of a subway train is forbidden.

21. _____ is very bad for the health.

22. _____ into a good university is his goal.

23. _____ on a good mattress is necessary for a good night's sleep.

24. The dog's _____ kept me awake last night.

25. _____ at this school has been a new experience for me.

6.3

GERUNDS AS OBJECTS OF CERTAIN VERBS

1. There are some verbs that cannot be followed by an infinitive. Compare:

Correct	Wrong
*I enjoy **eating**.*	*I enjoy to eat.*
*I finished **doing** my homework.*	*I finished to do my homework.*
*I miss **being** with my family.*	*I miss to be with my family.*

Some verbs that must be followed by a gerund are:

admit	deny	finish	miss	quit	risk
avoid	detest	give up	postpone	recall	stop (= quit)
consider	dislike	keep on	practice	recommend	suggest
delay	enjoy	mind	put off	resist	tolerate

2. An infinitive follows the verb *stop* if we mean *to stop for a purpose: I stopped **to get** a loaf of bread at the store on my way home; When I saw John on the street, I stopped **to talk** to him for a while.* However, a gerund must follow *stop* when the verb means *to quit: He's finally stopped (quit) **smoking** after twenty years.*

3. There are certain verbs that can be followed by a gerund or an infinitive; there is no difference in meaning. Compare:

Gerund	Infinitive
*I prefer **being** alone when I'm sick.*	*I prefer **to be** alone when I'm sick.*
*I like **dancing** the tango.*	*I like **to dance** the tango.*
*I plan **taking** another course.*	*I plan **to take** another course.*

Some verbs that may be followed by a gerund or an infinitive are:

attempt	continue	intend	plan
begin	dread	like	prefer
cannot bear (= tolerate)	hate	love	start
cannot stand (= tolerate)	hesitate	neglect	try

6.4

GRAMMAR EXERCISE   Name _____ Date _____

Focus: Gerund Phrases as Objects of Verbs

Supply appropriate gerunds in the blanks.

EXAMPLES: a. (be) Kim misses being with his family in Korea.
b. (close) Would you mind closing the door?
Note: In answer to example (b), *Yes, I would* means *I don't want to; No, I wouldn't* means *I want to.*

1. (run) The police yelled to the thief to stop, but he kept on _____. (be) I wouldn't enjoy _____ a policeman.

2. (tease) Timmy, would you please stop _____ the cat?

3. (tell) Would you mind _____ me what your problem is?

4. (invest) I wouldn't risk _____ in that company if I were you.

5. (hit) He was driving very fast and couldn't avoid _____ the dog.

6. (take) Don't postpone _____ care of this problem.

7. (worry) I wish you would stop _____ about your grades.

8. (help) Would you mind _____ me carry this carton?

9. (do) Would you mind _____ a little favor for me?

10. (smoke) The doctor recommends that she give up _____.

11. (be) His grandmother can't tolerate _____ in cold weather.

12. (do) Never put off _____ something until tomorrow when you can do it today.

13. (fall) He says he wouldn't risk _____ in love again.

14. (repeat) Would you mind _____ that question more slowly?

15. (work) Have you finished _____ on your project yet?

Now complete the sentences.

16. I didn't enjoy _____.

17. Would you mind_____?

18. Did you ever consider_____?

19. Has the thief finally admitted _____?

20. My lawyer suggested _____.

21. I dislike _____.

22. I hear that Bob has quit_____.

23. Don't postpone (put off)_____.

24. I don't recall (remember) _____.

6.5

GRAMMAR EXERCISE   Name _____ Date _____

      Focus: Gerund or Infinitive

Supply an appropriate infinitive or gerund in the blanks.

EXAMPLES: a. Doesn't everyone like being (to be) in love?
          b. I hate seeing (to see) children without enough food to eat.

1. When the weather is nice, we like _____ our breakfast in the garden.

2. I prefer _____ in a warm climate rather than a cold one.

3. We started _____ to the top of the mountain shortly after the sun had risen.

4. Your children really like _____ to the movies, don't they?

5. Their 16-year-old daughter has just recently started _____ out with boys.

6. Our little boy has recently begun _____ with a fork. Also, he has started _____ longer words when he speaks.

7. I don't like _____ to the dentist.

8. I hesitate _____ him this news because he might spread it around town.

9. They attempted _____ the top of the mountain but they failed because of a sudden storm.

10. Bobby, please try _____ quiet for a minute.

11. Many people prefer _____ by themselves.

12. Few people like _____ taxes.

13. Never neglect _____ care of your health.

14. Shall we continue _____ this exercise, or would you prefer _____ a break?

15. Everyone in the class has begun _____ a lot of progress.

16. I'm afraid that it's started _____ again.

17. Even though she works during the day, she's continued _____ at the university at night.

18. I can't stand _____ in a crowded room.

19. I plan _____ my studies after this course.

20. A lot of students dread _____ examinations.

6.6

GERUNDS AS OBJECTS OF PREPOSITIONS AND IN TIME PHRASES

1. Because they may function as nouns, gerunds and gerund phrases can also occur as objects of prepositions. Two usual patterns are: (a) verb + preposition + gerund (phrase): *He believes in **praying**; He believes in **praying to God**;* and (b) adjective + preposition + gerund (phrase): *I'm afraid of **falling**; He's very careless about **doing his homework**.*

2. Gerunds are often used in TIME PHRASES: ***Before leaving the room**, please turn off the lights; **After eating dinner**, we watched TV for a few hours.*

3. Be careful not to confuse a time phrase with a time clause. You may remember that a phrase never has a subject or a verb, but a clause always does. Compare:

Time Phrase	Time Clause
***When doing my homework**, I often have to use my dictionary.*	***When I do my homework**, I often have to use my dictionary.*
***Until coming to New York**, I'd never ridden on a subway.*	***Until I came to New York**, I'd never ridden on a subway.*
***Before leaving the room**, please turn off the lights.*	***Before you leave the room**, please turn off the lights.*

4. A frequent mistake that students make is to place a subject before a gerund in a time phrase. Compare:

Wrong	Correct
Before you leaving the room . . .	*Before leaving the room . . .*
While you doing your homework . . .	*While doing your homework . . .*
When he coming into the room . . .	*When coming into the room . . .*

6.7

GRAMMAR EXERCISE   Name _____ Date _____

Focus: Gerund Phrases as Objects of Prepositions

Make gerunds out of the base forms in the following list and supply them in the appropriate blanks. Study the prepositions carefully.

do	get	have	put	start	take
fall	give	kill	reach	steal	walk
find	go	make	run	study	work

EXAMPLES: a. She looks forward to <u>graduating</u> from the university.
   Reminder: (*To look forward to* means *to anticipate a future event with pleasure.*)
   b. They don't believe in <u>giving</u> their children a lot of money.

1. I'm not looking forward to _____ the final examination.

2. She's very interested in _____ chemistry.

Name _____ Date _____

3. We're all very tired of _____ so hard for so little money.

4. That customer always insists on _____ fast service.

5. I don't want to say anything; I'm a little afraid of _____ my foot in my mouth.

6. My boss is responsible for _____ an office of fifty people. He is capable of _____ a very good job.

7. The paper says the man is guilty of _____ his wife.

8. Don't worry about _____ a mistake in the next test.

9. We are planning on _____ to Spain next summer.

10. Because of the storm, they didn't succeed in _____ the top of the mountain.

11. She is incapable of _____ because of her arthritis.

12. The bad weather prevented us from _____ on the picnic.

13. The police have accused the woman of _____ the jewels.

14. I suspect my neighbor of _____ vegetables out of my garden.

Now supply a preposition as well as a gerund in the blanks.

15. I don't like mountain climbing because I'm afraid _____ _____.

16. Most of the students are interested _____ _____ another course.

17. I certainly am looking forward _____ _____ my vacation.

18. Our little boy is responsible _____ _____ care of the chickens.

19. Unfortunately, he hasn't succeeded _____ _____ a good job.

20. Do you ever get tired _____ _____ homework?

21. Selfish people insist _____ _____ everything for themselves.

22. The government says that man is responsible _____ _____ the revolution.

23. She plans _____ _____ graduate work next year.

24. We are thinking _____ _____ to Italy next spring.

25. The rain prevented me _____ _____ shopping.

6.8

Focus: *Be Used to* and *Get Used to*

1. *Be used to* means *be accustomed to: I'm not used to (accustomed to) the strange customs of the people in the mountains; North Americans are not used to (accustomed to) eating very spicy food.*
   Note: Do not confuse *be used to (accustomed to)* with *used to* + a base form for past custom: *When I was a little boy, I **used to enjoy** going fishing.*

2. *Get used to* means *become accustomed to: Are you getting used to (becoming used to) living in the United States? After living in Hong Kong for a year, he's finally getting used to (becoming used to) eating with chopsticks.*

Supply appropriate gerunds in the blanks.

EXAMPLES: a. Tazuko isn't used to <u>eating</u> American food.
            b. However, she is getting used to <u>eating</u> with a knife and fork.

1. I'm not used to _____ coffee without sugar.

2. He's been in New York for a year, but he still isn't used to _____ on the subways. But he's slowly getting used to the weather. He says he'll never get used to _____ in such a large and crowded city.

3. While I was living in England, I couldn't get used to _____ on the left side of the road.

4. I didn't enjoy living in England because I'm not used to _____ in such a wet climate.

5. While I was staying with a friend in Japan, I couldn't get used to _____ on the floor.

6. Their son is enjoying his experience at the university, but he still hasn't gotten used to _____ in a dormitory.

7. I'm not used to _____ English on the phone.

8. He's unhappy with his job because he isn't used to _____ for such a large company. But he thinks he'll get used to it.

9. My dog has finally gotten used to my new cat _____ in the house. Unfortunately, the cat hasn't gotten used to the dog.

10. When Carlos first came to the United States, he wasn't used to _____ out with American girls. But he got used to it very fast.

6.9

Focus: Gerunds and Gerund Phrases Following the Preposition *For*

A pattern consisting of the preposition *for* + a gerund phrase often occurs. Supply appropriate gerunds in the blanks.

EXAMPLES: a. Look at the rain! It's not a very good day for drying clothes, is it?
           b. It's a perfect day for taking a walk through the park.

1. I must apologize to you for _____ such a foolish question.

2. Thank you for _____ me to solve the problem.

3. I'm sorry, I must apologize to you for _____ so late.

4. Isn't it a perfect day for _____ pictures?

5. That old shirt makes a good rag for _____ the car.

6. I must thank you for _____ so kind to me during my illness.

7. There is no public transportation in my town, so I need a car for _____ to the store.

8. I'm angry at my neighbor's little boy for _____ all the apples off my apple tree in the backyard.

9. I'm angry at myself for _____ that stupid mistake.

10. Do you have a large pot for _____ lobsters?

11. I need a car for _____ errands. (*To run errands* means *to do little chores such as going to the store, bakery, or post office.*)

12. What a perfect day for _____ on a hike!

13. This is a wonderful evening for _____ dinner on the terrace.

14. Do you have a recipe for _____ apple pie?

15. I need the directions for _____ this radio set together. (*To put together* means *to assemble.*)

16. I also need the directions for _____ it apart. (*To take apart* means *to disassemble.*)

17. I'm surprised at myself for _____ such a foolish thing.

18. I need a good dictionary for _____ up new words.

19. I must apologize to you for _____ that rude remark.

20. I must thank all my friends for _____ me such a nice surprise birthday party.

21. I would like to thank you for _____ so kind; I appreciate everything you've done for me.

22. Thank you so much for _____ care of the problem.

6.10

GRAMMAR EXERCISE   Name _____ Date _____

Focus: Gerunds in Time Phrases

Supply appropriate gerunds in the blanks.

EXAMPLES: a. While coming to school, I was thinking about my last vacation.
           b. You should speak to your lawyer before making a decision.

1. Let's have another cocktail before _____ dinner.

2. I usually feel refreshed after _____ a nap.

3. It's a good idea to review before _____ an examination.

4. Please turn off the lights before _____ the room.

5. After _____ the shocking news, she fainted.

6. Don't you think the children should have breakfast before _____ the house for school?

7. How is the patient going to feel after _____ the medicine?

8. I often play the radio while _____ my homework.

9. Before _____ the house, you should check all the windows and doors to see that they're locked.

10. Before _____ the street, you should look both ways.

11. While _____ the mountain, I was thinking about nothing except my safety. I've always been afraid of falling.

12. When _____ a cake, be sure that nobody slams the door.

13. Your children should always brush their teeth before _____ to bed.

14. After _____ into bed, I suddenly realized I'd forgotten to lock the door.

15. Shouldn't Buddy wash his hands before _____ down to dinner?

16. That student must improve his English before _____ the university.

17. While _____ to the teacher's explanation, I was thinking about the person sitting across the room.

18. Before _____ someone for the definition of a word, you should look it up in a dictionary.

19. I felt much better about the situation after _____ a long conversation about it with a friend.

20. Before _____ any kind of medicine, be sure to read the directions on the bottle.

21. Before _____ any kind of contract, be sure to read the small print.

22. Before _____ on to the next exercise, let's take a break.

6.11

-ING FORMS OR BASE FORMS FOLLOWING CERTAIN VERBS

1. A base form or an -*ing* form may occur as the object of certain sense perception verbs. Some of the sense perception verbs are the following:

    feel   hear   notice   observe   see   smell   watch

    The (pro)noun between the verb and the -*ing* form (or base form) is called the subject of the -*ing* form: *Have you ever observed **ants*** (subject) *working* (or *work*)? *As I was standing in the bathroom, I felt **something*** (subject) *crawling* (or *crawl*) *over my foot.*

2. An -*ing* form after sense perception verbs emphasizes the duration of an event, whereas a base form after such verbs suggests the action was completed: *Did you see that pretty girl **sitting** under the umbrella (while we were walking on the beach)? Did you see her **sit** down (and then suddenly get up)? I saw someone **trying** to get into my neighbors' house (while I was looking out my window); I saw someone **try** to get into my neighbors' house (and then suddenly run away).*
    Important Note: An infinitive never occurs in this pattern. Compare:

Correct	Wrong
I saw him steal (stealing) the money.	*I saw him to steal the money.*

3. The verbs *make* (meaning *compel* or *force*) and *let* (meaning *allow* or *permit*) are always followed by a (pro)noun plus a base form. The (pro)noun in such a pattern may be referred to as the "doer" (performer or actor), the agent that performs the action: *The police **made the prisoner confess** her crime; You should **make your child eat** everything on his plate; They don't **let their daughter date** boys; Please don't **let the rain come** in; **Let me go.*** Never use an infinitive after *make* and *let.* Compare:

Correct	Wrong
Please let me go to the party.	*Please let me to go to the party.*
Don't make me tell a lie	*Don't make me to tell a lie.*

4. The verb *help* may be followed by a base form or an infinitive. Like *make* and *let*, *help* is always followed by a "doer": *Living with an English-speaking roommate **will help you improve** (or to improve) your conversation; I'll be glad to **help you do** (or to do) your homework.* In some cases, the doer is understood: *Would you like me to help* [*you*] *wash the car?*

6.12

GRAMMAR EXERCISE   Name _____ Date _____

Focus: -Ing Forms as Objects of Sense Perception Verbs

Fill in the blanks with -ing forms.

EXAMPLES: a. (beg) I felt terrible when I saw that poor old woman <u>begging</u> for money on the street.
  b. (work) When I was at the store, I saw my neighbor's son <u>working</u> there.

1. (have) I heard my neighbors _____ an argument last night.

2. (have) While walking in the park, I saw some boys _____ an exciting game.

3. (cook) I'm getting hungry because I smell something good _____ in the oven. (put) I saw you _____ it in.

4. (play) I heard the radio _____ in your room late last night.

5. (burn) Don't you smell something _____ in the kitchen?

6. (come) Do you see smoke _____ from that house?

7. (walk) On that lonely street late at night, I got frightened when I heard someone _____ behind me.

8. (sing) Don't you hear the birds _____ in the peach tree?

9. (live) Have you ever seen a lion _____ in its natural habitat?

10. (hit) I got angry when I saw Johnny _____ his sister.

11. (play) I like to watch children _____, don't you?

12. (cheat) The teacher saw a few students _____ during the examination. (do) He watched them _____ it out of the corner of his eye (without directly looking). All the students say he has eyes in the back of his head. (teach) I have watched him _____, and I believe they're right.

Now complete the sentences.

13. Did you see the thief _____?

14. Don't you hear the dog/cat/bird/baby _____?

15. Did you happen to notice the mailman _____?

16. Do you hear the rain/phone/wind _____?

17. Do you feel the earth _____?

18. Do you smell the turkey/cake _____?

19. Have you ever watched monkeys/lions/seals _____?

20. Have you ever heard someone _____?

6.13

GRAMMAR EXERCISE   Name _____ Date _____

Focus: *Make, Let,* and *Help*

Supply base forms after *make* and *let* and a base form or an infinitive after *help*.

EXAMPLES: a. (make) When I was a child, my mother used to make me <u>make</u> my bed.
            b. (get) The government mustn't let pollution <u>get</u> worse.
            c. (do) Please let me help you <u>do (to do)</u> your homework.

1. (make) Why are you always letting yourself _____ mistakes?

2. (carry) Would you please help me _____ this package?

3. (learn) A good teacher always enjoys helping his or her students _____.

4. (censor) We mustn't let the government _____ the newspapers.

5. (help) We must help the poor _____ themselves.

6. (set) When I was little, I used to help my mother _____ the table.

7. (do) Please don't make me _____ something that I shouldn't do.

8. (borrow) Dad, please let me _____ your car tonight.

Now supply base forms or infinitives of your own choice.

9. My boss makes me _____ all of the dirty work.

10. When I was a little boy/girl, I used to help my father _____ the cows. He used to let me _____ him _____ the chickens, too.

11. Please don't try to make me _____ you this secret.

12. I refuse to let myself _____ that kind of mistake again.

13. Why did you let yourself _____ such a foolish thing?

14. Does Timmy's father sometimes help him _____ his homework?

15. Would you please help me _____ where Paris is on this map?

16. Doctor, please don't make me _____ the hospital.

17. Many governments will not let the people _____ free.

18. We must help the United Nations _____ peace in the world.

19. We mustn't let the love for power and money _____ the ruling force in the world.

Now complete the sentences.

20. Mom, please let me _____.

21. I hope my boss doesn't make me _____.

22. Could you please help me _____?

23. Our teacher doesn't like to let us _____.

24. Why don't you help your mother _____?

25. Why don't your parents let you _____?

6.14

INFINITIVES FOLLOWING INFORMATION WORDS

1. Two-part direct objects consisting of an information word or words and an infinitive (phrase) follow certain verbs: *Do you know* **how to drive?** *I haven't decided* **where to go** *on my vacation.*

2. This pattern is also used with some verbs that require an indirect object: *The cop told* **me** *how to get to the bus stop; Can you advise* **me** *what subjects to take next semester?*

6.15

GRAMMAR EXERCISE   Name _____ Date _____

Focus: Infinitives Following Information Words

Supply appropriate infinitives in the blanks.

EXAMPLES: a. Can you advise me how <u>to deal</u> with this problem?
             b. Could you please show me how <u>to get</u> there?

1. I don't know which course _____ next semester.

2. Their son doesn't know what kind of career _____ for himself.

3. This map doesn't explain clearly how _____ to the mountains.

4. Have you decided what _____ about the problem with your boss?

5. I used to teach my dog how _____ tricks.

6. I don't know whom _____ to my next party.

7. I don't know what _____ this coming weekend.

8. Please don't tell me what _____.

9. Do you know how _____ rid of cockroaches?

10. I'm afraid I don't know how _____ with these problems.

11. I've forgotten how _____ her name. Do you know how?

12. I never learned how _____ a bicycle.

Now complete the sentences with your own words.

13. A friend of mine taught me how _____.

14. Please tell me how _____.

15. I can't decide where _____.

16. Could you teach me how _____?

17. Would you please show me how_____?

18. I don't remember how _____.

19. I have finally learned how _____.

20. The directions in the recipe don't say how _____.

6.16

Name _____ Date _____

Focus: *-Ing* Participles as Modifiers

Make *-ing* forms out of the base forms in the following list and supply them in the appropriate blanks.

ache	challenge	drive	grow	operate	win
advertise	depress	enlighten	interest	terrify	work
boil	develop	excite	iron	tire	
bore	dine	exhaust	learn	vote	

EXAMPLES: a. A very good friend of mine works for an <u>advertising</u> agency.
   b. Our family is getting larger, and we need a new <u>dining</u> table.

1. Have you got any _____ stories to tell us about your trip?

2. The movie was so _____ that we left in the middle of it.

3. Unfortunately, our son has never been on a _____ team.

4. I need to iron some clothes, but my _____ board is broken.

5. I've got to go to the dentist because I have an _____ tooth.

6. You shouldn't cook that kind of vegetable in _____ water.

7. It was _____ when our plane landed at Kennedy Airport.

8. Our trip across the Soviet Union by railroad (it took seven days) was _____, but it was long and _____.

9. Being in the store as the crime was taking place was a _____ experience for everyone.

10. The prophet gave an _____ lecture on the meaning of life.

11. Our son is a _____ boy and needs a lot of exercise.

12. The _____ nations of the world are demanding a bigger share of the natural resources.

13. Don't put the vegetables in the water before it reaches the _____ point.

14. Before you get your driver's license, you have to take a _____ test.

15. Has the patient entered the _____ room yet?

16. The unions in the United States represent the _____ people.

17. Billy, I'm sorry, but you won't be able to vote in an election until you've reached the _____ age.

18. All activities in a classroom should be a _____ experience for the students.

19. Trying to get to the top of the mountain was very _____.

20. Reading the sayings of Confucius can be very _____.

21. Getting a divorce was a _____ experience for both of them.

22. Taking the long hike yesterday was fun but _____.

23. I try to keep my _____ life separate from my private life.

GRAMMAR EXERCISE   Name _____ Date _____

Focus: Reviewing Prepositions with Gerunds

In the blanks, supply appropriate prepositions from the following list: about, for, from, in, of, on, to. First do this exercise as a quiz.

EXAMPLES: a. Isn't it a beautiful day <u>for</u> going sailing?
              b. Many people are afraid <u>of</u> falling in love.

1. Are you looking forward _____ retiring from your company?

2. The ancient Egyptians believed _____ praying to the sun.

3. Are you interested _____ taking another English course?

4. My lawyer is responsible _____ taking care of all my legal problems.

5. The papers say that the government is guilty _____ starting the war.

6. Why are you worried _____ losing your job?

7. The General insists _____ getting correct information from his subordinates. If he doesn't, he is capable _____ getting angry.

8. The people suspect the police _____ torturing the prisoner.

9. I'm planning _____ taking a vacation in Russia next spring.

10. The cold and wet weather this spring has prevented us _____ planting anything in our garden.

11. Unfortunately, the police didn't succeed _____ catching the bank robbers.

12. It's not always easy to get used _____ living in a foreign country.

13. Living in the Middle East was difficult for him because he wasn't accustomed _____ living in such a hot climate.

14. He and his wife are thinking _____ moving into a smaller house.

15. He's a very honest man and is incapable _____ cheating.

16. Does your wife ever get tired _____ taking care of the children?

17. I need a screwdriver _____ taking this radio apart.

18. I don't have the directions _____ putting this radio together.

19. I'm not looking forward _____ going to the dentist's tomorrow.

20. Many people are afraid _____ being in high places.

21. I'd like to thank you _____ being so kind to my family during this crisis.

22. Has your little girl finally gotten used _____ being in school?

23. I need at least one full day a week _____ running errands.

24. What countries do you plan _____ visiting on your next trip?

25. Will the new war prevent you _____ traveling in that part of the world?

26. I don't have to worry _____ cleaning the house because I've got a maid.

ADJECTIVE CLAUSES

7

7.1

ESSENTIAL AND NONESSENTIAL ADJECTIVE CLAUSES

1. An ADJECTIVE CLAUSE is a subordinate clause that modifies a noun or pronoun preceding it in the main clause of a sentence: *He **who laughs last** laughs best; The team **that wins the most games** wins the World Series.*

2. The noun or pronoun that is modified by an adjective clause is called the ANTECEDENT of that clause: *I have **a cat** that is very independent; I have **a dog** that doesn't get along with my cat.*
   Note: Adjective clauses are sometimes called RELATIVE CLAUSES. The British often refer to them as DEFINING CLAUSES.

3. An adjective clause frequently "splits" the main clause of a sentence: *People **who lie to others** often lie to themselves; People **who eat too much** will get heavy.*

4. Adjective clauses are most often introduced by the relative pronouns *who* (*whom* or *whose*), *which,* or *that. Who* or *that* refers to a person, and *which* or *that* refers to an animal or thing: *A person **who** (that) lies is called a liar; Animals **which** (that) are in cages are not happy; A machine **which** (that) cuts grass is called a lawnmower.*

5. When we are referring to animal pets, or when we are personifying an animal, we may use *who: I have **a cat who** is always cleaning itself; **Male lions who** are not lazy are rare; My neighbor has **a dog who** is always barking.*

6. A relative pronoun is often used as the subject of an adjective clause. It replaces the subject that originally appears in the sentence from which the clause is derived. Compare:

   *I have a cat. **My cat** is very independent = I have a cat **who** is very independent.*
   *I have a machine. **This machine** shreds paper = I have a machine **which** shreds paper.*
   *I know a woman. **She** has an advertising agency = I know a woman **who** has an advertising agency.*

7. There are two kinds of adjective clauses: ESSENTIAL and NONESSENTIAL CLAUSES. An essential adjective clause cannot be omitted from a sentence because the true meaning of the sentence would be lost; for example, if the adjective clause is omitted from the sentence *Children **who are sick** shouldn't go to school,* the remaining main clause *Children . . . shouldn't go to school* is false. Compare:

Essential Adjective Clause	False Statement
*Women **who are over sixty** cannot give birth to a child.*	*Women . . . cannot give birth to a child.*
*People **who are blind** cannot live by themselves.*	*People . . . cannot live by themselves.*
*Chickens **that have clipped wings** cannot fly.*	*Chickens . . . cannot fly.*

   Punctuation Note: Essential adjective clauses are <u>never</u> set off with commas.

8. A nonessential adjective clause may be omitted from a sentence because the truth of the statement would not be lost; for example, if the adjective clause is omitted from the sentence *Paris,* **which is the capital of France,** *is a beautiful city;* the remaining main clause *Paris is a beautiful city* remains a true statement. Compare:

Nonessential Adjective Clause	True Statement
New York, which is the largest city in the United States, is a fascinating place.	*New York . . . is a fascinating place.*
This machine, which cost a lot, makes paper out of wood.	*This machine . . . makes paper out of wood.*
H₂O, which is an easy formula to remember, is the formula for water.	*H₂O . . . is the formula for water.*

Punctuation Note: Nonessential adjective clauses are <u>always</u> set off with commas.

9. Nonessential adjective clauses may also be said to provide extra information that can be left in or out of a sentence: *John, who is 37 years old, is a medical doctor; Mary and John, who were married in 1967, have three children.*

10. An essential adjective clause is traditionally called a RESTRICTIVE CLAUSE because it restricts, singles out, or defines the antecedent in the main clause of a sentence. It refers to <u>some</u> of a class. A nonessential clause is traditionally called NONRESTRICTIVE because it does not restrict, single out, or define the antecedent. It refers to <u>all</u> of a class. Compare:

Essential (Restrictive), Some	Nonessential (Nonrestrictive), All
The typewriters that are not working well must be repaired.	*The typewriters, which are not working well, must be repaired.*
The windows that are dirty should be washed.	*The windows, which are dirty, should be washed.*

11. The relative pronoun *that* is the usual marker for essential clauses following an antecedent that refers to a <u>thing</u> and is never used to introduce nonessential clauses, which are introduced by *which* (see examples above).

12. While *who* or *that* may be used in an essential clause following an antecedent that refers to a <u>person</u>, it is considered by some better usage to use *who: People* **who** (sometimes *that*) *work hard deserve good pay.*

13. Although *that* or *which* may be used in an essential clause that refers to an <u>animal</u> or <u>thing</u>, *that* occurs more frequently: *I have a tractor* **that** (sometimes *which*) *needs new tires.*
    Reminder: (a) *Which* occurs in nonessential clauses where the antecedent refers to an animal or thing. (b) When an animal is personified, we may use *who: Pluto,* **who** *is sick, is a very old dog.*

14. *Whose,* the possessive form of *who,* sometimes occurs as an introducer of essential and nonessential clauses: *I have a neighbor* **whose cat is always climbing trees;** *Mary Smith,* **whose husband has recently died,** *wears only black.*
    Note: Adjective clauses following proper names are always nonessential: *Bob and Anna, who have no children, are going to adopt one; Christopher Columbus, who was an Italian, declared the New World a part of the Spanish Empire.*

15. Essential adjective clauses are often used to define a part of a class: *A cannibal* (a part) *is a person* (a class) *who eats the flesh of human beings.*

7.2

SENTENCE COMPLETION   Name _____ Date _____

Focus: *Who* and *That* as Subjects of Essential Adjective Clauses

Complete the following sentences with appropriate adjective clauses.

EXAMPLES: a. I know a man who makes a living by writing poetry.
              b. I have a neighbor that plays his radio all night long.

1. There is a student in my class who_____.

2. I have a teacher/doctor/lawyer/girlfriend/boyfriend who _____
_____.

3. I know a person in the government who _____.

4. They have a baby/cat/dog that _____.

5. When I was in elementary school, I used to have a teacher who _____
_____.

6. When I was little, our neighbors next door had a boy/girl who _____
_____.

7. I used to know a policeman/mailman/banker/an architect who _____
_____.

8. I know somebody/I don't know anybody who _____.

9. I have a brother/sister/cousin/aunt/uncle/nephew/niece who _____
_____.

10. There is a very old man/woman in the apartment below mine who _____
_____.

11. I don't like people who _____.

12. I sometimes see a student in the school cafeteria who _____
_____.

7.3

SENTENCE COMPLETION

Focus: *Which* and *That* as Subjects of Essential Adjective Clauses

Complete the following sentences with appropriate adjective clauses.

EXAMPLES: a. I have a TV which isn't working.
              b. They live in an area of the country that has terrible weather.

1. My dog has a bark that _____.

2. I want to find an apartment which _____

7.3 (Continued)

3. We don't let our children see movies that _____.

4. I have a good refrigerator, but I have a stove that _____.

5. I want to find a book/dictionary/atlas/encyclopedia that _____

_____.

6. The government needs to develop a program which _____.

7. I want to find a nice present that _____.

7.4

SENTENCE COMPLETION   Name _____ Date _____

Focus: *Who* or *That*

Complete the following sentences with adjective clauses introduced by *who* or *that*.

EXAMPLES: a. I know a man <u>who speaks five languages</u>.
b. I have a watch <u>that doesn't need winding</u>.

1. I have a TV set _____.

2. There is a clerk at that store _____.

3. Our children go to a school _____.

4. They have a teacher _____.

5. I know a waiter _____.

6. He works at a restaurant _____.

7. I know an actor/actress _____.

8. S/he played in a movie _____.

9. I know a doctor _____.

10. S/he works at a hospital _____.

11. I don't understand people _____.

12. I want to live in a place _____.

13. I have a landlord _____.

14. I like exercises _____.

7.5

GRAMMAR EXERCISE

Name _____ Date _____

Focus: *Whose* Introducing Essential Adjective Clauses

Supply appropriate verb or verb phrases in the blanks.

appear	be	come	have	sell	take
bark	burn	die	own	swim	work

EXAMPLES: a. I have a neighbor whose wife <u>works</u> for the government.
              b. I have a neighbor whose dog <u>is always barking</u>.

1. She is the woman whose child _____ sick in the hospital.

2. That's the man whose wife almost _____ in the fire last night.

3. I want you to meet the woman whose husband _____ the next President.

4. Do you know anyone whose husband or wife _____ for the government?

5. Mary Smith is the girl whose brother _____ the star of our football team.

6. Bob Jones is the fellow whose sister _____ a movie star.

7. I have a friend whose father _____ special connections in the government.

8. I know a man at work whose wife _____ from South America.

9. He has a doctor whose office _____ on Park Avenue.

10. I have a good friend whose hobby _____ collecting stamps.

11. Do you know the people whose house _____ down last night?

12. That is the girl whose photograph _____ in the newspaper yesterday.

13. I know a woman whose husband _____ a policeman.

14. The neighbor whose dog _____ complained to me about my cat.

15. Isn't that the woman whose husband _____ your boss?

16. There's the professor whose course I _____ last semester.

17. I have a friend whose mother _____ an opera singer.

18. Writers whose books _____ popular appeal make a lot of money.

19. I know a girl whose family _____ a house up in the mountains.

20. I know a guy whose father _____ a large factory.

21. I met the man whose wife _____ across the English Channel last year.

22. I asked the neighbor whose husband _____ a policeman what to do about the

     neighbor whose dog _____.

23. The teacher whose methods _____ popular with everyone does not exist.

24. I know a writer whose books _____ all over the world.

GRAMMAR EXERCISE   Name _____ Date _____

Focus: Essential Adjective Clauses Used in Definitions

Form -s forms from the base forms in the following list and supply them in the appropriate blanks.

catch	cut	dry	keep	own	tell	write
climb	detect	eat	lay	rob	tune	
cook	dig	fold	make	sharpen	wash	
cure	drive	grind	open	teach	work	

EXAMPLES: a. A vegetarian is a person who <u>eats</u> no meat.
              b. A piano tuner is a person who <u>tunes</u> pianos.

1. A washing machine is a machine that _____ clothes.

2. A dishwasher is a machine that _____ dishes.

3. A poet is a person who _____ poetry.

4. A can opener is a device that _____ cans.

5. A storyteller is a person (very often a writer) who _____ stories.

6. A bricklayer is a person who _____ bricks.

7. A bank robber is a person who _____ banks.

8. A coffee grinder is a device that _____ coffee.

9. An English teacher is a person who _____ English.

10. A shoemaker is a person who _____ shoes.

11. A lie detector is a device that _____ lies.

12. A dog catcher is a person who _____ stray dogs.

13. A home owner is a person who _____ a house.

14. A working person is a person who _____ for a living.

15. A folding chair is a chair that _____ up.

16. A grave digger is a person who _____ graves.

17. A bookkeeper is a person who _____ books.

18. A pencil sharpener is a device that _____ pencils.

19. A cook is a person who _____ for a living.

20. A doctor is a person who _____ sick people.

21. A lawnmower is a machine that _____ grass.

22. A taxi driver is a person who _____ a taxi in order to make a living.

23. A writer is a person who _____ for a living.

24. A mountain climber is a person who _____ mountains.

25. A clothes dryer is a machine that _____ clothes.

7.7

RELATIVE PRONOUNS AS OBJECTS OF VERBS AND PREPOSITIONS

1. As we have already discussed, relative pronouns may be used as subjects of adjective clauses: *The person **who stole** the money out of my purse was a stranger to me; The typewriter **that broke** yesterday wasn't in very good working order.*

2. Relative pronouns may also be used as the object of a verb: *The man **whom** she **met** at the party was to become her husband;* or as the object of a preposition: *The man **with whom** she fell in love soon fell in love with her.*

3. When a relative pronoun is the object of a verb or preposition, a formal or informal style may be used. Without any doubt, the informal style is most frequently observed in speaking. Only in formal writing does the formal style usually occur. Compare:

Formal	Informal
(Object of a Verb)	
*The man **whom she married** had been married before.*	*The man (who) **she married** had been married before.*
*The doctor **whom she visited** gave her the wrong prescription.*	*The doctor (who) **she visited** gave her the wrong prescription.*
(Object of a Preposition)	
*The woman **for whom I work** is from France.*	*The woman (who) **I work for** is from France.*
*The man **to whom I sent the letter** never sent back a reply.*	*The man (who) **I sent the letter to** never sent back a reply.*
*The table **on which he placed the vase** was an antique.*	*The table (which) **he placed the vase on** was an antique.*

4. In informal usage, when a relative pronoun in an adjective clause is the object of a verb or a preposition, the pronoun may be omitted. The clause then becomes what is called an UNMARKED ADJECTIVE CLAUSE: *The game (that) **we were at** was called off because of rain; The company (which) **I work for** is going out of business.*
Special Note: Study the use of postponed prepositions in informal usage.
Note: Since a clause always has a subject, a relative pronoun cannot be omitted from a clause when the pronoun is the subject of the clause: *He **who** laughs last laughs best; I have a car **that** drives like a dream.*

GRAMMAR EXERCISE

Name _____ Date _____

Focus: Relative Pronouns as Objects of Verbs and Prepositions

Supply appropriate verb forms in the blanks. Note the differences in formal and informal usage.

EXAMPLES: a. I want to buy a watch (that) I don't have to <u>wind</u>.
b. The person for whom he <u>works</u> is difficult.

1. The person (who) he _____ for is easy to get along with.

2. The person to whom he _____ was the president.

3. The person (who) he _____ with is always playing the radio too loud.

4. I don't enjoy going to movies (that) I can't _____.

5. I need to buy a car (that) my wife can _____ while I'm driving the family car.

6. The lawyer to whom I had _____ the letter replied within a few days.

7. The lawyer (who) I'd _____ the letter to never sent a reply.

8. The apartment under which I am _____ is vacant.

9. The apartment (that) I am _____ under is vacant.

10. I've got to find a job (that) I _____.

11. I have a refrigerator (that) I don't have to _____.

12. The man whom I _____ at the party was an engineer.

13. The man (who) I _____ on the ship when I was going to Europe was a doctor from Chicago.

14. The vacation (that) we _____ last year cost us a lot.

15. The decision (that) she _____ was made too hastily.

16. The woman to whom she is _____ on the phone is her boss.

17. The woman (who) she is _____ to on the phone is her boss.

18. The man for whom I am _____ in the next election isn't going to win because he's too liberal.

19. The man (who) I am _____ for in the next election doesn't have a chance.

20. The woman with whom he _____ in love was not the right woman for him.

21. The woman (who) he _____ in love with was the perfect woman for him.

22. The mushrooms (that) I _____ last night made me sick.

23. The doctor whom they had _____ never came.

24. The doctor (who) they had _____ finally arrived three hours later.

7.9

GRAMMAR EXERCISE   Name _____ Date _____

Focus: Unmarked Essential Adjective Clauses

Supply in the blanks appropriate past forms of the base forms in the following list.

borrow	drink	get	lose	plant	speak	write
break	enter	have	marry	receive	steal	
buy	find	invite	meet	serve	take	

EXAMPLES: a. The person I <u>went</u> to the party with was my roommate's sister.
   b. The tree I <u>planted</u> in the garden last year hasn't been doing very well.

1. The university our son _____ last September is one of the best in the country.

2. The medicine the patient _____ didn't do any good.

3. She married a man she _____ while she was traveling in France.

4. The thief took all of the money I _____ in my wallet.

5. The book I _____ from my neighbor wasn't his.

6. The dish I _____ last night had been a wedding gift from my mother-in-law.

7. The painting the thief _____ out of my apartment didn't belong to me.

8. The bike I finally _____ cost more than $200.

9. The algebra course Bob _____ last semester was too difficult for him, and he didn't get a passing grade.

10. The person I _____ to on the phone couldn't understand me.

11. The man she _____ at that party never called later.

12. The book I _____ for that course cost more than twenty dollars.

13. There was about $300 in the wallet I _____ yesterday.

14. The phone call I _____ last night worried me a lot.

15. The woman he finally _____ turned out to be the wrong choice.

16. Several people she _____ to the party never showed up.

17. The invitation I _____ didn't give the time that the party would begin.

18. The lawyer I _____ to about the problem didn't know what he was talking about.

19. The coffee I _____ for breakfast this morning tasted bitter.

20. The champagne they _____ at the wedding was flat.

21. I'm afraid that the letter I _____ to the company was full of mistakes.

22. The clothes I _____ with me on my last trip to Europe were too warm for that time of year.

7.10

Focus: Unmarked Essential Adjective Clauses

Supply appropriate base forms or -s forms in the blanks.

be	go	listen	read	smoke	use	want
drive	have	live	sit	take	vote	work

EXAMPLES: a. The man she <u>works</u> for isn't easy to get along with.
                   b. The typewriter I <u>have</u> was made in Germany.

1. The company her husband _____ for is the largest manufacturer of toys in the world.

2. The train he _____ to work is almost always on time.

3. Most of the students I _____ are from South America.

4. The medicine the patient _____ every day is for his heart condition.

5. The man John _____ with is from Australia.

6. The person I _____ to work with every day on the bus works in my office.

7. The woman she _____ for is easy to get along with.

8. The desk she _____ at is right next to mine.

9. The dictionary I _____ is out of date.

10. The children my grandmother _____ care of in the afternoons are very difficult.

11. The man she _____ in love with doesn't love her.

12. Usually, the person I _____ for in an election doesn't win.

13. The apartment they _____ in faces the river.

14. The car he _____ to work every day is an old Ford.

15. The shampoo I _____ is very expensive.

16. The hairdresser she _____ to charges a lot.

17. The furniture he _____ in his apartment he inherited from his grandparents.

18. The dentist I _____ to is excellent.

19. The radio station I _____ to in the mornings gives good traffic reports.

20. The cigarettes he _____ have a terrible smell.

21. The books and magazines Johnny _____ are usually about sports.

22. The car I _____ is second hand.

23. The church we _____ to is just around the corner.

24. The man I _____ for is always giving me a hard time.

25. The street they _____ on is one of the most beautiful in the city.

26. The dress she _____ on was a gift from her mother.

7.11

SENTENCE COMPLETION   Name _____ Date _____

Focus: Unmarked Essential Adjective Clauses

Complete the following sentences with appropriate unmarked essential adjective clauses. Pay careful attention to prepositions.

EXAMPLES: a. The program <u>I watched last night</u> was interesting.
              b. The man <u>I met at the party</u> knows my father.

1. The vacation _____.

2. The party _____.

3. The book _____.

4. The movie _____.

5. The train/bus/plane _____.

6. The French course _____.

7. The woman _____.

8. The teacher _____.

9. The bank _____.

10. The phone call _____.

11. The job _____.

12. The airline _____.

13. The company _____.

14. The politician _____.

15. The lawyer _____.

16. The doctor _____.

17. The religion _____.

18. The food _____.

19. The drinks _____.

20. The school/university _____.

21. The dog/cat/bird/monkey _____.

22. The house/apartment _____.

23. The dish/glass _____.

24. The test/quiz/examination _____.

25. The coffee/tea/milk _____.

26. The movie/program _____.

27. The advice _____.

28. The picnic/cookout _____.

29. The fair/fiesta/game _____.

7.12

RELATIVE ADVERBS INTRODUCING ADJECTIVE CLAUSES

1. The relative adverbs *when, where,* and *why* are sometimes used to introduce adjective clauses: *2001 will be the year **when we enter the twenty-first century**; It was in the morning **when the fire started**; The place **where his grandfather is buried** is in a large forest; They live in a small town **where there is no electricity**; Please give me a reason **why you made that mistake.**

2. *Before* and *after* are two other words that sometimes introduce adjective clauses: *She ran away the day **before she was to get married**; We left London the night **after our friends arrived.***

The Present (Past) Perfect Tense in Essential Adjective Clauses

3. When the object of a verb in a main clause is a noun modified by a superlative adjective (*This is the best wine*), it is frequently followed by an adjective clause containing *ever* in a verb phrase in the present perfect tense: *This is the best wine **I have ever drunk.*** This kind of clause is usually introduced by *that: She is one of the finest teachers (that) **I have ever had.***

4. The past perfect tense is also sometimes found in the same pattern: *It **was** the best movie (that) **I had ever seen**; It **was** the fastest car (that) **I had ever ridden in.*** (Note how the rule of sequence of tenses must be followed here.)

Pronunciation of Nonessential Adjective Clauses

5. When a comma occurs in a written sentence, a pause usually occurs when the sentence is spoken: *Because I was tired,* (pause) *I went to bed earlier than usual; When all of the children had finally gone to bed,* (pause) *we put all of their presents under the Christmas tree.*
There is also a drop in intonation and a slight pause before and after a nonessential clause: *Franklin D. Roosevelt,* (pause) *who was the President of the United States from 1933 to 1945,* (pause) *was a great and popular leader; Christmas,* (pause) *which most people like,* (pause) *is not my favorite holiday.*

7.13

SENTENCE COMPLETION   Name _____ Date _____

Focus: *Where* Introducing Essential Adjective Clauses

Complete the following sentences with appropriate adjective clauses.

EXAMPLES: a. I want to find a job where I can make a lot of money and don't have to work very hard.
  b. They want to find an apartment where they have enough room for their five children and themselves.
  c. My grandmother wants to find a nice place where she can retire.

1. We want to find a nice place in the mountains where _____

_____.

2. We're looking for a beach where _____.

3. I'm looking for a safe place in my apartment where _____

_____.

Name _____ Date _____

   4. We're looking for a restaurant where _____.

   5. I'm looking for a garage where _____.

   6. We want to find a nice place in the country where _____

   _____.

   7. Unfortunately, I don't have any room in my apartment where _____

   _____.

   8. I don't enjoy being in a place where _____.

   9. During our vacation in the middle of South America, we were in a place where _____

   _____.

   10. Have you ever been at a party where_____?

   11. Would you happen to know about a good store where _____

   _____?

   12. We're looking for a city/country/place where _____

   _____.

   13. I want to find a job/school/institute where _____

   _____.

   14. Do you know a nice place where _____?

   15. They want to find a good school where _____

   _____.

   16. Have you ever been in a house where _____?

   17. I would like to live in a place where _____.

7.14

SENTENCE COMPLETION

   Focus: The Present Perfect Tense in Essential Adjective Clauses

Complete the following sentences with appropriate adjective clauses that contain verb phrases with the present perfect tense and *ever*.

EXAMPLES: a. This is the most comfortable car that I've ever ridden in.
   b. This is the most difficult project I've ever worked on.

   1. My girlfriend/boyfriend has the most beautiful eyes _____.

   2. I think this is one of the saddest letters _____.

   3. Without a doubt, she is one of the nicest women _____.

   4. S/he is one of the best doctors/dentists/teachers_____.

   5. This is probably the best/worst food/champagne _____.

   6. This is probably the most sensational party _____.

   7. S/he has one of the most beautiful voices_____.

   8. That is one of the funniest stories _____.

   9. This is one of the most interesting/boring books _____.

  10. His pronunciation is one of the best/worst _____.

  11. New York is the largest city _____.

  12. I can't believe it! This is the most beautiful water _____.

7.15

SENTENCE COMPLETION   Name _____ Date _____

Focus: The Past Perfect Tense in Essential Adjective Clauses

Complete the following sentences with appropriate adjective clauses that contain verb phrases with the past perfect tense and *ever*.

EXAMPLES: a. It was one of the best movies <u>that I had ever seen.</u>
              b. It was one of the best programs on nature I'd <u>ever seen.</u>

   1. It was one of the best vacations _____.

   2. The trains in Japan were the fastest _____.

   3. The wine at the party was one of the finest _____.

   4. It was one of the most expensive restaurants _____.

   5. It was the most expensive car_____.

   6. It was the easiest/most difficult course _____.

   7. My grandmother's trip to Europe was the first time_____.

   8. It was the most terrible hurricane _____.

   9. He was the most famous person_____.

  10. It was one of the most beautiful weddings _____.

  11. It was one of the most interesting/boring books _____.

  12. It was the most exciting game _____.

  13. It was the loneliest place _____.

  14. It was the highest mountain _____.

  15. My conversation with the prophet was the most fascinating _____.

GRAMMAR EXERCISE   Name _____ Date _____

Focus: The Past Perfect Tense in Essential Adjective Clauses

Supply appropriate verb phrases in the past perfect tense in the blanks.

be	give	live	score	swim
buy	hear	meet	set	wear
forget	kidnap	prepare	steal	win

EXAMPLES: a. The horse that I <u>had bet</u> on didn't win.
  b. The woman who <u>had directed</u> the movie received a prize.

1. The house where they _____ for almost twenty years burned down.

2. The police found the purse which the thief _____.

3. Fortunately, I didn't need the clothes that I _____ to pack in my suitcase.

4. She wore the same dress at her wedding that her mother _____ at hers.

5. The police finally caught the man who _____ the fire.

6. She wore a beautiful dress at the party that her husband _____ her.

7. The house where he _____ born was destroyed in a hurricane.

8. She was upset because she couldn't find the watch that her mother _____ her.

9. Everyone was congratulating the player who _____ the most points in the game.

10. He was telling everyone about the girl that he _____ on his vacation.

11. When I finally sat down to dinner, I couldn't eat the food that I _____ for myself.

12. I met a man at the party who _____ across the English Channel.

13. I couldn't believe the story that I _____ about you.

14. The police finally caught the three men and one woman who _____ the millionaire's son.

15. I didn't eat the mushrooms that I _____ the day before because they didn't look right.

16. The information she was giving me was something that I _____ about already.

17. The air conditioner that I _____ just a few days before wasn't working right.

18. I was confused because I couldn't understand the explanation that the teacher _____ _____.

19. Everyone was shocked by the news of the President's death because he was a man who _____ the hearts of the people.

GRAMMAR EXERCISE   Name _____ Date _____

> Focus: Nonessential Adjective Clauses

In the blanks supply appropriate verb forms of the verbs in the following list: be, drive, have, live, stand, take, tell, write. Note the use of commas.

EXAMPLES: a. Germany, where I have never been, is a divided nation.
             b. Gary, who is a librarian, is an old friend of mine.
             c. His mother, who lives in California, is coming to New York for a visit.

1. The male lion, who _____ a lazy animal, seldom hunts for food.

2. Robert Jones, who _____ the president of my company, lives in Connecticut.

3. The Empire State Building, which _____ located in New York City, was opened in 1932.

4. Our teacher, who _____ in Los Angeles since 1972, is originally from Texas.

5. Adam and Eve, whom God _____ not to eat the forbidden fruit, were forced to leave the Garden of Eden.

6. My car, which I _____ for seven years, hasn't been working well recently.

7. Mary Smith, whose husband _____ my boss, is an old friend of my mother's.

8. My neighbors, who _____ married for almost thirty years, have recently told me they're going to get a divorce.

9. The pyramids, which _____ for more than five thousand years, were built by slaves.

10. *Romeo and Juliet,* which Shakespeare _____ almost five hundred years ago, is one of the most famous love stories of all time.

11. Maria, who _____ three courses in English since she arrived in the United States two years ago, doesn't have to take any more and is going to enroll at the university in the fall.

12. Her mother and father, who _____ in an apartment ever since they were first married, have finally decided to buy a small house in the country.

13. English, which _____ a relatively young language, is spoken all over the world.

14. Carlos, who _____ in England for fifteen years, speaks English like a native.

7.18

Focus: Commas with Nonessential Clauses

Set off with commas the adjective clauses in the sentences where they are nonessential.

EXAMPLES: a. People who live in glass houses shouldn't throw stones.
            b. Her pronunciation, which is almost perfect, is easy to understand.

1. Cows that are sick cannot produce good milk.
2. Children who are usually more honest than adults cannot lie well.
3. Chickens whose wings have been clipped cannot fly.
4. John F. Kennedy who was the President of the United States for only a short time was assassinated on November 22, 1963.
5. A child who is sick is a sad thing to see.
6. He who laughs last laughs best.
7. Her husband who is from Latin America refuses to help her in the house.
8. Men who have been spoiled by their mothers do not make good husbands.
9. Ducks who don't like water are very rare.
10. Ducks who are very fond of being in water are fun to watch.
11. Bill who doesn't have a sense of humor didn't laugh at my story.
12. Her husband who has recently inherited a great deal of money doesn't have to work.

7.19

SENTENCE COMPLETION

Focus: Expressing Contrast with Nonessential Clauses

Complete the main clauses in the following sentences, using the examples as a guide.

EXAMPLES: a. Bob and Mary, who have already had five children, *want two more.*
            b. His company, which is the largest in the city, *is going broke.*

1. Their daughter/son, who is only eighteen years old, . . .
2. Their grandfather, who has never been to school, . . .
3. Some man, whom she has never met, . . .
4. Our teacher, who never lets us chew gum in class, . . .
5. Their father, who was never sick a day in his life, . . .
6. Our school baseball team, which is not very good, . . .
7. Our cat and dog, who have always been bitter enemies, . . .
8. Frank and Mary, who have always appeared so happy together, . . .
9. Their daughter, who is a very beautiful young woman, . . .
10. Their son, who has always been a good boy, . . .
11. A friend of mine, who has always been very nice to me, . . .
12. My hometown, which has always been a very rich city, . . .
13. All of my house plants, which I'd carefully taken care of, . . .
14. John, who never did any of the homework for the course, . . .
15. English, which is a relatively young language, . . .

      Note: The above sentences could be transformed into sentences containing concessive *even though* clauses: *Even though (although, though) Bob and Mary have five children, they want two more.*

THE PASSIVE VOICE

8

8.1

VOICE

1. A verb phrase may be in the ACTIVE or PASSIVE VOICE: (active) *Columbus **discovered** America in 1492;* (passive) *America **was discovered** in 1492.*

2. An active verb phrase indicates that the subject of the sentence is the <u>doer</u> (actor) of the action; the subject itself generates the action: *I* (subject and doer) ***told** everyone the wonderful news; I* (subject and doer) ***watered** all of my house plants yesterday.*

3. A passive verb phrase indicates that the subject of the sentence is the <u>receiver</u> of the action generated by the verb: ***Everyone** (receiver) **was told** the wonderful news; All of my **house plants** (receiver) **were watered** yesterday.*

4. In the passive voice, we use a form of the verb *be* (as an auxiliary) and a past participle (as a main verb):

   (a) Present tense: *The New York Times **is published** every day of the year.*
   (b) Past tense: *Jesus **was born** in a manger in Bethlehem.*
   (c) Future tense: *A final examination **will be given** at the end of the semester.*
   (d) Present perfect tense: *Many discoveries in medical science **have been made** in the last twenty years.*
   (e) Past perfect tense: *The war **had been predicted** by a prophet many years earlier.*

8.1 (Continued)

5. Only those verbs that can take direct or indirect objects in the active voice may be used in the passive voice. Verbs that may take direct objects are called TRANSITIVE, and verbs that cannot take direct objects are called INTRANSITIVE. Compare how transitive verbs in the passive voice may be transformed into passive verb phrases. Note how the direct objects are transformed into subjects.

Active	Passive
*We laid **the plans*** (direct object) *carefully.*	***The plans*** *were laid carefully.*
*Someone raised **a question*** (direct object).	***A question*** *was raised.*
*He turned off **the light*** (direct object).	***The light*** *was turned off.*

6. Intransitive verbs cannot be used in passive verb phrases because they cannot take a direct or indirect object: *Everyone dies in the end* (we die by ourselves); *I am lying on my bed* (I am the doer of the action); *The sun rises every day* (the sun is the doer of the action, not the receiver).

7. A common mistake for students to make is to use an intransitive verb in a passive verb phrase. Compare:

Wrong	Correct
*Greta Garbo **was appeared** in many movies.*	*She **appeared** in many movies.*
*An earthquake **was occurred.***	*An earthquake **occurred.***
*The patient **was died** suddenly.*	*The patient suddenly **died.***

Note: Any good dictionary will indicate whether or not a verb is transitive or intransitive.

8. Like a direct object, an indirect object of an active verb becomes the subject when the verb phrase is transformed into the passive voice; *I told **her*** (indirect object) *the news* = ***She*** (subject) *was told the news* (by me); *The President gave **the Ambassador*** (indirect object) *the message* = ***The Ambassador*** (subject) *was given the message* (by the President).
In the above examples, the direct objects can also become subjects: ***The news** was told to her;* ***The message** was given to the Ambassador.*

9. When a passive verb phrase is used in a sentence, the PERFORMING AGENT (the doer of the action) is often not mentioned or not known: *The mail is delivered every day* (not mentioned); *The politician was assassinated* (not known).

10. When the performing agent is mentioned, it follows the verb phrase and is introduced by the preposition *by: The wireless was invented **by Marconi;** The electric light bulb was invented **by Thomas Alva Edison;** The guests were entertained **by a comedian.***

11. In negative passive verb phrases, the adverb *not* is placed after the initial verb or auxiliary in a phrase.

$$\text{The job} \begin{Bmatrix} \text{is not} \\ \text{was not} \\ \text{will not be} \\ \text{has not been} \\ \text{had not been} \end{Bmatrix} \text{done easily.}$$

12. Other adverbs also follow the initial verb or auxiliary in a passive verb phrase: *That kind of animal **is seldom** seen in captivity; He **has never** been examined by a doctor; We all hope that a world war **will never** be fought again.*

13. It is generally felt by most writers that the active voice is more direct and effective than the passive; however, although the active voice is more frequently used, the passive voice is preferred when (a) we do not know who performed the action: *The money **was stolen** from her purse; That building **was constructed** 100 years ago;* (b) we wish to draw attention to the receiver of the action: *Their son **was educated** at Harvard; Her husband **was given** a promotion and a raise;* and (c) it is desirable to maintain an impersonal tone as in textbooks, technical or scientific writing, and newspaper reporting: *The war **was won** with a great loss of lives; The development of this procedure **has been brought** about by the work of many scientists; Textbooks **are usually written** by teachers.*

GRAMMAR EXERCISE   Name _____ Date _____

Focus: Past Participles in Passive Verb Phrases

Supply appropriate past participles in the blanks. Reminder: A past participle is always the main verb in a passive verb phrase.

accompany	catch	discover	elect	forecast	kill	pick	raise
allow	crucify	do	execute	introduce	make	predict	report
bear	cut	drop	fix	invent	marry	publish	write

EXAMPLES: a. He was <u>raised</u> on a farm.
               b. Marie Antoinette was <u>executed</u> on the guillotine.

1. *Don Quixote* was _____ by Cervantes.

2. A decision hasn't been _____ by the government yet.

3. Two atomic bombs were _____ on Japan in 1945.

4. The telephone was _____ by Alexander Graham Bell.

5. Jesus was _____ almost two thousand years ago. He was _____ on the Cross.

6. My mother was _____ in her grandmother's wedding dress.

7. Smoking is not _____ in the front of the theater.

8. My radio was _____ in Japan.

9. My father was _____ to my mother at a party.

10. Rain was _____ for today, but it never came.

11. Radium and polonium were _____ by Marie Curie.

12. Frank was _____ to be chairman of the department.

13. This book was _____ in Englewood, New Jersey.

14. The garbage wasn't _____ up (collected) yesterday.

15. Young people are not _____ to see that movie unless they are _____ by adults.

16. Little has been _____ about the problem of pollution.

17. We won't be able to go out of town unless our car is _____.

18. The best perfume in the world is _____ in France.

19. My boss and I were talking on the phone, but we were _____ off (disconnected).

20. The book was _____ and _____ by the author herself.

21. Most books in the United States are _____ in New York.

22. Because of the charity ball, a lot of money was _____.

23. It was _____ by the fortune teller that Ellen would marry a wealthy man.

24. The crime wasn't _____ in the newspapers until the thief had been _____ by the police.

8.3

Focus: Affirmative Verb Phrases in the Passive Voice

In the blanks supply appropriate affirmative verb phrases in the passive voice. Make past participles out of the base forms given in the parentheses. Do not use any negative forms.

EXAMPLES: a. (speak) Approximately 4,000 languages <u>are spoken</u> in the world.
　　　　　　　b. (shock) All of us <u>were shocked</u> by the news.

1. (give) So far, no prize _____ to anyone.

2. (wash) The windows in my apartment _____ once a month.

3. (give) Everyone _____ an examination tomorrow.

4. (shoot) Abraham Lincoln _____ while he was sitting in Ford Theater in Washington, D.C.

5. (hang) John Wilkes Booth, the man who assassinated Lincoln, _____, along with some others, for his crime.

6. (invent) Movable type _____ by Guttenberg in the fifteenth century. (print) The first book that _____ by Guttenberg was The Holy Bible.

7. (fix) My color TV _____ twice since I bought it.

8. (make) Some of the best cars in the world _____ in England.

9. (water) The garden _____ every afternoon.

10. (make) My watch _____ in Switzerland.

11. (promote) She _____ three times since she started working for this company.

12. (fix) Your car _____ by the end of next week.

13. (serve) Usually, red wine _____ with red meat.

14. (feed) My cat _____ twice a day.

15. (fix) When I got to the watchmaker's, my watch _____.

16. (paint) This portrait of myself _____ by a famous artist.

17. (take) If I had spoken to my lawyer about the problem last month, it _____ care of immediately.

18. (kill) Millions of people _____ in World War II.

19. (fix) If I have enough money, my car _____ next week.

20. (cook) If the chicken _____ too long, it will get dry.

21. (change) In hotels, the sheets on the bed _____ every day.

22. (publish) That author's new book _____ next year.

23. (marry) My mother and father _____ on a ship.

24. (wash) The dishes _____ right after we finished dinner.

8.4

GRAMMAR EXERCISE   Name _____ Date _____

Focus: Negative Verb Phrases in the Passive Voice

Fill in the blanks with appropriate negative verb phrases in the passive voice.

EXAMPLES: a. (finish) The project <u>hasn't been finished</u> yet.
                      b. (build) Rome <u>wasn't built</u> in a day. (old saying)

1. (paint) The outside of our house _____ since we moved into it almost eleven years ago.

2. (give) I _____ a promotion in my company yet.

3. (serve) When I got home, dinner _____ yet.

4. (invent) The electric light bulb _____ until the latter part of the nineteenth century.

5. (compose) Some people feel that beautiful music _____ these days.

6. (tell) I was angry that I _____ the news before yesterday.

7. (make) Progress _____ until we have a new government.

8. (install) A good air conditioner _____ in my office yet.

9. (speak) In most Roman Catholic churches, Latin _____ during the Mass any more.

10. (write) The Bible _____ by one person.

11. (forbid) Our daughter _____ to go to the party, but she still didn't go.

12. (install) My new phone _____ until the end of next week.

13. (fix) When I got to the garage, my car _____ yet.

14. (solve) My problems _____ until I speak and write well.

15. (finish) If this job _____ by tomorrow, I will be fired.

16. (grow) Coffee _____ in the United States.

17. (deliver) Our new TV _____ until the end of the month.

18. (fire) I wish that I _____ from my job last week.

19. (see) He left town last year and _____ since then.

20. (deal) If that problem _____ with last week, I would have been in trouble.

21. (announce) The decision _____ by the government until the elections are over.

22. (hand) When I got to class, the material _____ out yet.

23. (declare) War _____ between those two countries yet.

24. (give) I _____ the message until it was too late.

25. (invite) I was angry because I _____ to the party.

8.5

Focus: Adverbs in Passive Verb Phrases

Fill in the blanks with passive verb phrases containing adverbs from the following list.

already	hardly ever	occasionally	rarely	seldom
always	just	probably	recently	usually

EXAMPLES: a. (deliver) Mail isn't usually delivered in the afternoon.
              b. (find) Inexpensive food is seldom found in the stores now.

1. (make) The best clothes _____ by hand.

2. (give) The final examination _____ tomorrow.

3. (defrost) My refrigerator _____ once a month.

4. (pay) Bills _____ at the end of the month.

5. (serve) When I got to the party, dinner _____.

6. (install) Telephones _____ in people's bedrooms.

7. (make) An important discovery in chemistry _____.

8. (take) Tax problems _____ care of by my lawyer.

9. (marry) When Jill married Jack, she _____ once.

10. (give) When I got to the meeting, the main speech _____.

11. (deliver) The mail _____ on Sunday.

12. (feed) Babies _____ about five times a day.

13. (use) Dictionaries _____ during tests in my class.

14. (install) A new phone system _____ in my office.

15. (hold) In hot weather, classes _____ in the playground.

16. (see) Young children _____ at the theater in London.

17. (fix) When I got to the garage, my car _____.

18. (marry) When I got to the wedding late, the bride and groom _____.

19. (wash) My apartment windows _____ once every two months.

20. (deal) That problem _____ with by my lawyer tomorrow.

21. (water) Our garden _____ three times a week.

22. (fire) People in my office _____ on Friday afternoons.

23. (hire) In my factory, new workers _____ in the spring and laid off (fired) in the fall.

24. (steal) Cars _____ when they are locked.

25. (give) A Nobel Prize _____ to an American next year.

26. (introduce) New car models _____ to the market in the fall.

8.6

THE PRESENT AND PAST CONTINUOUS TENSES

1. In passive verb phrases containing the present and past continuous tenses, we use a form of the verb *be* as the first auxiliary, the *-ing* form of the verb *be* as the second auxiliary, and a past participle as the main verb of the phrase.

   (a) Present continuous tense: *Lucy **is being sent** to bed because she's been naughty; A new apartment house **is being built** on the corner; The patient **is being given** oxygen now.*

   (b) Past continuous tense: *When we got to the reception, the guests **were being introduced** to the President; The children **were being put** to bed when I got home last night; When I first arrived in New York, the Verrazano Bridge **was being built.***

2. The adverb *not* follows the first auxiliary in a negative verb phrase: *Dinner **isn't** being served until the last guest arrives; They were angry because they were **not** being given a fair deal.*

8.7

PASSIVE VERB PHRASES CONTAINING MODAL AUXILIARIES

1. Passive verb phrases containing modals (and idiomatic substitutes like *have to*) are simply formed by placing *be* (as an auxiliary) and a past participle (as a main verb) after the modal: (can) *A lot of wonderful people **can be found** in the world;* (should) *This medicine **should be taken** three times a day;* (have to) *This letter **has to be sent** right away;* (may) *The patient **may be operated** on today;* (must) *The project **must be completed** before the first of June.*

2. To form the past tense of passive verb phrases containing modals, we place *have been* plus the past participle after the modal: (should) *The children **should have been put** to bed earlier last night;* (might) *The wrong kind of gas **might have been put** in the car;* (must) *That Persian rug **must have been made** with great care.*
   Note: It is customary to call *being* and *been* auxiliaries.

GRAMMAR EXERCISE   Name _____ Date _____

Focus: The Present Continuous Tense

In the blanks supply appropriate verb phrases (affirmative only) in the present continuous tense in the passive voice.

cancel	do	introduce	operate	publish	take
change	give	investigate	plant	repair	tell
develop	hold	make	postpone	serve	use

EXAMPLES: a. Champagne is being served at the wedding next Saturday.
            b. The problem is being taken care of right now.

1. Nothing _____ about the problem, even though it is getting serious.

2. A completely new and revolutionary method _____ in the laboratory now.

3. The project _____ until more money is found.

4. Because dinner _____ earlier than usual, we won't have time to have cocktails.

5. The game _____ because of the bad rain.

6. A story _____ to the children and soon they will go to bed.

7. We can't move the meeting to the other room because it _____ by some other people.

8. Rented typewriters _____ in my office for the time being because our regular typewriters _____.

9. The patient _____ on right now.

10. Would you please be quiet because an examination _____ in the other room.

11. Don't wory about a thing! Your schedule _____ today.

12. Lunch _____ in the main dining room now.

13. A lot of changes _____ by the new government.

14. Nothing _____ about the bad social situation in that part of the country.

15. We can't use our car today because it _____.

16. The company's new models _____ to the public very soon.

17. An important meeting _____ in the other room now.

18. A lot of new products _____ in my company now.

19. Everything possible _____ to locate the stolen goods.

20. That author's book _____ next year.

21. The crime _____ by the police.

22. A lot of new trees _____ on my street.

8.9

GRAMMAR EXERCISE   Name _____ Date _____

       Focus: The Past Continuous Tense

In the blanks supply appropriate verb phrases (affirmative or negative) in the past continuous tense in the passive voice.

| broadcast | do | give | install | marry | put | repair | tow |
| build | fix | hold | make | paint | rebuild | take | |

EXAMPLES: a. When I got back to my car, it <u>was being towed</u> away.
            b. When I first arrived in France on my last vacation, an important election <u>was being held</u>.

  1. When I got to the garage, my car _____.

  2. I was angry at my lawyer because the problem _____ care of properly.

  3. When my grandfather first came to New York, the Empire State Building _____

     _____.

  4. Even though an examination _____ that morning, I wasn't at all nervous, and neither was anyone else.

  5. Even though the patient _____ heavy doses of penicillin, his condition wasn't improving.

  6. I was angry at my boss because I _____ a fair deal.

  7. Many people were angry at the government because nothing _____ about the poor financial situation of the country.

  8. I wasn't wearing my watch that day because it _____.

  9. The children were a little upset because they _____ to bed earlier than usual.

  10. Just as I got to the church, the bride and groom _____.

  11. When I looked at the apartment that I might rent, it _____.

  12. An examination _____ when I got to class late the other day.

  13. When I turned on the radio, the news _____.

  14. A lot of wonderful movies _____ in Hollywood during the 1930's.

  15. When we first arrived in the city shortly after the earthquake, it _____.

  16. When I got to my office yesterday morning, a new air conditioner _____ in the window.

  17. We couldn't use our classroom yesterday because it _____.

8.10

GRAMMAR EXERCISE   Name _____ Date _____

Focus: Modal Auxiliaries and Related Idioms

Supply appropriate past participles in the blanks.

cook	do	fix	install	operate	pull	take	wash
deal	find	freeze	keep	pay	reveal	teach	water
defrost	finish	give	make	play	serve	tune	write

EXAMPLES: a. Everyone's taxes must be <u>paid</u> before April fifteenth.
               b. This kind of plant doesn't have to be <u>watered</u> very much.

1. This job has got to be _____ right away.

2. Fish should be _____ in a refrigerator.

3. Our piano should be _____ at least twice a year.

4. This problem had better be _____ care of at once.

5. This tape has to be _____ on a special kind of machine.

6. Buddy has got to be _____ a spanking for being so naughty.

7. This secret between you and me mustn't be _____ to anyone.

8. That blouse shouldn't have been _____ in hot water.

9. Fortunately, the patient didn't have to be _____ on.

10. A turkey has to be _____ for a long time.

11. Impossible! This beautiful letter couldn't have been _____ by such a young child.

12. This job has just got to be _____ before the end of the day.

13. Children should be _____ good manners.

14. This problem must be _____ with now.

15. This machine had better be _____ before it hurts someone.

16. Peace in the world must be _____.

17. Your homework should always be _____ in ink.

18. White wine should be _____ with fish.

19. A list of irregular verbs can be _____ at the back of this book.

20. Potatoes should be _____ in a cool and dry place.

21. Our new phone should be _____ in the bedroom.

22. Frozen food shouldn't be _____ again after it has once been defrosted.

23. There are some words that can't be _____ in the dictionary.

24. Before the invention of the printing press, books used to be _____ by hand.

25. Something should be _____ about this situation right now.

26. Unfortunately, my grandfather's teeth have got to be _____ out.

27. My refrigerator doesn't have to be _____.

8.11

Name _____ Date _____

Focus: Transforming Active Verb Phrases into Passive Verb Phrases

Transform the active verb phrases in the following sentences to passive verb phrases. Omit the performing agents. (A few phrases containing intransitive verbs may not be transformed.)

EXAMPLES: a. The surgeon will operate on the patient tomorrow. The patient will be operated on tomorrow.
   b. Indians in New Mexico made this rug by hand. This rug was made by hand.

1. I have to clean my apartment today. _____.

2. I've already washed all of the dishes. _____.

3. I don't have to defrost the refrigerator until next week. _____

_____.

4. He's fixing my car. He's fixed my car. _____.

5. I wish someone had introduced me to the President at the reception. _____

_____.

6. You must develop this film before the end of the year. _____

_____.

7. We often use the passive voice in textbooks. _____.

8. When I got to the party, they were already serving dinner. _____

_____.

9. They don't speak Spanish during the meetings. _____.

10. Warner Brothers introduced sound to the movies in 1927. _____

_____.

11. We never use notes during an examination. _____.

12. People don't speak English in that part of the world. _____

_____.

13. If there had been time, we would have finished the job. _____

_____.

14. I have to take my little boy to the dentist today. _____

_____.

15. We should review all of the past material. _____.

16. We're using rented equipment for the time being. _____

_____.

17. The doctor is delivering the baby now. _____.

18. If I hadn't done the job, my boss might have gotten angry at me. _____

_____ .

19. The government isn't developing good social programs. _____

_____ .

20. The director has recently changed my schedule. _____ .

21. They haven't developed a perfect mouse trap yet. _____ .

22. She's doing the job right now. She's already done the job. _____

_____ .

23. He didn't do the job properly. _____ .

24. The teacher was giving out material when I got to class. _____

_____ .

25. We're discussing the problem at the next meeting. _____

_____ .

26. The waiters are serving lunch now. _____ .

27. They usually deliver the mail twice a day during Christmas. _____

_____ .

28. I always wash this blouse in cold water. _____ .

8.12

YES-NO AND INFORMATION QUESTIONS

1. In a *yes-no* question, the subject of a sentence is put after the initial auxiliary in a passive verb phrase: *Are **you** going to be given a raise with your promotion? Have **you** ever been given penicillin? Had **the job** been completed by the time you left work? Should **the chicken** have been cooked longer? Could **a mistake** have been made in the last transaction? Does **anything** have to be done about the problem today?*

2. In an information question, the subject is also put after the initial auxiliary in a passive verb phrase: *Why has **the project** been postponed? When is **my schedule** being changed? How should **the package** have been delivered? How often does **your cat** have to be fed? Where can **the best food in town** be found? How many times has **your grandfather** been operated on?*

3. As with sentences containing active verb phrases, when an information word(s) is the subject of a sentence, the usual question form is not used: **What** has been done about the problem of pollution? **Who** has recently been given an award? **What** was being discussed when you left the meeting? **Who** is being transferred to another class?

8.13

GRAMMAR EXERCISE Name _____ Date _____

Focus: *Yes-No and Information Questions*

Supply appropriate past participles in the blanks. **Reminder:** A past participle is always the main verb of a passive verb phrase.

EXAMPLES: a. Have you ever been <u>married</u>?
             b. About how many languages are <u>spoken</u> in the world?

1. Where are the best cars in the world _____?

2. What kind of fruit is _____ in California?

3. How long ago was the Bible _____?

4. Where was this book _____?

5. What is often _____ in Spanish/Chinese/French/Greek/Armenian/Hungarian food?

6. Have you ever been _____ a scholarship/a bouquet of flowers?

7. Where in a hospital are patients _____ on?

8. How often is the mail _____?

9. When was America _____?

10. If you were being _____ a physical examination now, do you think you would be a little nervous?

11. Are you going to be _____ to the university next semester?

12. How many times have you been _____ to a political office?

13. How often does a month-old baby have to be _____?

14. Besides President Kennedy, what important men have been _____ since the end of the Second World War?

15. Have you ever been _____ in a church?

16. Where is the best coffee _____?

17. Where are most of the books in the United States _____?

18. Will you be _____ a grade when you finish this course?

19. When was *Romeo and Juliet* _____?

20. Were you _____ in a hospital or at home?

21. Where is English/Spanish/French/Portuguese _____?

22. Has English/Russian ever been _____ on the moon?

23. How often does a guitar/piano have to be _____?

24. Where should fish be _____?

25. What is being _____ about the problem of pollution?

26. How often does a cat have to be _____?

27. What should be _____ with the turkey on Thanksgiving Day?

8.14

Focus: Questions

Transform the following sentences into *yes-no* questions.

EXAMPLES: a. The patient has to be operated on. Does the patient have to be operated on?
            b. This formula should be changed. Should this formula be changed?

1. His car had to be taken to the garage. _____.

2. This procedure must be followed. _____.

3. He's being transferred. He's been transferred. _____

_____.

4. The refrigerator should have been delivered before yesterday. _____

_____.

5. This telegram has to be sent right away. _____.

6. The patient was being operated on when the lights went out. _____

_____.

7. The game had to be called off because of the rain. _____

_____.

8. The mail is being delivered twice a day now. _____.

9. The job could have been done yesterday. _____.

10. Tom has been told about the situation. _____.

On another piece of paper, transform the following sentences into information questions.

EXAMPLES: c. The concert will be held at *Carnegie Hall*. *Where will the concert be held?*
            b. The book has been revised *three times*. *How many times has the book been revised?*

11. This matter will probably be taken care of *tomorrow*.
12. She's been married *twice*.
13. The refrigerator has to be defrosted *twice a month*.
14. The best watches in the world are made *in Switzerland*.
15. The army is being sent to stop the rioting *now*.
16. Important letters are always sent *by special delivery*.
17. A recording of the new opera is being made *next year*.
18. That kind of animal is usually seen *at high altitudes in the Andes*.

19. *A new kind of weapon* is being rushed to the battlefront.
20. The children have to be taken to the doctor *tomorrow*.
21. Your car should have been fixed before *yesterday*.
22. That kind of radio can be found *at practically all stores*.
23. *John's* application has been accepted.
24. The mail is usually delivered *in the mornings*.
25. This letter has to be duplicated *at once* (immediately).
26. He's been defeated *twice* in national elections.
27. This letter has to be sent to *the president of the company*.
28. *Something* should be done about this problem.

8.15

CAUSATIVE FORMS AND GIVING INSTRUCTIONS

1. CAUSATIVE FORMS are used when one person causes another to perform a service—in other words, in giving instructions to someone else. The following two patterns are causative:

    (a) Causer (person who causes the action) + *have* (or *has* or *had*) + performing agent (doer or actor) + base form + object: **I have my gardener water** *the garden every afternoon;* **She had the butcher cut up** *five pounds of stew meat.*
    Note: Modals may precede *have* in this pattern: **I must have** *my teacher explain this procedure to me;* You **should have** *the police investigate this matter right away.*

    (b) When the doer is not mentioned, a past participle replaces the base form, and the object precedes the verb rather than following it: *The General had* (doer not mentioned) **the best troops sent** *to the front* (but *The General had the President send the best troops to the front*); *You should have* (doer not mentioned) **your eyes examined** (but *You should have your doctor examine your eyes*).

2. In the pattern illustrated in (b), *get* may replace *have: I got* (*had*) *my apartment painted before I moved in; Have you* **gotten** (*had*) *the radiator fixed yet; Did you* **get** (*have*) *new tires put on your car?*
    Note: *Get* never replaces *have* in the pattern illustrated in (a).

3. *Get* + object + infinitive is another causative form, which is used to express persuasion: *How did you* **get** (*persuade*) **the children to go** *to bed so early? How do you* **get** (*persuade*) **your dog to obey** *you?*

4. Since causative forms are used when it is necessary to take a particular course of action, *have to,* the idiomatic substitute for the modal *must,* may occur in the above patterns in all the tenses: (present tense) *I* **have to** *have my car tuned;* (past tense) *I* **had to** *have the gas station attendant put some water in the radiator;* (future tense) *I* **will have to** *have my car fixed;* (present perfect tense) *I* **have had to** *have new tires put on my car;* (past perfect tense) *I was disappointed because I* **had had to** *have my schedule changed.*

8.16

Name _____ Date _____

Focus: Causatives with *Have* + Doer + Base Form

Supply appropriate base forms in the blanks.

bring	check	deliver	fix	keep	look	retype	spray
change	clean	do	install	lengthen	put	shorten	take

EXAMPLES: a. I always have to have the store <u>deliver</u> my groceries.
  b. Her dress was too long, and she had her seamstress <u>shorten</u> it.
  c. My pants were too short, and I had my tailor <u>lengthen</u> them.

1. You must have your doctor _____ your blood pressure.

2. You'd better have the plumber _____ the leak in the bathroom.

3. I always have my accountant _____ my tax return.

4. You've got to have your lawyer _____ this contract before you sign it. You should also have your boss _____ it over.

5. I had the jeweler _____ a new band on my watch.

6. I've got to have my secretary _____ this letter.

7. You should have the dry cleaner _____ this dress before you wear it again. You should also have your seamstress _____ it.

8. I must have the post office _____ my mail while I'm away.

9. I had the phone man _____ the extension phone in the kitchen.

10. Let's have the waiter _____ us another round of cocktails.

11. I'm going to have to have the store _____ this package.

12. You should have your doctor _____ at the rash on your arm.

13. We've got to have the police _____ something about this problem.

14. I'd like to have the phone company _____ my number.

15. I had to have the mechanic _____ a new battery in my car.

16. We'd like to have the maid _____ our room before we get back.

17. Why don't you have your lawyer _____ care of this problem?

18. You'd better have your gardener _____ the lawn with insecticide before it dies. You should have him _____ it right away.

Now complete the sentences.

19. You should have your dentist/doctor _____.

20. I must have my attorney (lawyer) _____.

21. I ought to have my accountant _____.

22. I must have my landlord _____.

8.17

Name _____ Date _____

Focus: Instructions with *Have* + a Past Participle

Supply appropriate past participles in the blanks.

change	deliver	fix	make	pull	tune
clean	develop	install	paint	put	wash
cut	do	lengthen	press	shorten	X-ray

EXAMPLES: a. I have my apartment <u>painted</u> every three years.
b. I have to have the windows <u>washed</u> at least once a month.

1. She has to have her hair _____ at least once a month.

2. Her dress was too long/short, and she had it _____.

3. I've got to have that leak in the kitchen _____ soon.

4. I can't have an air conditioner _____ in that window because it faces a fire escape.

5. Having a tooth _____ out isn't a very pleasant experience.

6. She had her phone number _____ because she was receiving obscene calls from some stranger.

7. Why don't you have your phone _____ near the bed?

8. He has to have his hair _____ at least once a month.
   Note: A woman has her hair *done* or *set,* but a man only has his hair *cut.*

9. It costs quite a lot to have film _____.

10. I have never had to have my watch _____.

11. How often should I have my car _____.

12. I have to have these wrinkled pants _____ before I can wear them again.

13. She spends a lot of money on having clothes _____.

14. I'm very lucky. I've never had to have my TV _____.

15. Darn it! I wish I had had my car _____ before this weekend so that I could have gone out of town.

16. Because he doesn't know how to do it, he always has his income tax return _____ for him.

17. Only people with a lot of money can afford to have everything _____ for them.

18. The doctor says that I have to have my lungs _____.

19. I usually have all of my groceries _____ because I live on the sixth floor and there is no elevator.

20. I'm afraid I'm going to have to have a tooth _____ out.

21. She never has her hair _____. She does it herself.

22. I've recently had new curtains _____ for the bedroom.

23. Fortunately, I don't have to have anything _____ in my new apartment.

8.18

Name _____ Date _____

Focus: Instructions with *Get* + a Past Participle

Supply appropriate past participles in the blanks.

EXAMPLES: a. I've just got to get my teeth checked as soon as possible.
           b. Where do you get your shirts laundered?

1. Where's a good place to get a typewriter _____?

2. How much does it cost to get a piano _____?

3. I have to get a longer cord _____ on my phone.

4. The electricity in our house is inadequate so we have to get new wiring _____ in.

5. You'd better get your hair _____, it's beginning to look sloppy (not neat).

6. Have you gotten the schedule for the meetings _____ yet?

7. How much does it cost to get a tooth _____ out?

8. I want to get new curtains _____ for the bedroom.

9. Getting my terrible work schedule _____ took a lot of talking.

10. I had to wait for a couple of months to get my phone _____ because the phone company was so busy.

11. Getting that job _____ cost me a small fortune.

12. I made my landlord get the lock on my front door _____.

13. You'd better get that leak _____ before you have a flood in your kitchen.

14. I usually get my film _____ at Woolworth's.

15. It costs a lot to get clothes _____.

16. Have you ever had to get your watch _____?

17. It's very hard, and expensive, to get things _____ anywhere because of the high cost of labor.

18. How much did you have to pay to get those shelves _____ up on the wall?

19. I'd like to get my apartment _____ a different color.

20. You'd better get that faulty wiring _____ before you get a shock.

21. They have had to get a new roof _____ on their house.

22. How often do you get your piano _____?

23. How much do you have to pay to get your windows _____?

GRAMMAR EXERCISE   Name _____ Date _____

Focus: Persuasion with *Get* + an Infinitive

Supply an appropriate infinitive in the blanks.

clean	get	grow	lend	play	talk
do	give	install	marry	stop	watch
eat	go	keep	move	take	water

EXAMPLES: a. How did that teacher get such a lazy student to do her homework?

b. What's a good way to get a stubborn child to eat all of his dinner?

1. What did you do to get the phone company _____ your new phone so quickly?

2. How do you get your children _____ up their bedrooms every day? I can't get mine _____ anything.

3. How did your doctor get you _____ smoking?

4. What's a good way to get a stubborn mule _____?

5. How did you get the policeman not _____ you a ticket?

6. How do you get yourself _____ up so early in the morning?

7. How do you get your dog _____ off the bed?

8. How did you get your Dad _____ you his car?

9. How do you get your dog _____ barking when he hears people out on the street?

10. How did you get your neighbors _____ up their yard?

11. How are you going to get your boss _____ you a raise?

12. How do you get the flowers in your garden _____ so beautifully?

13. Who do you get _____ your house plants while you're away on vacations?

14. How do you get the children not _____ too much TV?

15. How do you get your children _____ to bed early on school nights?

16. How did you get your cat _____ scratching her paws on the furniture?

17. How did she finally get that stubborn man _____ her?

18. How did you get your dog _____ such wonderful tricks?

19. How did you get your parrot _____ so well that he sounds like a person?

20. How did you get your parents _____ you such a beautiful car for your birthday?

21. How did you get your lawyer _____ care of the problem so quickly?

1. The auxiliary (verb phrase) *be supposed to* combined with a base form may be used in two different ways:

   (a) *Be supposed to* meaning *it is believed that: French food **is supposed to be** the best in the world* (It is believed that French food is the best in the world); *Japanese trains **are supposed to be** the fastest in the world* (It is believed that Japanese trains are the fastest in the world).
   Note: *Be supposed to* is passive in construction: *French perfume is supposed* (by people) *to be the best in the world; California is supposed* (by people) *to be very nice.*
   Like a statement with *it is believed that,* a statement expressing a belief with *be supposed to* is often open to dispute. For example, hardly anyone would disagree with the statement *Good health is our most precious possession;* however, some people might disagree with the statement *French food is the best in the world.* An individual may respond to such a remark about French food with *Perhaps, but I believe Chinese food is better.*

   (b) *Be supposed to* meaning *be required to* or *be expected to: I am supposed to* (I am required to) *renew my passport; The train is supposed to* (it is expected to) *arrive at 3:10.*
   Note: Similar in meaning to *be expected to* is *be scheduled to: The train is supposed to* (scheduled to) *arrive at 3:10; The reception is supposed to* (scheduled to) *begin at five o'clock.*

2. In the passive voice the pattern is *be supposed to + be +* a past participle: *The meeting **is supposed to be finished** by now; This room **is supposed to be painted** green.*

3. When *be supposed to* is used to express a requirement, its meaning is similar to that expressed by the modal auxiliary *should: I'm not supposed to* (shouldn't) *smoke, but I do; I'm supposed to* (should) *be at school today, but I want to go to the beach instead.*

4. The past form of *be supposed to* (meaning requirement) is also similar in meaning to the past form of *should: I was supposed to be* (should have been) *at the meeting, but I decided to stay home; I was supposed to do* (should have done) *my homework, but I didn't.*

8.21

Name _____ Date _____

Focus: *Be Supposed to*

Supply an appropriate base form, or *be* + a past participle, in the blanks.

EXAMPLES: a.   This brand of coffee is supposed to <u>taste</u> better than most other brands.
      b.   The package was supposed to <u>be sent</u> by air freight, but it wasn't.

1. I'm supposed to _____ dinner with my family on Christmas Day, but I'd rather spend the day with you.

2. Women are supposed to _____ more emotional than men. What do you think?

3. I'm not supposed to _____ any salt in my food because I have high blood pressure.

4. The best cars in the world are supposed to _____ in England.

5. Red wine is supposed to _____ with red meat.

6. I'm supposed to _____ all of my bills on the first of the month, but I sometimes can't.

7. We're not supposed to _____ about our friends behind their backs.

8. The train was supposed to _____ at 3:15, and it was exactly on time.

9. What was supposed to _____ about the problem?

10. Little girls are supposed to _____ neater than little boys.

11. Smoking is supposed to _____ cancer.

12. My grandmother says that carrots are supposed to _____ good for the eyes.

13. The best coffee is supposed to _____ in Brazil.

14. The best photographic film is supposed to _____ in the United States.

15. The law says that all children are supposed to _____ to school, but a lot of young people don't.

16. We're not supposed to _____ our car in this place, so let's go somewhere else.

17. I'm not supposed to _____ my car fast, but I enjoy doing it.

18. Life in a warm climate is supposed to _____ better for our health than living in a cold climate.

19. This kind of wax isn't supposed to _____ on wood floors.

20. When I do my homework, I'm not supposed to _____ anyone to help me.

21. What are you supposed to _____ today? What were you supposed to _____ yesterday?

THE FUTURE PERFECT TENSE AND REVIEW

9

9.1

EVENTS PRECEDING EVENTS IN THE FUTURE

1. The FUTURE PERFECT TENSE is used for an event that precedes another in the future: *By the year 2000, many things **will have changed**; When you get home, I **will have already gone** to bed*. The form is also used to express the duration of an event prior to another in the future: *When he finally graduates from the university, he **will have been** in school for eighteen years. When she retires from the company, she **will have been** the president for twenty-seven years.*

2. *Will (shall)* + *have* + a past participle (as a main verb) are used to form a verb phrase in the future perfect tense. In the passive voice, the auxiliary *been* follows *have*.

	Singular	Plural
First person	I	we
Second person	you } will have (been) told	you } will have (been) told
Third person	he	they
	she	
	it	

Reminder: *Shall* in first person occurs most frequently in British English.

3. The adverb *not* follows *will* in a negative verb phrase: *When my roommate leaves for class tomorrow morning, I **will not** have gotten up yet; I'm afraid that when we get to the garage, our car **won't** have been fixed yet.*

4. The adverb *already* sometimes occurs in the future perfect tense and is usually found following *will* in a verb phrase; however, it can also be placed after *have*: *When we get to the church, the bride and groom will **already** have been married; By the time she enters the class, the semester will have **already** begun.*

5. The future perfect tense is usually accompanied by time expressions beginning with *when, on, at,* and *by*: ***When they celebrate their next anniversary,** they'll have been married for twelve years; **At this time tomorrow,** we will have already left for our trip to Europe; **On June 15,** we will have been in the United States for thirteen years; **By the end** of the party, everything will have been drunk and eaten.*

6. For the FUTURE PERFECT CONTINUOUS TENSE, *will have been* + a present participle is used to form a verb phrase. This tense is used to emphasize the duration of an event prior to another in future time: *By the time the rain finally stops, it **will have been raining** for about two weeks; On March 17, we **will have been living** in our house for exactly five years; When we finally get to Paris, we **will have been traveling** for more than a year.*
   Note: The future perfect tense (particularly its continuous form) does not occur as frequently as the other verb tenses; however, it is sometimes used, and it is advisable that a student new to the language become acquainted with the form.

GRAMMAR EXERCISE

Name _____ Date _____

Focus: The Future Perfect Tense

Fill in the blanks with appropriate verb phrase in the future perfect tense.

EXAMPLES: a. We <u>will have learned</u> many new things by the end of the course.
b. When Dad gets home, he <u>won't have eaten</u> dinner yet.

1. When Mom gets home at eleven o'clock, the children _____ to bed.

2. If you get to the party after eleven, I'm sure that all of the food _____.

3. By this time next year, my project _____.

4. When Billy gets home from the game, he'll probably be hungry because he _____ _____ his lunch yet.

5. Unfortunately, I'm afraid the play _____ by the time we get to the theater.

6. At the end of this year, I _____ away from home for exactly twelve years.

7. When my grandparents celebrate their next anniversary, they _____ married for fifty-seven years.

8. When this semester is over, I _____ many friends.

9. When we get to the party, dinner _____ yet.

10. By the time the president of the company retires, he _____ a great deal of money, and enemies.

11. When you see me again two years from now, I _____ my studies at the university.

12. By the time they leave Europe, they _____ in every country except the Soviet Union, Hungary, and Albania.

13. I'm sure that my lawyer _____ care of everything by the end of the month.

14. By the time you get to the hospital, your father _____ his operation, and you'll be able to find him in his room.

15. We _____ hundreds of exercises by the time we finish this book.

16. When I get home, the children _____ home from school yet, so I'll be able to relax for a while.

17. By the time we get to Vermont on our early winter vacation, all the leaves _____ _____ from the trees.

18. By the time our vacation is over, we _____ about seven rolls of film.

19. If you come at ten o'clock, the doctor _____ to the office yet, so I suggest that you come around eleven.

20. By the time we finally arrive in Bombay, we _____ on this plane for more than twenty hours.

21. It's so late that I'm afraid by the time we get to the wedding the bride and groom _____ _____.

22. When we get to the beach this afternoon, the sun _____ yet, so we'll be able to go swimming.

23. By the time we finish this course, we _____ most of the important features of English grammar.

24. When we finally leave this country, we _____ here for about three weeks.

25. By the time he retires after this last film, that actor _____ in about seventy-five movies.

26. Do you realize that we _____ each other for fifteen years this coming September?

27. We'll be able to have something to eat when we get to the airport because our plane _____ yet.

28. By the time we leave Egypt on this vacation, we _____ and _____ _____ many interesting things.

29. He's afraid that by the end of this party, he _____ and _____ _____ too much.

30. I think that by the end of this exercise, we _____ a little bit more about the future perfect tense.

31. By the time I get home late tonight, everyone _____ dinner and _____ to bed.

32. At this time next year, I _____ the university.

9.3

GRAMMAR EXERCISE   Name _____ Date _____

Focus: The Future Perfect Tense

Complete the following sentences with appropriate clauses containing verb phrases in the future perfect (continuous) tense.

EXAMPLES: a. By the time my father retires, he will have been working for fifty-three years.
           b. By the year 2000, the United States will have been independent for 224 years.

1. When my mother and father celebrate their next anniversary, _____
   _____.

2. When I get home tonight, _____.

3. By this time next year, _____.

4. By two o'clock this afternoon, _____.

5. I'm afraid that when I get to school, _____
   _____.

6. This coming September, _____.

7. When I wake up tomorrow morning, _____.

8. When I finally finish this course, _____.

9. When I get to work tomorrow morning, _____
   _____.

10. When I celebrate my next birthday, _____
    _____.

11. When we finish this book, _____.

12. When I leave the house tomorrow morning, _____
    _____.

13. When this meeting is over, _____.

14. When I finally get to bed tonight, _____.

15. When I leave work tonight around eight o'clock, _____
    _____.

16. When this century finally comes to an end, _____
    _____.

REVIEW QUIZZES

1.1

Name _____ Date _____.

Focus: Reviewing Prepositions

Supply appropriate prepositions in the blanks.

EXAMPLES: a. They live in the middle of the city.
b. *King Lear* was written by Shakespeare.

1. We enjoy Chinese food only once _____ a while.

2. I don't like to sit _____ the first row _____ seats _____ a theater.

3. There is a large sign _____ the side _____ my neighbor's barn.

4. _____ the time we got _____ school, class had already begun.

5. Most people were sleeping _____ their beds _____ the time _____ the earthquake.

6. I was raised _____ a farm, but my sister grew _____ _____ a city.

7. The thief entered the house _____ the window.

8. It is impossible to live _____ money.

9. Timmy, you should look _____ your dirty face _____ the mirror.

10. Would you rather live _____ the country or the city?

11. The President lives _____ 1600 Pennsylvania Avenue _____ Washington, D.C.

12. That person standing over there reminds me _____ my sister.

13. Santa Claus lives _____ the North Pole.

14. Let's take a trip _____ the world.

15. Hawaii is _____ the United States and Japan.

16. The earth is _____ a solar system. We are _____ the earth.

17. It is very hot _____ the Equator.

18. Your name is _____ the right-hand corner _____ the top _____ this page.

19. Some good friends _____ mine live _____ Park Avenue.

20. This is a secret _____ you and me.

21. The sun is 93 million miles _____ the earth.

22. Champagne will be served _____ the reception next Saturday.

23. How much money did you borrow _____ the bank?

24. We're going to take a trip _____ Spain _____ April.

1.2

Focus: Reviewing Tag Questions

Supply appropriate tag endings in the blanks.

EXAMPLES: a. You'd never talk about me behind my back, <u>would you?</u>
           b. Your sister and Jack haven't gotten married yet, <u>have they?</u>

1. You've got to go to the doctor today, _____?

2. You'd like to eat out tonight, _____?

3. Bob has never been in Europe, _____?

4. The final examination is being given tomorrow, _____?

5. The patient is being operated on today, _____?

6. You'd rather live in your native country, _____?

7. John put his shoes in the closet, _____?

8. You have to take another course, _____?

9. You've taken your medicine, _____?

10. Your neighbors never give parties, _____?

11. Your teacher doesn't have a car, _____?

12. It's raining outside, _____?

13. You won't be at the meeting tonight, _____?

14. I'm not making a mistake, _____?

15. I'm saying the wrong thing, _____?

16. This letter should be sent by air mail, _____?

17. That kind of refrigerator has to be defrosted, _____?

18. The refrigerator hasn't been defrosted yet, _____?

19. He's being given a promotion, _____?

20. You couldn't tell a serious lie, _____?

21. The twentieth century is quickly coming to an end, _____?

22. You've made a lot of new friends in your class, _____?

23. That man is always making a fool out of himself, _____?

24. Time has gone fast this month, _____?

25. You'll be here tomorrow, _____?

26. You don't enjoy working at night, _____?

27. She should stop smoking, _____?

28. This job has to be finished today, _____?

29. The manuscript has been submitted to the publisher, _____?

Name _____ Date _____

Focus: Reviewing *And, But, Too,* and *Either*

Supply appropriate words in the blanks.

EXAMPLES: a. I didn't enjoy the movie, and my sister <u>didn't either</u>.
            b. My neighbor has a color TV, and I <u>do too</u>.
            c. He speaks English well, but his brother <u>doesn't</u>.

1. The kitchen has to be painted, and the bathroom _____.

2. My neighbor's car was made in Japan, and mine _____.

3. She makes a lot of money, but her husband _____.

4. English is spoken in Canada, and French _____.

5. Our son's bike cost a lot, and our daughter's _____.

6. The refrigerator has to be fixed, and the stove _____.

7. She's had a university education, but her sister _____.

8. He's being given a promotion, but his boss _____.

9. We've been given a promotion, and everyone else in the company _____.

10. I've never been in the Orient, but my parents _____.

11. They had to borrow money in order to pay their taxes last year, and we _____.

12. They were invited to the party, but we _____.

13. I was at the last meeting, but you _____.

14. She won't be in school next semester, and I _____.

15. The female lion isn't lazy, but the male _____.

16. Their daughter doesn't go to school, and their son _____.

17. He was born at home, and I _____.

18. He has to pay a lot of taxes this year, but his wife _____.

19. They'll be at the game next Saturday, but we _____.

20. Mary wore her mother's wedding dress when she got married, and her sister _____.

21. The President was at the reception, and his wife _____.

22. Their son is in high school, and ours _____.

23. You'll never make a million, and I _____.

24. His wife can't be at the next meeting, and he _____.

25. I'm paid once a month, and everyone else in the office _____.

26. I thank you for being so helpful, and my wife _____.

27. The French flag is red, white, and blue, and the American flag _____.

28. He's never had an operation, and she _____.

29. He doesn't believe in Santa Claus, but his little sister _____.

Name _____ Date _____

Focus: Reviewing *And, But, So,* and *Neither*

Supply appropriate words in the blanks.

EXAMPLES: a. I'm not going to take a vacation this year, and neither <u>is</u> he.
b. I have to take another course, and so <u>do</u> you.
c. She took the final examination, but I <u>didn't</u>.

1. Our cat has to be fed twice a day, and so _____ our dog.

2. He should stop smoking, and so _____ she.

3. My radio's being repaired, and so _____ my TV.

4. She's been given a promotion and raise, and so _____ he.

5. I've tried hard during the course, and so _____ you.

6. The refrigerator doesn't have to be fixed, but the stove _____.

7. He's not going to be here tomorrow, and neither _____ I.

8. She was at the last meeting, and so _____ he.

9. He'll never get married again, and neither _____ she.

10. Their children are going to summer camp this year, and so _____ ours.

11. He has to take another course, but I _____.

12. I can't work miracles, and neither _____ you.

13. I wasn't at that game, and neither _____ you.

14. The last quiz wasn't difficult, and neither _____ this one.

15. The kitchen has to be cleaned up, and so _____ the bathroom.

16. She'd rather live in her native country, and so _____ I.

17. I'd like to take another course, and so _____ you.

18. I'd better keep quiet in this discussion, and so _____ you.

19. I didn't do the right thing, and neither _____ you.

20. She'll be at the party, and so _____ I.

21. I'm not wrong in this matter, but you _____.

22. I wasn't sleeping during the movie, but my wife _____.

23. You don't like the government's decision, and neither _____ I.

24. I'm angry at my boss, and so _____ everyone else.

25. We bought a new car last year, and so _____ our neighbor.

26. He has to drive to work, but his wife _____.

27. I've got to pay taxes, and so _____ you.

28. I'm not going to live forever, and neither _____ anyone else.

29. Our children are still going to school, but theirs _____.

1.5

Name _____ Date _____

Focus: Reviewing Verb Tenses

In the blanks supply appropriate forms of the verbs given in the parentheses.

EXAMPLES: a. (be) They <u>have been</u> in Chicago for twenty years.
            b. (see) I <u>saw</u> a wonderful movie last night.
            c. (go) We <u>didn't go</u> anywhere special on our last vacation.

1. (take) Fortunately, that problem _____ care of yesterday.

2. (listen) Sh! Someone _____ to our conversation.

3. (fix) I'm not wearing my watch because it _____.

4. (happen) Nothing much _____ when I got to the meeting.

5. (be) My parents _____ in Los Angeles two weeks from today.

6. (make) I _____ only two mistakes in the last quiz.

7. (sleep) I was tired yesterday because I _____ well the night before.

8. (do) Nothing _____ about the problem until tomorrow.

9. (be) This _____ an easy quiz so far.

10. (take) Unfortunately, just as we got to the airport, their plane _____ off.

11. (go) They _____ to the movies only once in a while.

12. (send) They _____ any Christmas cards last year.

13. (get) I _____ up at 7:30 every morning.

14. (fix) When I got to the garage, my car _____ yet.

15. (give) When I got to class late yesterday morning, a quiz _____.

16. (reveal) I promise that I _____ this secret to anyone.

17. (make) I was angry that I _____ such a foolish mistake.

18. (leave) I think Bob _____ for Paris at this very moment.

19. (graduate) Our daughter _____ from the university yet.

20. (live) Mary _____ with her family, is she?

21. (win) Unfortunately, our team _____ any games last year.

22. (quit) He _____ his job a couple of weeks ago.

23. (live) He _____ by himself since his recent divorce.

24. (do) We _____ twenty-four sentences so far.

25. (baptize) He _____ when he was three days old.

26. (go) She _____ to the doctor once a year for a physical examination.

27. (land) I predict that by the year 2000, man _____ on Mars.

28. (eat) Please don't call around 6:00 tomorrow evening because we _____.

29. (come) This quiz _____ to an end.

1.6

Focus: Reviewing Mixed Forms

Supply appropriate words or phrases in the blanks.

EXAMPLES: a. <u>Did</u> you have a good time at the party last night?
           b. <u>Although</u> she has a lot of money, she's an unhappy woman.

1. She _____ in London since 1974.

2. Do you enjoy _____ to the movies by yourself?

3. Don't you think this water is _____ cold to swim in?

4. I was completely tired out, but I went to the party _____.

5. It was _____ a cold night that we didn't go out.

6. How often _____ your best friend _____ to school?

7. When Columbus arrived in the New World, he thought he _____ in India.

8. Would you mind _____ your radio off?

9. A lot of things _____ in the world right now.

10. A good friend of mine lives _____ 335 Sutton Place South.

11. I'm not looking forward to _____ to the dentist tomorrow.

12. I wish I _____ the richest person in the world.

13. I'm _____ tired that I want to go home.

14. The teacher told us _____ our homework _____ ink.

15. We'll go out as soon as the rain _____.

16. Do you know how many days _____ in February?

17. I _____ this quiz so far.

18. What's a good way to _____ of cockroaches?

19. That horse sure runs _____, _____?

20. Before _____ the room, please turn the light _____.

21. Could you please tell me what time _____?

22. The doctor insists that the patient _____ the hospital at once.

23. If I _____ sick yesterday, I would have gone home early.

24. The thief didn't enter the house _____ the door, _____?

25. They're living _____ a furnished apartment _____ the time being.

26. I'll ask her about that problem when she _____ back.

27. He has to go to work every day, and _____ his wife.

28. They _____ in love with each other since they were children in school.

29. My lawyer suggested that I _____ the contract immediately.

LIST OF COMMONLY USED IRREGULAR VERBS

Base Form	Past Form	Past Participle
arise	arose	arisen
awake	awoke, awaked	awaked, awoke, awoken
be	was	been
bear	bore	borne (*meaning* to carry) / born (*meaning* to bear a child)
beat	beat	beaten, beat
become	became	become
begin	began	begun
bend	bent	bent
bet	bet	bet
bite	bit	bitten, bit
bleed	bled	bled
blow	blew	blown
break	broke	broken
bring	brought	brought
broadcast	broadcast, broadcasted	broadcast, broadcasted
build	built	built
burst	burst	burst
buy	bought	bought
cast	cast	cast
catch	caught	caught
choose	chose	chosen
come	came	come
cost	cost	cost
deal	dealt	dealt
dig	dug	dug
do	did	done
draw	drew	drawn
dream	dreamed, dreamt	dreamed, dreamt
drink	drank	drunk
drive	drove	driven
eat	ate	eaten
fall	fell	fallen
feed	fed	fed
feel	felt	felt
fight	fought	fought
find	found	found
flee	fled	fled
fly	flew	flown
forbid	forbade	forbidden
forget	forgot	forgotten (*British* forgot)
freeze	froze	frozen
give	gave	given (*British* got)
go	went	gone
grind	ground	ground
grow	grew	grown

Base Form	Past Form	Past Participle
hang	{ hung { hanged (*meaning* being hanged by the neck until dead)	hung hanged
have	had	had
hear	heard	heard
hide	hid	hidden
hit	hit	hit
hold	held	held
hurt	hurt	hurt
keep	kept	kept
kneel	knelt, kneeled	knelt, kneeled
knit	knit, knitted	knit, knitted
know	knew	known
lay	laid	laid
lead	led	led
leap	leaped, leapt	leaped, leapt
leave	left	left
lend	lent	lent
let	let	let
lie (to recline)	lay	lain
lie (not to tell the truth)	lied	lied
light	lit, lighted	lit, lighted
lose	lost	lost
make	made	made
mean	meant	meant
meet	met	met
mistake	mistook	mistaken
overcome	overcame	overcome
pay	paid	paid
put	put	put
quit	quit	quit
read	read (*pronounced* "red")	read (*pronounced* "red")
ride	rode	ridden
ring	rang	rung
rise	rose	risen
run	ran	run
say	said	said
see	saw	seen
seek	sought	sought
sell	sold	sold
send	sent	sent
set	set	set
shake	shook	shaken
shine (intransitive)	shone	shone
(transitive)	shined	shined
shoot	shot	shot
show	showed	shown, showed
shrink	shrank, shrunk	shrunk
shut	shut	shut
sing	sang	sung
sink	sank, sunk	sunk
sit	sat	sat

Base Form	Past Form	Past Participle
sleep	slept	slept
slide	slid	slid
speak	spoke	spoken
speed	sped, speeded	sped, speeded
spend	spent	spent
spin	spun	spun
spit	spit, spat	spit, spat
split	split	split
spread	spread	spread
spring	sprang, sprung	sprung
stand	stood	stood
steal	stole	stolen
stick	stuck	stuck
sting	stung	stung
stink	stank	stunk
strike	struck	struck
swear	swore	sworn
sweep	swept	swept
swim	swam	swum
swing	swung	swung
take	took	taken
teach	taught	taught
tear	tore	torn
tell	told	told
think	thought	thought
throw	threw	thrown
undergo	underwent	undergone
understand	understood	understood
wake	woke, waked	woken, waked, woke
wear	wore	worn
weave	wove	woven
weep	wept	wept
win	won	won
wind	wound	wound
withdraw	withdrew	withdrawn
withhold	withheld	withheld
wring	wrung	wrung
write	wrote	written